What's Public About Charter Schools?

What's Public About Charter Schools?

**Lessons
Learned
About Choice
and
Accountability**

Gary Miron
Christopher Nelson

CORWIN PRESS, INC.
A Sage Publications Company
Thousand Oaks, California

For information:

Corwin Press, Inc.
A Sage Publications Company
2455 Teller Road
Thousand Oaks, California 91320
E-mail: order@corwinpress.com

Sage Publications Ltd.
6 Bonhill Street
London EC2A 4PU
United Kingdom

Sage Publications India Pvt. Ltd.
M-32 Market
Greater Kailash I
New Delhi 110 048 India

Printed in the United States of America

A catalog record for this book is available from the Library of Congress.

ISBN 0-7619-4537-7 (c.)—ISBN 0-7619-4538-5

This book is printed on acid-free paper.

02   03   04   05   06   07   7   6   5   4   3   2   1

Acquisitions Editor: Rachel Livsey
Editorial Assistant: Phyllis Cappello
Production Editor: Olivia Weber
Cover Designer: Tracy E. Miller

Contents

Preface

Colleagues often refer to us as charter school researchers and evaluators. This label doesn't really sit well with us. Instead, we think of ourselves as researchers of school reforms and school reform processes, of which charter schools are only one instance. Indeed, the charter school movement is only the most recent—and perhaps best known—of a long series of attempts to restructure our public school systems.

Restructuring burst onto the educational agenda during the 1980s, largely in response to such factors as (a) a perceived linkage between educational performance and lackluster economic growth, (b) skepticism about centralized government programs, (c) a concern for preserving traditional cultural values, and (d) a more general trend toward introducing market forces into the delivery of public services. In the United States, restructuring gained prominence largely in response to such reports as the well-known *A Nation at Risk* in 1983. However, efforts to restructure public schooling took on similar faces in a whole array of countries, most noteworthy the United Kingdom, New Zealand, and Sweden. Like these restructuring efforts, the charter school concept involves decentralization, choice, competition, and privatization.

The charter school movement, however, has achieved a level of saliency and prevalence in this country that earlier reforms failed to achieve. This, combined with the fact that the charter concept combines a host of ideas from earlier restructuring movements, means that the charter movement provides a unique opportunity to observe these various components working in concert. Thus, while this book is ostensibly about charter schools, it should be relevant to a wide range of current school reforms, both in the United States and elsewhere.

Most of the research reported in this book comes from some four years of research on charter schools in Michigan. Much of the material has appeared in technical reports associated with these projects. Our aim in this book is twofold. First, we seek to make this research more accessible to nonexperts, including policymakers, school administrators, and parents. In doing so, we have no doubt glossed over details that our colleagues in the research community will find important. These readers are referred to our technical reports for such detailed information (Horn & Miron, 1999, 2000). In other sections, our presentation is probably too technical for some readers. We suggest that these readers turn to the summaries at the end of each chapter before reading the more technical material.

Our second aim in writing the book is to consider some of the larger normative and conceptual issues surrounding charter schools. These issues are perhaps best summarized by the book's title, *What's Public About Charter Schools?* Charter schools, like other attempts at school restructuring, may be viewed as an attempt to create a new type of school—a hybrid that combines elements traditionally associated with both public and private schools. Throughout, we seek to evaluate the extent to which this new hybrid is serving the core purposes of public education. The public-private issue is of increasing relevance in the United States, as members of the new Bush administration seek to further privatize elements of the American education system. In the end, we hope to have not only illuminated some issues in the debate over charter schools, but also some of the larger issues associated with privatization in education.

The book's focus on Michigan charter schools raises an important question: What can citizens and policymakers in other states and countries hope to learn from the Great Lakes State?

Michigan is not a typical case when it comes to charter schools. Indeed, it is regarded by most observers to have one of the most permissive charter laws in the country. For reasons we will detail in Chapter 3, opening a charter school is easier in Michigan than in most other states. Moreover, Michigan charter schools make much more thorough use of privatized services than in any other state. Thus, we are not claiming that Michigan is in any way representative of charter schools here or abroad. Instead, its value lies in the fact that it provides important lessons for those in other states who are considering either adopting strong charter laws or strengthening existing laws. Michigan, in short, may provide a tale of things to come as we continue our experiment with charter schools and privatization. Readers should bear in mind that, as an outlier, our conclusions about Michigan do not necessarily apply to all charter schools and charter school laws.

Outline of the Book

The book proceeds as follows. The first three chapters provide both a theoretical framework for, and the descriptive context of, the charter school reform in Michigan. The first chapter explores the meaning of "public" and "private" and also introduces and explains the *formalist* and *functionalist* views of public-ness that undergird the book. We are grateful for the contributions of Christopher Lubienski—both in thought and written word—to this chapter. Chapter 2 describes the historical and political backdrop that led to the charter school reforms. Chapter 3, in turn, describes the Michigan charter school law and the growth of the movement in the state. Chapter 4 concludes the group of background chapters with an analysis of charter school finance in Michigan. In particular, we seek to determine whether the financial playing field is even between charter and noncharter public schools. We thank F. Howard Nelson for sharing his expertise and knowledge in the area of charter school finance.

The remainder of the book seeks to evaluate the public-ness of Michigan charter schools according to the definitions introduced in the first chapter. Chapter 5 explores issues of equity and access (including service to special education students) through an analysis of the characteristics of charter school students in Michigan, while Chapter 6 examines the characteristics of the schools' teachers. Chapter 7 assesses the extent to which Michigan charter schools are developing and implementing innovative practices in curriculum, instruction, and governance. Like the terms *public* and *private,* the concept of "innovation" is a conceptual minefield. Thus, we hope this chapter will help clarify the debate on innovation in charter schools, as well as provide useful evidence on the subject. Chapters 8 through 10 complete the empirical analysis through discussions of student achievement, customer satisfaction, and the role of private education management organizations (EMOs).

Chapter 11 concludes the book with a summary of the evidence and an answer to the question, "What's public about charter schools?" As is typical of academics, our answer is a little bit complicated. The schools appear to be doing a reasonably good job of creating communities of teachers with commonly held educational viewpoints and of providing educational alternatives that satisfy their customers. However, the evidence suggests that many of these goals are being accomplished at the expense of equitable access to the schools and student achievement gains. Moreover, the schools are leveraging only limited changes and improvements in noncharter schools, and are often not subject to effective oversight. In short, the schools are public in some senses, but not others.

We hasten to add that any criticism of charter schools must be cognizant of traditional public schools' failures on many of these same dimensions. Moreover, as yet we see no reason to believe that the faults we find in Michigan's charter school experiment are inevitable. Indeed, Chapter 11 includes a number of safeguards and suggestions—many of which are drawn from other states—that we believe will better ensure that charter schools serve the public interest.

In the end, we certainly hope that readers will be convinced of our arguments and, where possible, act upon our recommendations. Failing that, we will be satisfied merely to have made a sound contribution to the charter school and school choice debate, both by clarifying some key conceptual issues and by providing new evidence.

Acknowledgments

This book was truly a collaborative effort. First, it was collaboration between the authors, each of whom brings rather different perspectives to the issue of charter schools (one from comparative education, the other from political science and policy analysis) but who are united in the search for effective ways to reform schools. We also gratefully acknowledge F. Howard Nelson, who wrote the bulk of Chapter 4 on charter school finance, and Christopher Lubienski, who contributed to the first chapter and who stimulated our thinking on issues of public and private in education.

No project of this magnitude could be completed without stimulating professional colleagues. While we cannot name all who contributed to the project, we wish to single out Chia-Lin Hsieh and Carolyn Sullins, who helped organize and analyze the survey data and who provided critical comments on portions of the book. We are also grateful to Carla Howe, Deborah Lehmann, Kimberly Reynolds, and John Risley for excellent research assistance and to Sally Veeder for editing early drafts. We also thank Daniel Stufflebeam, director of The Evaluation Center, which has supported our work, and Jerry Horn for his guidance throughout the research process in Michigan.

We were also fortunate to have received helpful comments and suggestions from a number of colleagues, including Clive Belfield, Louann Bierlein-Palmer, Richard Berquist, Katrina Bulkley, Joseph Kretovics, Natalie Lacireno-Paquet, Christopher Lubienski, Catherine Maloney, Catherine Awsumb Nelson, F. Howard Nelson, Monica Pini, and Janelle Scott. We alone, however, bear responsibility for the contents of the book, its conclusions, and any errors of fact or judgment that remain.

Finally, we thank our families—Anna, Axel, and Nils, and Catherine, Jay, and Graham—for tolerating our late nights at the office and our seemingly interminable ramblings on the subject of charter schools.

Kalamazoo, Michigan
November, 2001

About the Authors

Gary Miron has a diverse background in the field of education. He worked as a public school teacher in Michigan in the mid-1980s. Later he worked as an educational researcher and university instructor in the field of education. Currently, he is Principal Research Associate at Western Michigan University's Evaluation Center. There, he has completed or is working on a variety of school reform evaluations, including evaluations of charter schools in Michigan, Pennsylvania, Connecticut, Illinois, and Cleveland. In Connecticut and Cleveland, he has been involved in providing training and technical assistance to charter schools aimed at helping them develop and implement accountability plans and self-evaluations. He has also conducted a study of student achievement gains in schools operated by Edison Schools Inc.

Before joining The Evaluation Center, Dr. Miron worked at Stockholm University, where he had completed his graduate studies. While in Sweden he conducted a study on the national voucher reform in the early 1990s and later took part in a study of school restructuring in Europe. He has researched and written on such topics as educational evaluation, special needs education, educational planning and policy, multimethod research, charter schools, and school reform.

Christopher Nelson is Senior Research Associate at Western Michigan University's Evaluation Center, where he works on large-scale evaluations of state charter school laws. He is project manager for evaluations in Pennsylvania and Illinois, and has contributed to evaluation reports on charter schools in Michigan, Connecticut and Cleveland. Before joining The Evaluation Center, Dr. Nelson was on the faculty of the H. John Heinz III School of Public Policy and Management at Carnegie Mellon University, where he taught courses on evaluation methodology, policy analysis, and public organizations. While in Pittsburgh, Nelson worked on a number of regional education policy studies, including a large-scale assessment of workforce readiness among high school students, and a study of early-grade literacy. In addition, he played a leading role in the development of an education policy indicator system that is still in use today. Nelson holds an M.A. and Ph.D. from the University of North Carolina at Chapel Hill, and a B.A. summa cum laude from the University of Minnesota, where he was elected to Phi Beta Kappa.

1

Charter Schools and Privatization

With Christopher Lubienski

On Tuesday, October 5, 1993, Michigan Governor John Engler stood in front of an assembly of state legislators with a 20-gauge sawed-off shotgun and voiced his support for school choice. Engler brandished the gun, "confiscated from a student, to dramatize school violence and promote his plan to allow parents more leeway in choosing the schools their children attend" (Basheda, 1993, p. 8a). According to the armed governor (Engler, 1993a):

> The total funding level of schools will be determined by how many students they can retain or attract. The schools that deliver will succeed. The schools that don't will not. No longer will there be a monopoly of mediocrity in this state . . . because our kids deserve better.

The unusual spectacle did not end there. Engler asked a 9-year-old student, Rory, to stand up from his reserved seat in the gallery. Rory's family wanted to transfer him from their small rural school district to one with a gifted program, but their request was denied by the home district seeking to retain per-pupil funds. "It was a small district," according to Rory's father, and "children are dollar signs in their system."

The connection between Rory's plight and the shotgun was telling. Engler was portraying a public school system in a deep state of crisis due to its governance structures—"Public education is a monopoly, and monopolies don't

Dr. Christopher Lubienski is an assistant professor in Historical, Philosophical, and Comparative Studies in Education, Iowa State University. He has researched and written about school choice, privatization, and the role of market mechanisms in school reforms.

work" (quoted in King, 1993). The link was clear: Public schools fail in promoting academic excellence just as they fail to promote character and values because they rely on a captured clientele. Shielded from competition, they have no incentive to respond to the preferences of parents. Engler declared: "It's because of experiences like yours, Rory, that we need real change. This plan's for you" (see Basheda, 1993; Engler, 1993a).

Engler was a principal figure in a loose coalition launching a comprehensive choice system for public education in Michigan in the 1990s. Charter schools—or "public school academies," as they are called in Michigan—represent a central element in these education reforms.

One of the most widely discussed reforms in education, charter schools are a new breed of public school—a hybrid that mixes elements of traditional public schools (universal access and public funding) with elements usually associated with private schools (choice, autonomy, and flexibility). The movement is part of a larger set of national and international trends toward subjecting the delivery of public services to market forces.[1] This, its proponents hope, will make education and other public services more efficient and responsive. It is, in short, an attempt to harness private interests and institutions in the service of public interests.

Unlike more strident privatization efforts like school vouchers, however, charter schools enjoy broad-based support among both liberals and conservatives. For liberals, charter schools provide a way to embrace notions of choice and competition—popular in the abstract—without moving to a full voucher system. For conservatives, charter schools serve as a stalking horse for vouchers—a modest first step in acclimating the public, skeptical of the details of voucher plans, to the virtues of choice and competition in education. While polling evidence suggests that Americans are still relatively unfamiliar with charter schools (Public Agenda, 1999), it is clear that the concept is much less controversial than vouchers.

The fact that the charter concept is so politically ambidextrous has contributed, no doubt, to the movement's impressive growth over the past decade. Indeed, the movement has grown from 2 charter schools in Minnesota in 1992 to more than 2,300 schools in 37 states and the District of Columbia as of the 2001-02 academic year. In spite of this impressive growth, charter schools comprise only 0.2 percent of public schools nationwide. If the movement were to continue at its historical rate of growth, however, the number of charter schools could grow to nearly 10,000 by the year 2010.[2] While this is unlikely, it does serve to illustrate the impressive rate at which the charter movement has expanded.

With the charter school movement nearing its 10-year anniversary and charter schools high on the new president's education agenda, it seems appropriate to pause to take stock of what we have learned from the first decade of charter school experience. This book provides an in-depth examination of the charter concept as it has been operationalized in one of the nation's most populous states—Michigan. Having one of the oldest and strongest charter school laws in the country, Michigan provides important insights into how a similarly robust charter school movement might affect the delivery of public education in other states and nationally. Thus, close examination of the Michigan case will offer important insights to policymakers in states considering the option of new charter school laws, in states considering amendments to existing laws, and to national policymakers seeking to influence state-level charter school policy and practice.

In examining charter schools through the lens of Michigan, we pay special attention to the charter concept's mix of public and private elements. How successfully have charter schools balanced public and private? To what extent have charter schools managed to harness private interests and institutions in the service of public educational goals? In short, what's public about charter schools?

The remainder of this chapter both explores the charter concept in detail and introduces the basic notions of "public" and "private" used throughout the book. Readers should bear in mind that our discussion of the charter concept is a distillation of the movement's stated goals and the mechanisms by which it seeks to accomplish these goals. In later chapters we assess how the *actual* operation of Michigan charter schools measures up against these abstract ideas.

What Are Charter Schools? A Crash Course in the Charter Concept

At the heart of the charter concept lies a bargain.[3] Charter schools will receive enhanced autonomy over curriculum, instruction, and operations. In exchange, they must agree to be held more accountable for results than other public schools. Standing at the center of charter school accountability is the charter document itself. A charter is an agreement between a school and an authorizer—the public body that grants the charter. The charter document prescribes the conditions under which the school will operate and the goals it must accomplish in order to remain in operation. Schools that fail to live up to the promises set forth in the charter risk being closed—either through failure to get their charter renewed or, in extreme cases, immediate revocation of the charter and closure.

Figure 1.1 illustrates the essential components of the charter concept using what policy analysts and evaluators call a "logic model." Logic models identify the goals of a policy design and the instruments and techniques used to achieve those outcomes. The remainder of this section elaborates this logic model by discussing how the charter concept restructures schools' environments, the "opportunity space" created by this restructuring, and the mechanisms by which the schools are held accountable.

Restructuring Schools' External Environments

The charter school logic model shown in Figure 1.1 contains three parts. On the far left are a set of policy changes—brought about mostly through changes in state law—that alter the legal, political, and economic environment in which charter schools operate. We call these "structural" changes because they seek to fundamentally alter the conditions under which schools operate. The point of these structural changes, however, is not to prescribe charter school actions in great detail but to enhance school autonomy. We may think of these structural changes as creating an opportunity space in which charter schools may experiment (RPP International, 1998).

Thus, the charter concept is rather different from other education reforms in that it seeks not to prescribe specific interventions but to change the conditions under which schools develop and implement educational interventions. This has led some critics to charge that the charter concept is an "empty vessel" or an "all-things-to-all people" reform (see, e.g., Wells et al., 1998). To others, this aspect of the reform is liberating for schools, since it allows them to select interventions most appropriate for a given group of students.

Figure 1.1 Illustration of the Charter School Concept

One of the most important ways in which the charter concept seeks to change schools' external environments is through *choice*. Charter schools are schools of choice in that, with some exceptions, students from any district or locale may attend any charter school.

According to the theory, choice improves schools through two distinct mechanisms (Hoxby, 2000). The first is through competition. Most charter schools receive the lion's share of their funding through voucher-like allocations that travel with pupils. If a student chooses to attend a charter school, that school receives a fixed-sum payment. As a consequence, schools that fail to attract and retain students will, in theory, go out of business. Since charter schools cannot gain a leg up on competitors by lowering their "prices," they must compete primarily on quality (Solmon, Block, & Gifford, 1999). Thus, the charter concept postulates that, other things equal, competition for students will raise the quality of charter schools and that schools failing to compete on quality will be forced to close.

Second, choice also works through a sorting process. Where there is a wide variety of schools from which to choose, and where each provides a different mix of services, customers will choose the mix of services that best meets their educational preferences. The result will be schools that cater to a relatively narrow range of educational preferences. Choice advocates (see, e.g., Chubb & Moe, 1990; Hill, Pierce, & Guthrie, 1997) argue that such sorting by educational preferences will reduce the amount of time schools spend resolving conflicts among school stakeholders, leaving them more time and energy to devote to developing and implementing educational programs. Choice advocates also argue that the very act of choice will leave students, parents, and teachers disposed to work harder to support the schools they have chosen.

Yet another way in which the charter concept seeks to restructure schools' environments is through a mix of *deregulation* and a new form of *accountability*. Traditionally, public schools have been accountable primarily for the educational processes they employ. These include curricula, teaching methods, and the structure of the school calendar. The implicit assumption behind this sort of accountability is that state- and district-level policymakers possess enough knowledge to prescribe inputs and processes that are likely to generate favorable student outcomes. Charter proponents—indeed, critics of "big government" in general—charge that central policymakers, in fact, have no such knowledge; and that one-size-fits-all approaches to education should be replaced by approaches that empower teachers and principals to prescribe inputs and processes on their own. This new accountability holds charter schools accountable for outcomes—many of them articulated in charter documents—and then employs deregulation to allow them to choose their own means for arriving at those goals. Charter proponents, in short, contend that school-level personnel are in the best position to assess and respond to specific students' needs.

Defining the Bounds of the Charter School "Opportunity Space"

The charter concept's deregulation of school processes, however, is far from complete. All charter school statutes require that the schools continue to abide by laws concerning civil rights, the safety and health of their students, and standards of fiscal accounting. Some laws require charter schools to adhere to state educational performance standards, take state assessments, and the like. Most laws set certain policy goals against which we may evaluate how charter schools use their autonomy. Thus, it is clear that the grant of autonomy to charter schools is no blank check.

Another way in which most charter school laws limit the opportunity space in which the schools operate is by defining a number of "intermediate" goals. In doing so, charter school laws seek to encourage (or even require) the schools to use their autonomy in certain ways. One such intermediate goal (found in the middle box of Figure 1.1) is the enhancement of opportunities for parental and community involvement. As an empirical matter, one might expect that parents who choose schools would be more engaged than those who do not. Beyond that, proponents of the charter concept contend that such involvement is a valuable resource that will ultimately lead to higher student achievement and other positive outcomes. Indeed, nearly four decades of research on student achievement has found that family and community characteristics can explain much of the variation in student achievement as measured by standardized tests. Thus, one might suspect that schools that work with home and community will be able to leverage improvements in student outcomes.

A second intermediate goal in most charter school laws is enhanced professional autonomy and opportunities for teachers. Charter schools are schools of choice for teachers as well as parents and students. It is reasonable to suppose, therefore, that teachers who choose to work at a school based on their agreement with the school's vision will be more willing to go the extra mile for the school. The call for teacher autonomy is in many ways grounded in the claim that the best educational interventions are targeted to the needs of individual students and that teachers are in the best position to select and implement interventions appropriate to particular students. Moreover, a body of research literature suggests that teacher collaboration and collegiality is correlated with a more positive learning climate and, ultimately, higher student achievement (Lee & Smith, 1996; Louis, Marks, & Kruse, 1996; Marks & Louis, 1997).

A third intermediate goal for charter schools is that they will develop innovations in curriculum, instruction, and governance. Put another way, proponents argue that charter schools will function as public education's R&D sector. As such, the benefits of charter schools will extend to noncharter students as traditional public schools adopt and emulate these innovations.

Finally, some charter school advocates hope that the schools will provide rich laboratories for experiments in the use of privatized services. According to these advocates, schools will run more efficiently by "buying" rather than "making" such goods as lunches, nursing and dental services, and special education services (see, e.g., Hill et al., 1997). One of the most controversial forms of privatization has been the use of private education management organizations (EMOs). The level of EMO involvement ranges from the provision of just one or two services to full operation of the school, including payroll, accounting, selection and supervision of staff, and the development and implementation of the school program. Nationally, between 20 and 25 percent of all charter schools are believed to be operated by for-profit EMOs (see Chapter 10 for more details). While advocates claim that use of EMOs has made charter schools more effective, critics question whether EMO-managed schools retain their "public" quality and whether they produce the results they promise (see, e.g., Miron & Applegate, 2000).

Accountability for What? The Question of Outcomes

The concept of accountability lies at the heart of the charter concept; indeed, it is the price the schools pay for their autonomy. As we have seen, charter proponents have in mind a particular kind of accountability—one that emphasizes accountability for outcomes over accountability for inputs and processes. This, however, begs two additional questions. The first is "accountability for which outputs and outcomes?" That is, which outcomes shall serve as the primary indicators of charter school quality? The second question is "accountability to whom?" That is, who will decide whether charter schools are making sufficient progress toward their goals? We begin with the first question.

As we have seen, the charter concept identifies a number of intermediate goals for which charter schools are to be held accountable (teacher autonomy, parental and community involvement, etc.). The most commonly noted "final" outcomes are student achievement and customer satisfaction. Thus, Figure 1.1 places these two constructs at the far right-hand side of the logic model. The representation in Figure 1.1, however, fails to capture the level of controversy over which outcomes charter schools ought to be accountable for.

The first conflict is over how important the intermediate outcomes are in relation to the final outcomes. Often, advocates of charter schools, choice, and privatization couch their discussions of educational outcomes in terms of efficiency. This view is usually contrasted to the more traditional view that public education should, in addition to producing bottom-line academic outcomes, serve as an agent of political and civic socialization and as a tool of social change, particularly on equity and distributional issues.

Choice proponents' emphasis on efficiency is not surprising given that many such advocates have backgrounds in business and economics and are used to having ready access to bottom-line accounting data. It is also linked with reformers' desire to make schooling less political and less bureaucratic. Yet, a little reflection on the concept of efficiency suggests that talking about educational goals in terms of efficiency only serves to obscure more fundamental differences in opinions about the ultimate goals of education. As Stone (1988) has argued,

> Efficiency is a comparative idea. It is a way of judging the merits of
> different ways of doing things. It has come to mean the ratio between
> input and output, effort and results, expenditure and income, or cost
> and resulting benefit. (p. 49)

While efficiency focuses our attention on bottom-line outcomes over inputs and processes, it can tell us nothing about which outcomes are worth pursuing. Thus, far from resolving questions about what we ought to do, the concept of efficiency presumes that we have already agreed on outcomes. Technical efficiency, in short, can help us decide how to get somewhere, but it cannot tell us where we should go.

So where should public education take us? Proponents of charter schools and privatization often seek to narrow the range of goals for public education (Lubienski, 2001), in the most extreme cases, to achievement as measured on standardized tests. For some, this narrowing is a moral imperative. Christian conservatives, for instance, often view choice and privatization as a way of breaking what they see as the dominance of secular culture and values in traditional public schools. When combined with efforts to reduce the separation of church and state, such a narrow focus on achievement and test scores creates a space in which religious communities can create a set of civic institutions that better comport with their own moral values. Put another way, such actors often seek to narrow the range of outcomes for which schools are *publicly* accountable in order to create more space for a set of parallel *private* educational activities.

For others, the narrowing of publicly enforceable educational goals is less a moral than a pragmatic decision. Here the claim is that schools function more effectively when they focus on a narrow range of activities. Often, such goals are reflected in clear and concise mission statements. Those who hold this position are often not fundamentally opposed to the broader range of goals that traditional public schools seek out (e.g., equity, citizenship education, etc.). Rather, they believe that schools have been torn in too many directions by a panoply of cross-cutting mandates (see, e.g., Chubb & Moe, 1990).

The second conflict is over how policymakers and citizens should balance the values of student achievement and customer satisfaction. While many charter advocates argue that both are important, some laissez faire market conservatives view customer satisfaction as the paramount aim of public programs and agencies. Advocates of this position hold that a policy decision or outcome is good only if its customers think it is good and continue to "vote with their feet" for the service. Proponents of this position also maintain that it is the customers—parents, guardians—and not public officials who are best suited to know what is good for children. The conflict over the importance of customer satisfaction is represented by the fact that it appears in Figure 1.1 as both a final and an intermediate outcome.

Accountability to Whom? The New Politics of Education

To ask the question "accountability for what," however, raises still another question: Who shall decide whether charter schools are making sufficient progress toward their goals? This is the question of "accountability to whom?"

At the heart of this question lies a debate over the nature of education as a social and economic good. Traditionally, education has been viewed as a "public good." Advocates of choice and privatization, by contrast, generally regard education as essentially a private good (Englund, 1993; Lubienski, 2000). In layman's terms, a public good is a good in which the public has a clear stake. Public policy analysts have formalized this notion somewhat by defining public goods as those goods that have significant "spillover" costs and benefits ("externalities") associated with them.[4] As English philosopher John Stuart Mill characterized the distinction, a public good or action is one that has "other-regarding consequences," whereas a private act is one that has only "self-regarding consequences" (Mill, 1989). Or, to paraphrase U.S. Supreme Court justice Oliver Wendell Holmes, my private right to swing my fist ends where your chin begins. Few, if any, goods are purely public or private; most fall somewhere on a continuum between the two. Thus, whether education (or any other good) is public or private is open to some debate.

Clearly, education possesses characteristics of both public and private goods. Private good dimensions of education include the human capital skills that individuals acquire in school and take with them to the job market. Public good dimensions include the inculcation of a set of civic values and a common core of cultural meanings. However, one and the same aspect of education may have both public good and private good characteristics. The human capital skills just mentioned are consumed not only by the individual who carries them but also, through positive externalities, by other citizens who benefit from the wealth and cultural value generated by that individual. Similarly, cultural and civic values can also be consumed by individuals as they derive personal pleasure from participating in politics and from enjoying cultural artifacts (e.g., museum trips). Levin (2000) summarized the ambiguity of the public/private good distinction in education as follows:

> The problem is that schooling takes place at the intersection of two sets of rights, those of the family and those of society. The first is the right of parents to choose the experiences, influences and values to which they expose their children, the right to rear their children in the manner that they see fit. The second is the right of a democratic society to use the educational system as a means to reproduce its most essential political, economic and social institutions through a common schooling experience. (p. 4)

Whether education is construed as a public or private good has tremendous practical consequences. Generally, policy analysts argue that public goods are best distributed through democratic majority rule while private goods are best distributed through market processes.[5]

Traditionalists, while not denying the private good aspects of education, generally emphasize the public good aspects. This is not surprising given that they are also more likely to view public education as having broad social goals such as equity and socialization. Drawing upon an intellectual framework from the field of economics, these traditionalists point out that markets generally do a poor job of producing public goods. This is because of the "free-rider" problem, according to which each individual has a incentive to sit back while others produce public goods.[6] Such situations, according to this framework, are prime examples of market failure and cry out for intervention through democratic processes. In short, the fact that education is a public good, along with the fact that markets generally underproduce public goods, necessitates that schools are accountable to the entire citizenry—or at least most of it.

Advocates of choice and privatization do not deny the public good aspects of education but argue that the private good components are more important. This comports with their narrower view of the goals of public education. These advocates also argue that government intervention through majority rule is just as likely to create problems as to correct any market failures.

Critics of traditional government-run public schools cite two sets of problems with control by majority rule, one moral and the other practical. The moral argument notes that wherever there is not a unanimous majority behind a public decision, majority rule produces winners and losers. Thus, as Chubb and Moe (1990) observed, "in this sense, democracy is essentially coercive. The winners get to use public authority to impose their policies on the losers" (p. 28). Transactions in a well-functioning market, by contrast, enable each person to improve his or her welfare, since no rational person would engage in a market exchange unless it left him or her better off. Thus, where democratic politics necessarily subjugates the will of the minority to that of the majority, markets—in theory, at least—create only winners and are therefore more compatible with the values of individual autonomy and choice.

The practical argument against democratic control of schools is more complicated. Critics often begin by noting that schools are hindered by the excessive bureaucracies they labor under. By limiting school officials' flexibility to adapt to the needs of their particular students and communities, such bureaucratization limits their effectiveness. Many critics ascribe these problems to "provider capture," or the tendency for schools to be under the influence of teachers' unions and others who insist on stifling regulations in order to ensure their own job security. Others (e.g., Chubb & Moe, 1990; Hill et al., 1997) place the blame for this bureaucratic sclerosis on the features of democratic politics. Chubb and Moe (1990), for instance, claimed that bureaucratic structures arise when majorities seek to insulate their victories against future coalitions through rules and regulations.

> The best way for groups to protect their achievements from the uncertainties of future politics, is through formalization: the formal reduction or elimination of discretion, and the formal insulation of any remaining discretion from future political influence. (Chubb & Moe, 1990, pp. 42-43)

The key to the bureaucracy problem, on this argument, is not rogue elephant bureaucracies but democratic politics itself. The solution, therefore, is to replace democratic control with an alternative answer to the "accountability to whom" question.

The alternative control mechanism suggested by choice-based reforms like charter schools is market accountability. Unlike democratic/political accountability, market accountability requires that schools be evaluated primarily by individual consumers (parents and students). The principal mechanism of accountability is the threat that customers will vote with their feet by leaving the school. Given that state funding under charter laws is tied to the individual student, large enrollment losses could mean financial insolvency and, ultimately, closure.

Market accountability, then, effectively suspends normal democratic processes. Instead of having to convince majorities of their worth, schools must satisfy one customer at a time (Lubienski, 2001). Moreover, market accountability places most of the influence over schools in the hands of parents and students, while minimizing the role of other stakeholders. Chubb and Moe (1990) characterized the difference as follows:

> Under a system of democratic control the public schools are governed by an enormous, far-flung constituency in which the interests of

parents and students carry no special status or weight. When markets prevail, parents and students are thrust onto center stage, along with the owners and staff of schools; most of the rest of society plays a distinctly secondary role, limited for the most part to setting the framework within which educational choices get made. (p. 35)

By placing students and parents (not democratic majorities) at the heart of school accountability, the charter concept seeks a transformation in the politics of education.

What's Public About Charter Schools?

Charter schools, as we noted at the beginning of the chapter, are a hybrid form of school, combining elements of traditional public schools with those usually associated with private schools. Like vouchers and other more strident forms of privatization, charter schools are schools of choice, which means that they risk closure if they fail to attract and retain "customers." Proponents of choice and privatization—in education and elsewhere—argue that market-based systems work by creating incentives for private sector actors to produce goods valued by the public. This argument is perhaps best crystallized in the title of a book by former Council of Economic Advisors chair Charles Schultze—*The Public Use of Private Interest* (1977). Critics, however, have charged that charter schools are not really public at all and that charter school laws use public funds to subsidize private behavior, with few redeeming public purposes.

This issue is especially relevant in Michigan, where nearly three fourths of all charter schools are operated by private education management companies (EMOs). Thus, one of the key questions we wish to raise in this book is whether charter schools retain enough of their public character to be considered public schools. In short, what's public about charter schools?

The issue of public versus private is far from academic.[7] On November 1, 1994, the issue nearly stopped Michigan's new experiment with charter schools dead in its tracks. On that day, a Michigan circuit court declared that public school academies, in spite of their name, were not public after all. As a consequence, the court held that public funding of the schools was unconstitutional. At the center of the dispute lay the Michigan constitution's "parochiaid" amendment, which was approved by referendum in 1970. The amendment, among the strongest of its kind in the country, expressly prohibits government support of non-public schools. Specifically:

No public monies or property shall be appropriated or paid or any public credit utilized, by the legislature or any other political subdivision or agency of the state directly or indirectly to aid or maintain any private, denominational or other nonpublic, preelementary, elementary, or secondary school. (Art. VIII, sec 2)[8]

The plaintiffs argued that the charter school law violated this constitutional provision. They also argued that the charter school law represented an unconstitutional delegation of authority over public schooling. Citing the Michigan constitution's requirement that "the legislature shall maintain and support a system of free public elementary and secondary schools," the plaintiffs argued that the legislature had essentially abdicated its responsibilities to private sector entities.

In rendering their decisions, the Michigan courts had little legal precedent to go on. Indeed, no constitutional provision, statute, or court case has provided a clear definition of "public" in the case of schooling. Plaintiffs, in their legal briefs, relied heavily on a 1989 opinion of the state's attorney general regarding public aid to an Indian school. Citing a 1945 court case from the state of Connecticut, the opinion articulated a two-part test to determine whether a school is public. First, the school must be under the "exclusive control" of the state. Second, the school must be "free from sectarian instruction" (Michigan Office of the Attorney General, 1989).

A Michigan trial court agreed with the plaintiff's use of the two-part test from Connecticut and that Michigan charter schools failed the first of the two tests (the court did not address the second test). For the justices signing the majority opinion, the most damning fact was that the law allowed privately- and self-selected boards to control the schools. The opinion acknowledged that the law allowed authorizers to determine the manner in which board members were selected and that the authorizers (usually public universities or school boards) are themselves public bodies. However, the fact that the boards were generally constituted *before* the charter application led the justices in the majority to conclude that charter schools were, ultimately, *not* under the "exclusive control" of the state. Two years later, a Michigan appeals court upheld the lower court's decision, concluding that the schools are "run by an essentially private entity, outside the realm of public control" (Michigan Court of Appeals, 1996, p. 5), and thus violate the law.

The Michigan Supreme Court (1997) took the opposite view in considering a 1997 appeal. Echoing dissenters in the lower court decisions, the high court challenged the lower court justices' reading of the charter school law. The majority opinion disagreed that the charter school law constituted an improper delegation of authority. More important, it challenged the assertion that schools are public by virtue of being under the "exclusive control" of the state. Specifically, the majority opinion noted that while the constitution requires that the legislature "maintain and support a system of free public elementary and secondary schools," there is, in fact, no requirement that those schools be under its "exclusive control." Having rejected the notion that schools must remain under the state's *exclusive* control, the opinion went on to demonstrate three mechanisms by which the state maintains effective partial control. First, the schools' charters may be revoked by authorizing bodies for failure to live up to their promises. Second, since the authorizers are themselves creatures of the state, this comprises an effective form of partial control. Finally, the justices noted that the state controls the flow of money to charter schools.

The supreme court majority also addressed the lower courts' concern that charter schools are essentially under the control of private boards. Here, the court disagreed with the lower courts' rulings that control over the *selection* of board members was insufficient. Control over process, according to the justices, provides ample opportunity for control, and the legislature may change that process at any time.

Formalist and Functionalist Views of Public-ness

Though the lower court and supreme court opinions arrived at very different conclusions on the Michigan charter school law's constitutionality, both sides of the argument appear to have accepted a common set of tacit assumptions. In particular, all three opinions accepted the notion that charter schools involve a delegation of legislative authority to lower-level units and that whether these units are public or not hinges mainly on the extent to which the people and their elected representatives retain control over them.

Since issues of delegation and control are properties of institutional forms, we refer to this view as the formalist view of public-ness. This view holds that schools (or other institutions) are public if they are either publicly owned or controlled by citizens or their duly constituted representatives. On this definition, a charter school is public if there is some chain of political authority and influence that links voters to school decisions. This linkage may be mediated through various elected representatives, including school board members, state legislators, and others (Lubienski, 2001).

Choice proponents, however, suggest a more flexible *functionalist* definition that more closely resembles the economic definition discussed above. On this view, a school (or other institution) is public not by virtue of lines of authority and chains of influence, but by whether it performs important public functions. This view is fully consistent with the notion of "the public use of private interest"—no matter who owns charter schools and no matter who controls and manages them, they are public so long as they serve public purposes (i.e., produce positive externalities), such as raising student achievement.

Once again, this view is illustrated by a judicial decision, this time from the state of New Jersey. In a 2000 decision, the New Jersey Supreme Court responded to an appeal over a case involving two local school districts' challenges to the granting of charters in their catchment areas. Unlike Michigan, charters in New Jersey may be granted only by the state department of education, with local districts acting in an advisory capacity. As in Michigan, plaintiffs invoked the notion of delegation. In particular, school officials disputed decisions to locate charter schools in their districts on the grounds that the state's charter school law constituted, among other things, "an improper delegation of legislative power to a private body" (New Jersey Supreme Court, 2000).

As we have seen, the Michigan courts, when faced with a similar question, presented arguments about institutional forms and mechanisms of control. More generally, the Michigan courts sought to determine whether charter schools were an appropriate *means* by which the legislature could deliver public education. The New Jersey courts, by contrast, were less concerned with whether charter schools were a permissible tool in and of themselves and more concerned with whether charter schools might reasonably produce appropriate public *outcomes*. Thus, the court reasoned that,

> The choice to include charter schools among the array of public entities providing educational services to our pupils is a choice appropriately made by the Legislature so long as the constitutional mandate to provide a thorough and efficient system of education in New Jersey is satisfied. (New Jersey Supreme Court, 2000)

In short, although government should *support* public education, there is no need for government to *run* it.

Unlike the formalist view of public-ness, the functionalist view focuses less on how education is delivered and more on whether the techniques used serve important public functions. This definition has the important consequence of opening the delivery of public education up to organizations that have traditionally been considered private. In the words of former Michigan state board of education president, W. Clark Durant (1997),

> . . . we must also have multiple educational providers who have the motivation of ownership and accountability. Let's have public corporations for a new kind of public education. Let's allow educational entrepreneurs to raise capital in the public markets . . . enormous resources are available. . . . Banks and financial service companies might start a school of business and finance. Automobile makers and their suppliers might start a school for engineers and other related professions. Our houses of faith can create and/or expand existing schools to offer a program to touch the heart and not just the mind. (pp. 363-364)

Thus, private schools can serve the public in the same way that private restaurants can nourish their patrons as well as any government program feeds the public, or in the same way that for-profit media outlets complement public broadcasting in providing knowledge of public affairs to the public. As for traditional public schools, this perspective holds that they are best understood not as "public schools" but as "government-run schools" (Lubienski, 2001).

Looking Ahead

The remainder of this book seeks to assess just how public Michigan charter schools are according to both the formalist and functionalist definitions. On the formalist side of the equation, we examine the extent to which charter schools remain accountable to citizens and their elected representatives. On the functionalist side, we assess whether Michigan charter schools are serving the public purposes their proponents claimed they would, including equity, student achievement, professional opportunities for teachers, innovation, and customer satisfaction. Before turning to those issues, however, the next two chapters provide important information on the policy climate that produced the Michigan charter school law and an overview of the law's major components.

Notes

1. See, for instance, Savoie (1994) for a survey of the privatization of a variety of public services in the United States, Canada, and Great Britain. Other relevant sources include Miron (1997), Walford (1996), and Whitty, Power, & Halpin (1998).

2. The number of charter schools as a proportion of all public schools was derived by dividing the total number of charter schools in 2001 reported by the Center for Education Reform [on-line: http://www.edreform.com] by the total number of public schools as reported by the National Center for Education Statistics (NCES; 2000). Projections were derived by estimating a quadratic regression on past growth rates and then making out-of-sample predictions based on the estimates. Details are available from the authors.

3. This discussion draws upon a large number of sources on the charter school concept and policy theory. These include: Budde (1988), Bulkley (1999), Finn, Manno, & Vanourek (2000), Hassel (1999), Kolderie (1990), Nathan (1996), RPP International (1998), Wohlstetter & Griffin (1998), and Wohlstetter, Wenning & Briggs (1995).

4. This discussion simplifies the policy analytic definition somewhat. Most policy analysis and economics textbooks define public goods in terms of two conditions, both of which are related to the notion of externalities. First, the good must be "nonrival"; that is, the addition of other consumers must not affect the good's

usefulness to those already consuming it. This property is also known among economists as "jointness of supply." Second, a public good is "nonexcludable"; that is, it is impossible or impractical to exclude free-riders from enjoying the good. Private goods are goods that lack these two qualities. Readers may consult Olson (1965) and Stiglitz (1988) for more complete discussions of these concepts.

5. This is because the externalities associated with public schools implies that one person's decision to consume a good (or a certain amount of a good) commits other individuals to consume similar levels of the good. Consider, for instance, the regulation of toxic chemicals. Air pollution is a strong candidate for democratic decision making since individuals in a given area must all consume the same amount of air pollution, regardless of their individual preferences.

6. The free-rider problem is a consequence of positive externalities. If you are engaged in an action (e.g., cleaning the house) from which I can benefit without contributing, then I will have an incentive to let you do the cleaning while I sit back and enjoy its benefits.

7. Kemerer & Maloney (2001) have explored the complexity of the legal issues defining the public versus private nature of education. Their work also examines the legal issues regarding accountability in independent private schools, in public schools operated by private companies, and in publicly funded voucher programs.

8. Michigan Constitution of 1963 [http://www.state.mi.us/migov/Constitution]

2

Shifting From Public to Private: Historical and Political Backdrop

In many respects, the charter concept may be viewed as old wine in new bottles. It is a mixture of other reforms that had been present in the "policy primordial soup" (Kingdon, 1995) for many years before the nation's first charter law was enacted in 1991. What is unique about charter schools, therefore, is not this or that element, but rather the *combination* of elements.

In this chapter we examine the context and forces out of which this new breed of public education emerged. As will quickly become apparent, we must look far and wide—to other countries, as well as other states—to find the intellectual and political roots of the charter concept. Morever, we shall see that in Michigan the charter concept is part of a larger policy pendulum, oscillating between an emphasis on private or public provision of education. Indeed, the impact of charter schools in Michigan must be understood against this mosaic of evolving reforms.

Charter Schools in the National and International Context

Charter schools represent one of a number of reforms that fall into the category of school restructuring. Restructuring has no precise or generally agreed-upon definition, largely due to the fact that the term has become an important political instrument and that groups support it for a variety of sometimes contradictory reasons (Cibulka, 1990; Henig, 1994). The term is borrowed from economics and usually refers to structural reforms that include decentralization, increased school choice, the application of market forces, deregulation, privatization, and the use of new steering mechanisms such as a central curriculum and central examinations (Miron, 1997). The concept of restructuring was forged, in large measure, during the economic crises of the 1970s and 1980s.[1] A common response to these crises—often prescribed by "structural adjustment" plans—was a move toward privatization and away from government provision of key social services (see, e.g., Naim, 1993). Over time, these ideas spread from economics to social and educational policy.[2]

Drawing upon these intellectual roots, school restructuring applies many of the same basic concepts as economic restructuring. In all, restructuring encompasses a wide variety of reforms and employs an interesting mixture of centralizing and decentralizing elements. On the one hand, restructuring emphasizes devolution of authority to local units of governance, increased school choice, competition, deregulation, and privatization. On the other hand, this is often tempered with centralized steering or funding mechanisms such as a national and state curricula and examinations. The movement toward school restructuring has been bolstered by the frustration of policymakers who wish to reform schools. School restructuring focuses on structural changes that alter the control and governance of schools. This, in turn, is believed to allow new opportunities to change the inner workings of schools.

A number of countries introduced restructuring at approximately the same time (see Fiske & Ladd, 2000; McEwan & Carnoy, 2000; Miron, 1993; Walford, 1996; Whitty, Power, & Halpin, 1998; Wylie, 1994). Starting in 1987, the Tory government in the United Kingdom took steps to weaken the local education authorities (LEAs) in England and Wales and strengthen the involvement of the national government. Over time, a variety of "sticks" and "carrots" were used to convince schools to opt out of the LEAs and become charter-like "grant-maintained schools," receiving funding directly from the newly established Funding Agency for Schools. A national curriculum was developed and a national examination used to rank schools according to their average test scores. The grant-maintained schools program was part of a larger range of reforms that encouraged the use of market forces and allowed greater private involvement in public schools. As Boyd (1993) has shown, there was extensive cross-Atlantic policy borrowing between the United Kingdom and the United States, which was itself beginning to consider similar reforms.

Similarly, Sweden and New Zealand were able to accomplish—at least in legislation—what Margaret Thatcher and Ronald Reagan could only have dreamed of for their respective school systems. Shortly after the conservative coalition of parties formed a government in Sweden in 1992, it introduced a national voucher reform (Miron, 1993). And in New Zealand, Social Democrats (and later the conservative Nationalist Party) enacted and implemented a school-based management reform to allow greater autonomy and accountability in the country's schools (Fiske & Ladd, 2000; Wylie, 1994). The reforms in Sweden and

New Zealand are remarkable because those countries had been widely perceived as bastions of left-leaning politicians and social democratic thinking.

As Apple (1996, 2001) has written, restructuring has been championed by a broad coalition, which he terms the "new right," including neoliberals, neoconservatives, authoritarian populists (i.e., Religious Right), and the new middle class. Each member of the coalition emphasizes different aspects of the concept. Neoliberals have seen in restructuring's emphasis on school choice and competition an opportunity to affirm their core belief in free choice and human liberty. For these advocates, choice is a good unto itself, irrespective of its consequences. Neoconservatives and religious populists, while less concerned with choice as an end in itself, see in restructuring's emphasis on decentraliza tion and deregulation an opportunity to remove government restrictions on the creation of schools that emphasize moral values and religion. Finally, members of the professional middle class often view restructuring as a way to improve the return on their investment in public education.

The fact that charter schools and other forms of school restructuring appeal to such a broad range of political and ideological groups has led some to charge that the concept is an empty vessel (Wells et al., 1999). Perhaps the most convincing testament to the movement's political flexibility is the fact that restructuring programs have survived changes in party control of government in several nations. New Zealand's 1989 reform, for instance, was initiated by the Social Democrat party, but was extended (with revisions) by the conservative Nationalist party upon its return to power. The Social Democrats in Sweden vowed to eliminate vouchers if returned to power. Yet they made only minor adjustments to the program when they regained power in 1994. Finally, the Labour government in the United Kingdom has proceeded with a number of reform ideas initiated by the Tories. For example, they continue to promote school choice, specialization of schools, and privatization, even though they have moved the grant-maintained schools back under the control of the LEAs and have eliminated that National Finance Agency.

While restructuring is still quite controversial, there is more agreement across the political spectrum over charter schools, and over some elements of restructuring, such as site-based management. Debates continue to focus on fundamental questions of how a society should balance the often competing values of efficiency, equity, and liberty (Guthrie & Koppich, 1993). As discussed in Chapter 1, advocates of charter schools usually seek to give greater (though not exclusive) weight to efficiency and liberty considerations than do advocates of traditional public schools.

The Public-Private Pendulum in Michigan

In Michigan, charter schools are part of a longstanding debate over the appropriate balance between public and private forces in the state's education system. The charter school movement may be viewed as part of a recent swing from a public-dominated education system to one that increasingly involves elements of the private sector. An understanding of the place and impact of charter schools on public education in Michigan requires that we briefly explore this historical pendulum.

The Shift From Private to Public

Like other states, Michigan's education system at the turn of the century was a largely decentralized, unregulated system that included many private and parochial schools. In spite of the fact that these schools were not government-run, however, many served what are today considered public functions.[3] Indeed, many nominally private schools were set up by churches and other local benefactors to serve poor, previously undereducated populations.

Over time, this system of largely private education evolved into the network of government-run schools we see today. Indeed, many of the erstwhile private schools converted into fully public schools. To a large extent, this shift toward government administration of the state's schools was a response to larger social and economic forces created by the dawn of the industrial and technological age, demographic changes, and the changing role and status of the extended family and social networks. The shift was also part and parcel of the larger expansion of governments—both in the United States and abroad—into the business of fostering and improving the public welfare and social equality (Higgs, 1987).

The 1960s saw some movement toward privatization, as groups wishing to divert public funds to private schools made some inroads. If anything, however, this was the exception that proved the rule. When there was an attempt to provide direct aid to private and parochial schools as outlined in Public Act 100 (more popularly known as the parochiaid bill), a strong coalition formed and successfully amended the state's constitution to restrict *any* form of public aid—direct or indirect—to private schools. This amendment, known as the parochiad amendment, was successfully passed in the November 1970 election, with the support of 57 percent of voters. This amendment provided one of the strongest legal barriers to public subsidy of private schools in the country and marked the farthest swing toward public dominance in the state's public-private pendulum in educational policy. But change was just around the corner.

Privatization by Other Means: The Pendulum Swings Back

In the wake of the parochiaid amendment came a number of attempts to remove the constitutional obstacle to providing public funding of private schools. Proposal H in 1978 sought to institute a system of school vouchers in the state. However, the measure was rejected by 74 percent of the voters. Another more recent voucher bid, Proposal 1, would have provided vouchers to students in districts with a graduation rate of two-thirds or lower and to districts that approved vouchers through a school board vote or a public referendum.[4] This measure was defeated in 2000 with 70 percent of the voters opposed.

The failure of these vigorous and highly visible attempts at privatization in no way signals defeat for the idea, however. A number of other less controversial and less strident reforms have effectively introduced competition, choice, the use of market mechanisms, and deregulation, and have partially shifted control of schools from local districts to state agencies. In doing so, the reforms have accomplished many of the goals of the restructuring movement discussed above. More generally, these reforms have also marked a shift from the formalist to the functionalist understanding of what it means to be a public school (see Chapter 1). These reforms also represent a shift from seeing education as a "public good" to seeing it as a "private good" (Englund, 1993; Levin, 2000; Lubienski, 2000). We briefly summarize three such reforms.

Intradistrict choice and magnet schools. In 1991, Michigan adopted an open-enrollment law that promoted choice within districts (i.e., intra-district choice). Magnet schools introduced another form of intra-district choice during the 1980s and 1990s. Magnet schools are district schools or learning centers with a particular profile and curriculum designed to attract students of different racial backgrounds from throughout the district. In this way, magnet schools serve as one response to racial segregation in school enrollment. The federal government has provided grants to districts wishing to establish magnet schools, and the number of magnet schools and districts that establish magnets has grown dramatically during the late 1980s and 1990s. Today magnet schools are still used to reduce racial isolation,[5] but they are increasingly seen as superior options within the public sector for all students.

School finance reform. The second reform came with the passage of Proposal A in 1994. This provision shifted funding for all public schools from reliance on local property taxes to reliance on the state sales tax, which was increased from 4 percent to 6 percent. Under this system, funding to districts is based largely on head counts, as opposed to local property values. An important consequence of the new system is that money follows students and thus introduces market mechanisms and signals to school finance.[6]

Schools of choice. A third reform related to charter schools was the so-called schools of choice reform, which was implemented in 1996. While the reform at first allowed families to choose schools within a given intermediate school district (ISD), it was later expanded to allow for choice among schools in contiguous ISDs. Before this time, intra-district choice was available to interested families, but seldom exercised. While *intra*-district choice remains a local issue, *inter*-district choice was spelled out in the state-sponsored schools of choice program. Under this program, districts are required to announce the number of places open, accept applications, and then choose students based on a lottery. More than 26,000 students took part in the schools of choice program during the 2000-01 school year.

Clearly, these three reforms are all linked by a common desire to increase choice among schools and to introduce market forces into the operation of schools. As such, they reflect the same forces that led to charter schools and helped pave the way toward the impressive growth in the state's charter movement (see Chapter 3). It also seems clear that attempts to implement further reforms will be proposed—and perhaps adopted—in the future. One such reform might be a universal tuition tax credit plan. Proposed by the Mackinac Center in 1997, the plan would allow Michigan taxpayers to claim a tax credit against certain state taxes for tuition paid on behalf of public or non-public K-12 students.[7] While the plan was never brought before voters in a referendum, many anticipate that the tuition tax credit plan will be reintroduced in the coming years, especially given the recent failure of the voucher proposal.

The education system in Michigan—like the education systems in other states and countries—experienced a number of shifts in policy objectives over the past century. These shifts can be mapped out in the proposed and enacted legislation, amendments to the Constitution, and court rulings. Appendix A provides a comprehensive and detailed review of major developments and milestones that have affected the public-private balance in the Michigan education system.

The Emergence of Michigan's Charter School Law

Michigan's charter school law was one of the first and is regarded as among the strongest charter school laws in the country. Following in the footsteps of Minnesota (1991) and California (1992), Michigan's charter law (Public Act 362) was passed in 1993, along with similar laws in Colorado, Georgia, Massachusetts, New Mexico, and Wisconsin. Michigan currently has more charter schools than the other states in the "class of 1993" and more charter schools than any other state, save for Arizona and California. The next chapter provides more detail on the structure of Michigan charter schools. For now, we conclude this chapter by exploring some of the specific political forces and actors that helped initiate the state's experiment with charter schools. These actors include the governor, the state board of education, the state superintendent of education, a number of think tanks and interest groups, and one particular state university.[8] Examining the movers and shakers behind Michigan's charter school reforms provides a richer sense of the goals behind charter schools and other reforms than one can glean from merely reading statutes and other formal pronouncements.[9]

The governor. The driving force behind Michigan's charter school reform was Governor John Engler. A Republican elected in 1990, Engler has gained national visibility as an education reformer. The governor's three consecutive four-year terms have allowed him to plan and implement a wide range of reforms, many of which have been described above. In spite of his apparent lack of support for the 2000 voucher proposal, Engler has consistently supported reforms and efforts to promote choice and weaken the public school establishment. In advancing charter schools, Engler (1993b) predicted "nothing less than a renaissance of public education in Michigan" that, by then end of the decade, would make "Michigan schools . . . the envy of the world."

State board of education. Another key actor in the creation of charter schools in Michigan was the state board of education. During the 1990s, the board was instrumental in its public advocacy of drastic and immediate school reform, primarily through the mechanisms of choice, competition, and charters. Constitutionally, the board is responsible for overseeing public and non-public elementary and secondary education in Michigan. But it also wields influence over the tone of public debates on education through public meetings and statements. A number of board members have been very influential in advocating reforms to the state's public schools, particularly W. Clark Durant III. Durant, who had a stint as board president, took a publicly combative stance in attacking the public school establishment and espousing change. He even directed a failed effort to eliminate school districts in favor of publicly traded "Public Education Corporations." He is a founding board member of the Education Leaders Council, which is affiliated with the pro school choice Center for Education Reform.

State superintendent of public instruction. As the chief education officer in the state, the state superintendent of public instruction was also a key player in the charter reform. One particularly important superintendent was Arthur Ellis, who held the office between 1995 and 2001. A former president of Central Michigan University, Ellis was appointed by Governor Engler to serve as director of the Michigan Department of Commerce before becoming state superintendent. In 2001, he stepped down as superintendent, leaving leadership of the state board (now dominated by Democrats) to Thomas Watkins, who was selected by the board as state superintendent. Watkins had served under a former Democratic governor and is seen by many as an advocate of public education. The work of the state board of education has come under attack by Governor Engler since Ellis left office.

Think tanks and interest groups. The Mackinac Center for Public Policy, based in Midland, Michigan, is a state-based think tank started by Engler and others to advance free-market solutions in public policy. The Center, which has recently entered into a partnership with The Goldwater Institute of Arizona, promotes privatization across a number of issues, particularly education. For instance, it advocates the universal tuition tax credit discussed above. The Mackinac Center is largely funded by contributions from the Dow (of Dow Chemical fame) and DeVos (of the Amway fortune) families, as well from foundations and corporations (see Lubienski, 2001). The organization uses research by its staff and associated scholars in popularizing the philosophical groundwork for privatization reforms. These efforts come largely in the form of opinion pieces and research reports directed at shaping public opinion.[10]

Another group, the TEACH (Towards Educational Accountability and Choice) Michigan Education Fund was also instrumental in promoting the original charter school legislation in Michigan. The group made clear that its support for school choice goes well beyond charter schools, seeing charters as only a stepping stone to a more "radical" version of a pure, free-market model (DeWeese, 1994; Lubienski, 2001). TEACH Michigan, which is now known as Michigan Learning, has supported various forms of school choice as well as a change in the state constitution that would have removed restrictions on state support for non-public schools.

The Michigan Association of Public School Academies (MAPSA) lobbies local, state, and federal policymakers on issues of concern to charter schools. According to the group's Web site, "MAPSA promotes the vision and benefits of charter schools, underscoring individual and collective successes."[11] Although MAPSA claims to be a statewide association, many charter schools are not members. In 2001, MAPSA's governing board was comprised of nine members: four executive officers of for-profit EMOs; two school representatives from EMO-operated schools; two representatives from private conversion charter schools; and James Goenner, former president of MAPSA and current director of Central Michigan University's charter school office.

Public universities. As we shall see in the next chapter, one of the more striking features of Michigan's charter school movement is the role of public universities, which have the opportunity to sponsor charter schools. Central Michigan University (CMU) has played a particularly important role in the reform. The university housed the Michigan Resource Center for Charter Schools, which during its first two years alone received a half million dollars in state funding. In May 2001 this resource center was replaced by CMU's Charter Schools Development and Performance Institute, which was funded by a nearly $1 million federal grant. CMU's charter school office and resource center have provided a springboard from which individuals have gone on to serve as program officers in authorizing agencies, administrators in EMOs, charter school founders, and lobbyists. The university and its surrounding community have at various times been home for many critical actors in the charter school reform, including Governor Engler and former state superintendent Arthur Ellis.

Central Michigan University's political muscle is perhaps evident in a provision of the charter school law that restricts any state university from granting more than half of the charters from the state university sector. This provision was inserted due to legislators' concerns that CMU would move quickly and, perhaps recklessly, in promoting the governor's reform.

The dominance of CMU in the charter school reform is exemplified by the list of recipients of leadership awards from the first statewide meeting of the charter school association. Then-state superintendent of education Ellis, who is a former president of CMU, gave an award to the then-current president of CMU (Leonard Plachta) recognizing the role of CMU in the charter school reform. The new president of the charter school association (MAPSA), Dan Quisenberry, gave an award to James Goenner, director of the CMU charter school office (former president of MAPSA). A leadership award was also given to the director of a private-conversion charter school authorized by CMU. One last leadership award was given to Richard McClellan, a lawyer who was involved in the formation of Governor Engler's administration in 1990 and in the drafting the charter school law a few years later. McClellan and the firm he works for, Dykema Gossett, provided legal counsel to CMU's charter school office even during the state audit in 1997 when the CMU charter school office asserted attorney-client privilege and refused to release 34 documents. Here we have a state university deterring the state auditor general's office from obtaining documents about a publicly funded public school (Michigan Office of the Auditor General, 1997).

Conclusion

Like restructuring movements in other states and nations, the political coalition that spearheaded Michigan's charter school reform has included groups that represent both the neoliberals' support for markets and privatization as well as the neoconservatives' and religious right's desire to carve out a larger space in public schools for moral and religious instruction. Finally, the accountability inherent in the charter school concept and the state's increasing emphasis on state standards and state testing is in line with the demands of the professional and managerial middle class, which tends to support measures to improve the efficiency of government programs. This coalition of groups has successfully swung the policy pendulum in the state (back) toward a greater emphasis on private interests and institutions. More profoundly, these groups have proffered a new view of public education, one that is more open to control and ownership by nongovernmental institutions. Through a variety of reforms and arguments, these groups have sought to make way for charter schools in Michigan—and to use charter schools to leverage other similar reforms. In the next chapter we examine more closely Michigan's charter school law and the growth and development of the schools opened under its auspices.

Notes

1. Other noted factors behind restructuring include: (i) worldwide economic restructuring and emergence of post-industrial knowledge societies, (ii) cultural revitalization, (iii) decreasing legitimacy of the state, (iv) concerns about declining achievement levels, and (v) ideological and political factors (Cibulka, 1990; Johnston, 1990; Miron, 1997).

2. See also Cibulka (1990) and Johnston (1990).

3. This claim, however, has been controversial in the historical literature. See, for instance, Beadie (1999), Bowles & Gintis (1976), Church & Sedlak (1976), Kaestle (1983), Katz (2001), and Ravitch (1978).

4. Proposal 1 also would have required teacher testing in public schools and non-public schools that redeem vouchers.

5. Some studies, however, have questioned whether magnet schools are an effective tool of desegregation. See, for instance, Crain (1993), and Moore & Davenport (1990).

6. Within districts, however, decisions about the allocation of funds are made by district officials and are largely based on needs as assessed by the district, not market signals.

7. Readers may find the proposal online at [http://www.mackinac.org].

8. Lubienski (1998) has described in detail some of these organizations and links them to school reform efforts dealing with privatization and choice.

9. Readers interested in a more extensive treatment of the Michigan charter statute's political history may consult Hassel (1999) and Bulkley (1999).

10. The quality of the research conducted by the Mackinac Center has been criticized in an academic review by Cookson, Molnar, & Embree (2001). The authors also criticize the center's studies for failing to clearly distinguish ideological presuppositions from the results of empirical research.

11. The Web site for MAPSA is [http://www.charterschools.org]

3

The Charter School Reform in Michigan

In the last chapter we examined the origins of the Michigan charter school law, both in the larger international restructuring movement and in the policy and political history of Michigan itself. In this chapter we examine the legislative and regulatory framework of the Michigan law in detail. Along the way we make comparisons with the laws of other states and discuss the particular ways in which the Michigan law operationalized the charter concept outlined in Chapter 1. Having set out the legal framework, we provide a brief overview of the growth of Michigan's charter movement since the law's inception.

The Charter School Concept in Michigan

Chapter 1 provided a "crash course" in the charter concept. At the heart of the charter concept, as we saw, lies an autonomy-accountability bargain—schools receive enhanced autonomy over operations in exchange for agreeing to be held more accountable than other schools for results. This accountability, in turn, can come through both market and (through oversight) political mechanisms. While it is sensible to talk of a single "charter concept" in the abstract, each state has given the concept a slightly different operationalization (Bulkley, 1999; Hassel, 1999; Millot, 1994; RPP International, 1998).

In this section we discuss how the Michigan charter school law addresses such topics as (a) the goals of charter schools—in particular, the ones for which they are held publicly accountable; (b) school structure and how this affects their autonomy; and (c) accountability, particularly as it pertains to authorization and oversight.[1] Along the way we compare Michigan's law with those of other states. As we shall see, Michigan's charter school law is "hard-wired"[2] to encourage the rapid creation of a large number of charter schools.

Goals

Like most public laws, Michigan's charter school law sets out a number of goals. Such statements of intent allow citizens and evaluators alike to judge whether a law has accomplished its objectives.

Like virtually all charter school laws in the country, one of the most prominent goals in the Michigan law is the improvement of student achievement. Indeed, this goal lies at the heart of the autonomy-accountability bargain. Because it is a "bargain," the concept implies that the grant of autonomy is conditional—schools shall receive and maintain their autonomy *as long as* they produce results. As suggested in Chapter 1, discussion of accountability often begs the question, "accountability for what?" As the law makes clear, to a significant extent charter schools' progress toward meeting their goals is to be measured using the state's assessment system.

Related to student achievement is the goal of school-level accountability. Accountability, while certainly including performance on examinations, is not limited to it. Central to the charter concept is the notion that schools are held accountable for goals set out in each particular charter agreement. Accountability, moreover, can come either through traditional political means (i.e., oversight by democratically elected local and state officials) or through market mechanisms. As discussed in Chapter 1, market accountability consists of the extent to which charter schools' consumers vote with their feet for or against the school. As we shall see in Chapter 4, Michigan provides relatively little money to charter schools beyond the basic per-pupil grant. From this we might infer that the charter concept as operationalized in Michigan contemplates a substantial role for market accountability. This emphasis on market accountability is apparent in two other goals set out in the statute: (a) to provide parents and students greater choices among public schools; and (b) to determine whether state funds may be more effectively, efficiently, and equitably utilized by allocating them on a per-pupil basis and directly to the school.

As discussed in Chapter 1, the charter school concept's emphasis on outcomes and performance is not complete. Indeed, most charter laws also state a number of intermediate goals designed to encourage schools to use their autonomy in particular ways. As is typical of charter laws across the country, two such goals in the Michigan statute are to stimulate innovative teaching methods (see Chapter 7) and to create new professional opportunities for teachers (see Chapter 6). The emphasis on professional opportunities for teachers is related to the notion of school autonomy and local control, as it envisions a situation in which school personnel design the school and its curriculum to meet the needs of particular local student populations. The goal of innovation, in turn, is generally interpreted to mean that the schools are encouraged to generate practices that are worthy of emulation by noncharter schools. As we earlier noted, many advocates view charter schools as public education's R&D sector.

School Structure

The autonomy-accountability bargain implies that if schools are to be held more accountable for results, they should also be given more freedom in determining how to accomplish these results. Accordingly, the Michigan charter school law contains a number of provisions designed to carve out a space in which the schools may operate autonomously.

The Michigan law prescribes three paths to charter school status. Charter schools in Michigan may include converted public schools, converted private schools, and new start-ups. In this way, the Michigan law is relatively permissive. At least one state, Mississippi, allows only public conversions. Other states, such as Georgia, allow public conversions and start-ups, but do not allow private conversions. This provision, then, is part and parcel of the overall swing in Michigan's education policy pendulum toward private education detailed in Chapter 2.

Charter schools in Michigan are expected to operate at a single site and provide the configuration of grades specified in their application. However, some charter operators in Michigan are skirting this requirement by housing students in some grades at other locations and, in some cases, in other districts. Some states, such as Arizona, explicitly allow charter operators to open multiple school sites with the same charter.

Once started, charter schools are regarded by law as separate school districts and receive both a building and district classification code from the state department of education. As such, charter schools bear the responsibilities delegated to other local education authorities, such as the provision of special education. However, they also enjoy fiscal autonomy and the responsibility for debts and financial decisions that go with it. For instance, they may purchase and own buildings and properties in their own name; and they are exempt from all taxation on their earnings and property. In some states, by contrast, charter schools are legally a part of their host districts, thereby lacking autonomy over—and responsibility for—spending priorities and other fiscal decisions.

Charter school autonomy does not come as a blank check, however. Like most charter school laws, Michigan's law includes a number of constraints on charter autonomy, many of which may be viewed as an attempt to ensure that these quasi-public institutions continue to use their autonomy to pursue public goals. Examples include the Freedom of Information Act and the Open Meetings Act.[3]

Michigan's charter school law is not particularly strong in the granting of regulatory waivers. Whereas many charter laws grant all charter schools blanket waivers from a wide range of regulatory requirements, Michigan charter schools must seek such waivers on a case-by-case basis, just like other public schools. Many other charter laws, by contrast, require that charter schools comply only with health, safety, and civil rights laws.

The Michigan law, like most others, also requires that charter schools be organized and administered under a board of directors in accordance with adopted bylaws. The schools must also be organized as nonprofit entities.

Other legal requirements for Michigan charter schools involve teachers. Michigan charter schools can employ only teachers who are state certified. Exceptions to this rule permitted for districts are all valid for charter schools. Michigan is much stricter than other states in regard to teacher certification, since most other charter school laws only require a portion (e.g., 75 percent) of the teachers be certified. Michigan's certification requirements do not, however, cover university or community college faculty teaching at schools sponsored by those institutions.[4] Moreover, unlike many other states, charter schools authorized by school districts are subject to district collective bargaining agreements. This requirement has proved to be a paper tiger in light of the fact that only 7 percent of existing charter schools were authorized by local districts.

Perhaps the most notable restrictions on Michigan charter schools concern the recruiting and enrollment of students. Charter schools cannot charge tuition and are not allowed to select students based on "intellectual or athletic ability, measures of achievement or aptitude, status as a handicapped person, or any other basis that would be illegal if used by a school district" (Sec 380.504 [2]). However, charter schools may limit admission to students within a particular grade or age range. The schools must hold a public lottery or other random selection process when the number of applicants exceeds the available places. Students previously enrolled are exempt from the lottery, and siblings of enrolled students are given priority. The principle of openness, in terms of recruitment and selection of students, is one of the things that differentiates the charter concept from vouchers and is one of the things that, in theory, helps maintain the schools' public character.

Authorization, Oversight, and Governance

In Chapter 1 we noted that the charter concept involves a transformation in, among other things, the way schools are governed. At the heart of the transformation lies an emphasis of the "private good" characteristics of education over its "public good" characteristics. As we saw, public goods, since they affect a large range of interests and individuals, are usually governed through a process that involves large, heterogeneous groups of citizens. The reconceptualization of education as a private good, therefore, goes hand-in-hand with a narrowing of the politics of education. The most radical form of this narrowing is market accountability, in which schools are held accountable for satisfying one consumer at a time.

Important as market accountability is to the charter concept, it is far from the only form of accountability. Like traditional public schools, charter schools are also subject to political accountability, which involves subjecting school decisions to the influence of citizens and their elected representatives. In Michigan, as elsewhere, schools receive their charters from authorizing bodies that, in turn, are responsible for ensuring that the schools live up to their obligations under their charter agreements. Moreover, Michigan's charter school law, like those in most states, requires that charter schools be governed by a local board.

Authorization. Charter schools are typically granted five-year contracts that may be issued by one of four types of authorizing agencies: (i) the board of a K-12 school district, (ii) an intermediate school district board, (iii) the board of a community college, or (iv) the governing board of a state university. Where many groups are seeking charters, they are issued on on a competitive basis. Unsuccessful applicants to local school boards can either petition the board to place the question of issuing a contract on the ballot for the next school election or apply to another authorizing agency. Authorizers may also approve charters contingent upon amendments and revisions. Among the more common revisions is the range of grades offered by the proposed school. In some cases, requests have been made to revise the school's name and mission.

The diversity of potential charter authorizers in Michigan is one of the factors that marks it as a strong charter school state. In states with weaker laws, such as Illinois and Kansas, charters may be granted only by local school districts, often subject to a clearance process at the state board of education to ensure compliance with state law. In Michigan, sponsor type determines from where charter schools may recruit students. Local school districts, intermediate school districts, and community colleges may charter only schools that will operate within their boundaries, while state universities can charter schools anywhere in the state.[5]

Oversight. The authorizer has the responsibility for overseeing a charter school's compliance with the charter and all applicable laws and can retain up to 3 percent of the state school aid received to cover the costs of providing oversight. The charter may be revoked by the authorizer for any of the following reasons: (i) failure to meet the educational goals set forth in the contract;[6] (ii) failure to comply with applicable laws; (iii) failure to meet generally accepted public sector accounting principles; or (iv) the existence of one or more other grounds for revocation as specified in the contract (380.507 [1]). The decision to revoke a contract is final and is not subject to review by any court or state agency.

An authorizer may contract with another authorizer to oversee any school it charters, but the oversight must be sufficient to ensure that the authorizing body can certify that the school is in compliance with statutes, rules, and the terms of the contract. This option was not used until the 2001-02 school year when a Native American community college in the state's Upper Peninsula began chartering schools downstate. In this case, the college arranged for Ferris State University to oversee the schools for the community college. The state board may suspend the power of an authorizer to grant new charters if it finds that the authorizer is not engaging in appropriate and continuous oversight.

Like other public schools, charter schools are subject to the leadership and general supervision of the state board of education. However, a number of factors make this a dubious connection. One is poor communication between authorizers and the state. The other is the state's poor record in submitting a mandated descriptive annual report on charter schools. Thus far, only one report, on the 1997-98 school year, has been submitted—and the report was not released until 1999 (Michigan Department of Education, 1999a).

Governance. Charter schools in Michigan, as elsewhere, are governed by local boards. Unlike traditional schools, where board members are elected by voters, charter school board members are appointed by the authorizer. As public bodies themselves, the authorizers theoretically provide a link between voters and charter schools. However, the connection is clearly more indirect and weaker than in traditional school districts. In practice, board members are selected by the schools' founders, often with an eye toward finding representatives of certain viewpoints. Often school founders recommend themselves to the authorizer as board members. When board members leave, replacements are selected by existing board members.

The selection of board members by authorizers and founders, along with the selection of replacements by existing board members, serves to narrow the range of interests represented by charter school boards.[7] This, as we saw in Chapter 1, is part and parcel of the charter concept's reconceptualization of education as a private good.

In sum, Michigan's charter school law is widely regarded as one of the strongest (i.e., most permissive) in the nation. As we have seen, the law allows many paths by which applications can gain charters, with school districts, public universities, and intermediate school districts all authorized to grant charters. Moreover, both public and private schools may convert to charter schools. However, the law is more restrictive than some with respect to the granting of waivers and teacher certification. Overall, the Center for Education Reform, which maintains perhaps the most widely cited ranking system of charter schools, ranks Michigan's law as third strongest, after Arizona and Delaware.[8]

The Growth and Development of Michigan Charter Schools

In this section—and in the remainder of the book—we seek to determine whether the development of Michigan's charter schools reflects the characteristics and goals of the state's statute. Put another way, to what extent has the actual implementation of the law reflected its formal structure?

The question of implementation is complex and multifaceted. There are many criteria against which to evaluate implementation. In this section we focus on the extent to which charter schools have provided Michigan families with a set of public school choices. Those who study consumer choice often divide the discussion into a quantitative and a qualitative element. The quantitative element involves the number of choices available in the marketplace. Thus, we examine the growth in the *number* of charter school students. The qualitative element involves differences in the *type* of products offered. In this connection, we examine trends in the school size, target population, and mission. Later chapters examine other aspects of the law's implementation, including student and teacher characteristics, student achievement, systemic impact, and customer satisfaction.

Growth in the Number of Schools and Students

Perhaps the simplest way to assess the implementation of Michigan's charter school law is in terms of the number of schools opened. Surprisingly, this basic question turns out to be rather difficult to answer with any precision in Michigan. To be sure, getting an accurate count of charter schools in any state is made difficult by the characteristics of many charter schools. These include the fact that some schools close shortly after opening, others receive charters but never open, and still others have changed locales since opening. Other complicating factors include turnover in school officials responsible for reporting data to the state, cutbacks in the Michigan Department of Education, and the fact that some schools have taken advantage of a loophole in the statutory cap on the number of schools by operating several school sites under a single charter. Some counts include a school operated by Wayne State University that was actually established under a separate piece of legislation. This school opened in 1991, which was two years before the charter school law was even passed. Michigan has been a state known for high-quality and readily accessible school data. Nevertheless, in terms of data on charter schools, it has failed to provide reliable data on the number of charter schools in operation during any given year.

These caveats aside, it is undeniable that the number of charter schools has grown rapidly since the law's inception. According to our best count, the number of schools in operation rose from 41 during the 1995-96 school year to

184 by 2000-01. Altogether there were 192 charters granted by the 2000-01 school year, but eight of them have since closed (just before the start of the 2001-02 school year another two closed). Additionally, there have been at least three other schools that have appeared on various lists because they initially received a charter, but they have never opened.

The growth is also impressive when viewed in terms of the number of students enrolled. Total enrollments increased from 5,100 during the 1995-96 school year to 56,500 in 2000-01. Figure 3.1 illustrates the growth of charter schools in Michigan both in terms of the number of schools and in the number of students these schools enrolled.

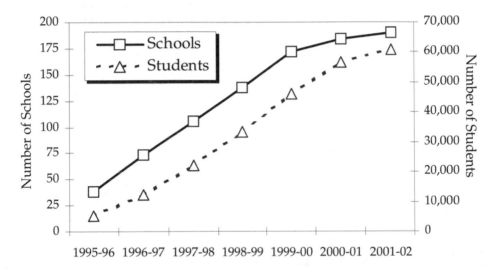

Figure 3.1 Growth in the Number of Charter Schools in Michigan

One factor responsible for growth in the number of students has been an increase in the average size of charter schools. Much of this growth has come as charter schools have added more grade levels over time. For instance, many schools that initially served Grades K-4 now serve Grades K-8. Indeed, the average size of charter schools has grown from 135 students in 1995-96 to 320 in 2000-01. Michigan charter schools are thus considerably larger than charter schools nationwide. A recent national study (RPP International, 2000) put the median charter school size across the nation at 137; the median charter school size in Michigan is 288. Perhaps more striking, the average Michigan charter school is not much smaller than the average noncharter public school in the state (480 students). Much of the growth in average charter school size appears to be due to EMO schools. According to recent enrollment figures, the average EMO-run charter school enrolls 360 students, compared with 204 for non-EMO charter schools. In short, Michigan charter schools are generally not the small, intimate settings envisioned by the movement's founders.

Figure 3.1 also shows that the rate of growth in charter schools, while fast at first, has slowed in recent years. On average, 35 new schools were opened each year until 2000 when the cap on state university-sponsored charter schools was met. Since then the rate of growth has slowed to less than 10 per year (see Figure 3.2). No doubt, the decline in the movement's growth is largely due to the legislative caps on the number of schools. The number of charter schools sponsored by state universities was capped at 85 by 1996, 100 by 1997, 125 by 1998, and 150 thereafter. Due to the fixed cap, only 7 of the 15 schools opened for the 2000-01 school year were chartered by state universities. We know of no university-sponsored schools opened during the 2001-02 school year.

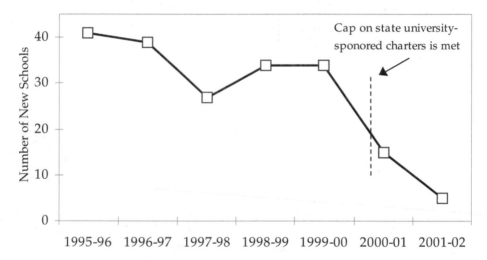

Figure 3.2 Growth in the Number of New Charter Schools in Michigan

A related factor slowing the growth in the number of charter schools is a statutory cap on the number of charters granted by any one state university. The law states that the number of such schools shall not exceed 50 by 1996; thereafter, no single state university could sponsor more than half the total number of charters issued. This statutory provision was in reference to Central Michigan University, which played a strong role in implementing this reform.

It is striking how quickly the statutory caps were reached in Michigan. This no doubt reflects many of the provisions in the charter school law that have earned it the reputation as one of the strongest in the nation. One such provision is the wide range of potential charter authorizers; a total of 23 such entities have granted charters since the beginning of the movement. Moreover, unlike other states, local districts may not veto the creation of a charter school.[9] In total only

7 percent of the charter schools currently operating are sponsored by local districts, and 12 percent are sponsored by intermediate school districts or service agencies.

Private education management organizations (EMOs) have also served as an engine of charter school growth. While charter schools were intended by many to provide an opportunity for local educators and community members to start their own schools, individuals and businesspeople from across the nation soon learned of the opportunity in the state. In a few cases, individuals relocated to Michigan to start their own schools. In other cases, for-profit EMOs began identifying communities where they could start schools of their own. In Chapter 10, on EMOs, we will explore these companies in greater detail.

Another factor driving the growth in the number of charter schools is the political climate. The governor has pushed the reform through the persons he has appointed to governing boards of state universities (which can grant charters) and through incentives (and, in some cases, threats) to these boards. The former president of Eastern Michigan University, for instance, told the state's first charter school meeting in 1998 that he was opposed to charter schools. But after the governor threatened his university with cuts in allocations he said that he had "mixed feelings" about charter schools. The university has since begun sponsoring charter schools. Administrators at several other state universities shared similar stories during interviews we conducted in 1997 and 1998.

In spite of impressive growth in the number of charter schools and students, Michigan's charter movement remains a small portion of the state's public school system. As of the 2000-01 academic year, charter schools enrolled approximately 3.7 percent of all public school students in Michigan, up from 0.3 percent in 1995-96. Still, even this small slice of the public education pie puts Michigan third in terms of overall share of public school enrollment, after the District of Columbia (13 percent) and Arizona (11 percent), and well ahead of the national average of 0.8 percent (RPP International, 2000).[10] State averages, however, mask the fact that in some regions of the state charter school enrollment comprises a much larger share of public school enrollment. In the southwest Michigan city of Holland, for instance, charter schools enrolled 17 percent of all public school students as of 1999. In some rural districts, moreover, a single charter school can enroll as many as 38 percent of public school enrollments in the local district, as was the case with Boyne Falls in the northen Lower Peninsula.[11] By contrast, in Detroit, which has the largest number of charter schools, only 6.6 percent of total public school enrollments are in charter schools. Figure 3.3 provides a map showing all charter schools open as of the 1999-2000 academic year. Here, too, one can see that some regions of the state, particularly the large urban areas, have a significant number of charter schools while vast portions of the state have no charter schools at all.

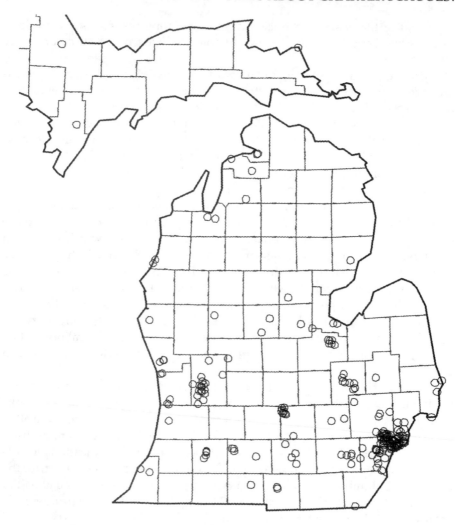

Figure 3.3 Location of Michigan Charter Schools

Characteristics of the Schools

In the previous section, we examined the quantitative aspect of choice in Michigan charter schools and found that there has been impressive growth in the number of charter-related choices for students and parents. However, a large number of choices might be cold comfort to those seeking alternatives unless those schools represent a wide variety of educational offerings. We turn now to the qualitative aspect of choice and to examining school missions and target populations.

As discussed earlier in this chapter, there are several pathways to the creation of a charter school. These include conversion of existing public and private schools and new start-ups. For the purposes of our analysis, we distinguish four types of charter schools.

Converted private schools. Private school conversions (which include parochial schools) were most common among the first schools chartered in the state. In fact, some authorizing agencies initially considered applications only from these schools. More recently, they have become less prevalent, making up approximately 14 percent of all charter schools today. This still places Michigan ahead of the national average of 10 percent (RPP International, 2000).

Converted public schools. A handful of charter schools in the state were formerly public schools that opted to become charter schools. In all cases that we are aware of, these were former alternative high schools. Thus far, there have been only eight public school conversions, which accounts for 4 percent of the charter schools. Nationally, 17.7 percent of charter schools are public conversions (RPP International, 2000).

"Mom and Pop" schools. Other charter schools in Michigan have been started by individuals or small groups of concerned adults. These schools, because of their small size and limited economic clout, have often struggled to secure buildings and facilities. Moreover, authorizers are granting fewer charters to these schools, perhaps because they require more assistance and are usually more vulnerable to shifts in enrollments. Many of these schools have over time been taken over by EMOs. During the initial years of the reform, this was the biggest group of schools. Currently, only about 10 percent of the charter schools remain in this category.

EMO-operated schools. EMO-operated schools have also been referred to as "franchise" or "cookie cutter" schools. EMOs have started these schools or have been invited to take over the management of the schools. Typically, EMO-operated schools must follow the established curriculum and management prescribed by the company. Nearly all charter schools opened in recent years were started and are operated by EMOs. Altogether, nearly 73 percent of all charter schools are currently operated by EMOs (see Chapter 10 for more information about EMOs).

The individual leaders and groups of people drawn to the reform come from extremely varied backgrounds. The charter school reform has attracted home schoolers and de-schoolers.[12] It has attracted "hippies" as well as groups from the Religious Right. It has also attracted "back to basics" groups and those that want high technology and computers to be heavily involved in instruction. In many cases, charter school founders are dissatisfied with district offerings, including large class sizes, the absence of certain types of courses, and safety and discipline issues. In some cases, these schools are created by those who wish to expose students to certain cultural and moral values or to inculcate good citizenship. For some of the private conversions, a key motivation is the desire for a more stable financial base. Over time, however, grassroots and small "mom and pop" groups have been less likely to initiate charters. In large part, this is due to the fact that university authorizers often will not consider proposals without EMO involvement.

The variety in school founders is reflected in the schools' missions, target populations, and instructional foci. While some schools cater only to elementary grades, a few provide only upper secondary education. Some schools have a strong desire not to grow in size, while others intend to expand as soon as they can. Some schools advocate Total Quality Management and its emphasis on testing, while at the other extreme are schools that openly oppose any form of testing. We explore charter schools' educational offerings more thoroughly in Chapter 7.[13]

There is also considerable variation in the types of students targeted by charter schools' programs. While some schools target at-risk students in inner-city districts, others resemble elite suburban schools and private school academies. While overall, charter schools enroll a similar proportion of low-income and nonwhite students as their host districts, there are pockets of segregation in the state's charter schools. Charter-noncharter disparities in special education enrollment is even more noteworthy. Perhaps the most striking difference between charter and noncharter schools is that the former overwhelmingly target students in lower and middle grades. This trend is especially apparent in EMO-run charter schools. Chapter 5 contains a more thorough analysis of demographic patterns in Michigan charter schools.

Conclusion

This chapter has provided an overview of the Michigan charter school law and the growth of charter schools since its passage. Michigan's charter law, as we have seen, is in most respects among the most permissive in the country. Among the features encouraging the growth of charter schools are the fact that many types of entities may grant charters and that many types of organizations, groups, and individuals may seek charters. Growth patterns suggest that, in terms of the sheer number of schools, Michigan has lived up to its reputation as a hot spot for charter school development.

In spite of the impressive growth in the number of charter schools and students, charter schools remain a fairly small part of Michigan's public school system, enrolling just under 4 percent of all public school students in the state. Much of this, of course, is related to the cap on the number of schools sponsored by public universities—one of the main engines of charter school development in Michigan. In the concluding chapter of the book, we consider the wisdom of the cap on the number of charters and other issues of policy design and implementation. For now, however, we turn to the issue of charter school finance.

Notes

1. Our goal in this section is not to provide a comprehensive review of the Michigan charter school law. Readers interested in a more detailed exposition may consult Bulkley (1999) and Hassel (1999).

2. For a discussion of the concept of hard-wiring as it pertains to policy design, see McCubbins, Noll, & Weingast (1987) and Moe (1989).

3. Bierlein (1997) notes that the public school aspects of charter schools are the "protection for students and public funds."

4. We are not aware of any faculty from authorizing entities teaching in charter schools. In fact, many faculty, particularly in colleges of education, have been hostile to the charter school concept and the manner in which the reform has been implemented. We have, however, seen university staff, from the respective charter school offices, step in as administrators to keep troubled charter schools afloat.

5. When the governor was unsuccessful in persuading the state's legislature to lift the cap on the number of charter schools that could be sponsored by state universities, he found a loophole by allowing a Native American community college in the state's Upper Peninsula to sponsor charter schools run by Mosaica Inc. in urban centers nearly 400 miles away. It was argued that since this community college could serve Native Americans throughout the state, its jurisdiction was statewide rather than the community in which it was located.

6. The charter or contract must include the charter school's educational goals, a description of the school's compliance and educational performance monitoring methods, procedures for revoking the contract and grounds for revoking the contract, and requirements and procedures for annual financial audits.

7. Horn & Miron (1999) discuss and compare the roles and functions of charter school boards with the boards of traditional pubic school districts.

8. Other studies that have evaluated or rated state charter laws include Bierlein, (1997), Mintrom & Vegari (1998), and RPP International (2000).

9. In some states this local "veto" may be overridden by appeals to state boards of education (e.g., Illinois) and special charter appeals boards (e.g., Pennsylvania). However, sometimes districts do have incentives to grant charters in spite of their concerns. For example, one district superintendent explained that the reason his board granted a charter was that "they knew that if they didn't grant the charter Central Michigan University would." By sponsoring the school,

the district could retain 3 percent of the state funding and could exercise some oversight of the school, which would not be allowed if a state university granted the charter.

10. We calculated the proportion of charter school students as a percentage of total public school enrollments in Arizona and Washington, DC based on the most recent figures (i.e., 2000-01 school year) for total charter school enrollments and the most recent total enrollments for the state. In both cases this involved data for the 2000-01 year. The figures were obtained from the Arizona Department of Education [http://www.ade.state.az.us/] and the District of Columbia Public Schools [http://www.k12.dc.us/dcps/home.html].

11. Glomm, Harris, & Lo (2000), moreover, found that district enrollments were positively and statistically significantly related to the number of charter schools in a district, controlling for a number of other factors.

12. "De-schooling" refers to the ideas of Ivan Illich spelled out in *Deschooling Society* (1971). Illich argues for the disestablishment of schooling, which he saw as a model of our centralized consumer society. Instead he advocated for nonformal and informal approaches to education and the development of educational webs or networks. For Illich, schooling and education were opposing ideas.

13. Readers may also consult our technical reports on Michigan charter schools (Horn & Miron, 1999, 2000), which include detailed school-by-school tables. These report are available on-line at [http://www.wmich.edu/evalctr/].

4

Charter School Finance

With F. Howard Nelson

Charter schools are, as we argued in Chapter 1, a new kind of public school, including, as they do, elements traditionally associated with both public and private schools. One of the most important ways charter schools differ from other public schools is in the charter concept's attempt to bring a measure of market accountability into the public education sector. Charter school funding is largely based on the number of students that the school enrolls. Consequently, charter schools that fail to attract and retain students will go out of business.

Not surprisingly, charter school finance has been a subject of intense debate and controversy, with charter proponents claiming that the schools get too little and critics claiming that they get too much. In this chapter we explore charter school finance in Michigan with an eye toward determining whether funding levels are adequate for the accomplishment of the schools' missions. It is important to emphasize at the outset that an appropriate analysis of charter school finance must go well beyond simple claims about whether charter schools get more or less money than noncharter public schools. Instead, the real question centers on whether charter schools get more or less than noncharter public schools that offer *comparable services to similar students*.

As we shall see, case studies of the finances of a small number of representative Michigan charter schools (based on data from the 1999-2000 academic year) provide evidence that while charter schools get less money per

---

Dr. F. Howard Nelson is a Senior Associate Director at the American Federation of Teachers and principal investigator on the National Charter School Finance Study. Two of his colleagues, Ed Muir and Rachel Drown, also provided assistance in preparing this chapter.

pupil than traditional public schools, they still receive more than traditional public schools receive for similar programs and similar students. This is largely a consequence of the fact that many Michigan charter schools "specialize" in low-cost, basic elementary education, with few students requiring special educational services.

Later in the book we suggest that the financial incentives built into Michigan's system of charter school finance have important consequences for patterns of student enrollment (Chapter 5) and teacher employment (Chapter 6), and might have implications for charter schools' ability to innovate and leverage reform in other schools (Chapter 7) and effectively raise student achievement (Chapter 8). In Chapter 11 we seek to relate the analysis of charter school costs to these outcomes and explore policy options to change the aforementioned incentives.

Along with attempting to assess whether the financial playing field is level between charter and noncharter public schools, the chapter provides important contextual information on charter school finance in Michigan. First, we present a brief overview of how the state funds charter schools. As we shall see, the state's system of charter school finance provides clear incentives for charter schools to avoid high-need and high-cost students. Next, the chapter provides aggregate data on the finances of all Michigan charter schools and finds, among other things, that the proportion of charter school expenditures on instruction-related items is considerably lower than in noncharter public schools and has declined over time. Recognizing the limitations of aggregate data, however, we present in-depth case studies of revenues and expenditure patterns for four representative charter schools. The chapter ends by comparing charter and noncharter schools offering similar services. Here, we conclude that charter schools enjoy cost and revenue advantages over noncharter public schools.

How Michigan Funds Charter Schools[1]

The charter school concept features an attempt to create a quasi-market for public education—at least among charter schools. A key element of this quasi-market is a funding system in which funding follows the student. Under such a system, charter schools must recruit and retain students in order to remain fiscally viable.

Michigan charter schools receive the per-student foundation allowance of the school district in which the school building is physically located. As of 1998-99, this amount was not to exceed $5,962.[2] In 2001-02, this amount is not to exceed $6,500. Unlike charter schools in a number of other states (e.g., Pennsylvania) public funds are distributed directly from the state, with local school districts making no direct payments to charter schools. As in other states, the money follows the students to the school at which they are enrolled.[3] The state, moreover, pays for students moving to charter schools from private schools.

In addition to the state foundation grant, charter schools may apply for and receive other types of state and federal grants. For example, charter schools can apply for federal and state categorical funding (grants made for specific educational purposes) on the same basis as school districts. Additionally, federal start-up funding is available to the schools, which as of 1999-2000 provided planning grants of at least $40,000 per school and implementation grants of up to $100,000 per school. While the state provides no facilities assistance, Michigan law specifically allows charter schools to issue tax-exempt securities.[4]

Charter schools are eligible for special education funding on the same basis as school districts, but a two-year funding lag creates a financial disincentive for offering special education programs. State special education funding covers only about 20 percent of actual special education costs. The remainder of the costs are typically drawn from the each school's general operating funds. In most areas of Michigan, ISDs coordinate, fund, or provide many special education services.[5]

The remainder of this chapter examines how much charter schools receive in revenues, how much they expend, and how these compare with the finances of noncharter public schools. Most of the analysis presented is based on case studies of representative charter schools. Before turning to the case studies, however, we briefly present aggregate data on expenditures in Michigan's charter schools in order to provide a broad context of comparison for the case studies. Our purpose here is to provide a general sense of the patterns and trends in expenditures among charter schools.

General Fund Expenditures

Charter schools and other reforms that bring elements of privatization to the provision of public services often promise to deliver those services more efficiently. In particular, advocates of these reforms often claim that market competition will attack the "bureaucracy problem" by reducing the amount of administrative overhead found in traditional public sector institutions.

To assess whether Michigan charter schools spend public funds more efficiently than noncharter public schools, we compared the proportion of expenditures devoted to instruction with that of noncharter public schools. Table 4.1 shows trends in charter school spending from 1995-96 through 1999-2000, the most recent year for which information is available. The analysis focuses on the general fund, which captures almost all charter school financial activity, including facility costs.[6] The table shows that charter schools spend a smaller proportion on instruction than host school districts do, especially on

Table 4.1 General Fund Expenditures

	1995-96	1996-97	1997-98	1998-99	1999-00	Change
Host school districts						
Instruction–added needs	12.6%	13.3%	14.0%	13.6%	13.5%	0.9%
Instruction–all other	49.8%	49.9%	48.9%	48.7%	48.5%	–1.3%
Support services	37.6%	36.8%	37.1%	37.6%	38.0%	0.4%
Current operating–$	$6,254	$6,338	$6,411	$6,696	$7,074	$820
Capital projects	$206	$192	$193	$239	$222	$16
All charter schools						
Instruction–added needs	4.1%	3.8%	3.0%	3.7%	4.0%	–0.1%
Instruction–all other	52.9%	51.6%	49.3%	48.7%	45.8%	–7.1%
Support services	43.0%	44.6%	47.8%	47.6%	50.1%	7.1%
Current operating–$	$5,033	$5,497	$5,961	$5,831	$6,511	$1,478
Capital projects	$528	$731	$516	$503	$553	-$25
Leona Group						
Instruction–added needs	0.4%	0.3%	2.0%	3.0%	4.7%	4.3%
Instruction–all other	56.8%	53.4%	44.8%	43.6%	41.7%	–15.1%
Support services	42.7%	46.3%	53.1%	53.4%	53.5%	10.8%
Current operating–$	$6,111	$5,744	$5,865	$5,651	$5,978	–$133
Capital projects	$861	$1,177	$612	$355	$123	–$738
National Heritage Academies						
Instruction–added needs	0.5%	3.8%	5.6%	4.0%	4.4%	3.9%
Instruction–all other	30.1%	34.5%	43.4%	37.9%	39.2%	9.1%
Support services	69.3%	61.7%	51.0%	58.1%	56.4%	–12.9%
Current operating–$	$5,393	$5,643	$6,225	$6,217	$6,346	$953
Capital projects *	$1	$8	$57	$0	$60	$61
Edison Schools Inc.**						
Instruction–added needs	-	-	-	-	4.7%	-
Instruction–all other	-	-	-	-	45.1%	-
Support services	-	-	-	-	52.6%	-
Current operating–$	-	-	-	-	$6,498	-
Capital projects	-	-	-	-	$119	-

Source: *Bulletin 1014*, Michigan Department of Education.

* Costs for capital projects cover facilities and equipment. Many schools, such as those operated by National Heritage Academies, lease facilities and sometimes equipment from the EMO or a sister company. In these instances, the capital costs are likely reported with operating costs, which explains the low or nonexistant expenditures on capital projects.

** Edison operated only two charter schools in Michigan in 1997-98 and three in 1997-98. Since then one of the charter schools has ended its contract with Edison.

programs for added needs (primarily special education and compensatory education). This finding is highlighted in Figure 4.1, which graphs trends in instructional expenditures as a percentage of total expenditures from 1995-96 to 1999-2000. Over time there has been a slight decrease in the proportion of charter school spending devoted to instruction. In part, this may be explained by some instruction-related activities being encompassed by management agreements, which may be recorded as support services.

As noted in Chapter 1 and detailed in Chapter 10, one of the most notable features of Michigan's charter school movement is the prevalence of schools operated by education management organizations (EMOs). Accordingly, both Table 4.1 and Figure 4.1 break out the expenditure data for three of the most prevalent EMOs in the state. The three EMOs profiled in Table 4.1 spend even less on instruction than the average for all charter schools. Schools managed by National Heritage Academies and the Leona Group used about 45 percent of spending for instruction in 1999-2000. Edison Schools Inc. (for which only one year of data was available) devoted about 50 percent of spending to instruction. The Leona Group shows a pattern of declining expenditures for instruction-related activities, while National Heritage Academies showed increasing expenditures on instruction. Edison Schools Inc. spent about $200 per pupil more than National Heritage Academies and about $500 per pupil more than the Leona Group. This largely confirms findings from other studies of charter school finance in Michigan.[7] Defenders of management companies, however, argue

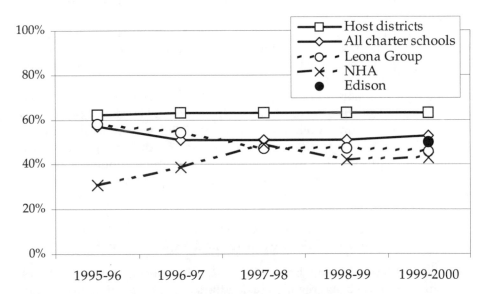

Figure 4.1 Percentage of Expenditures on Instruction-Related Activities
Note: Instructional costs include "added needs" and "all other" costs from Table 4.1.

that the inclusion of charter school rent and facility leases in the business office expenditure category explains—in part—the high administrative costs. Because these data look only at expenditures and not revenues, it is not possible to determine which company is financially more successful (or troubled).

In some sense, charter schools' relatively high administrative costs are not surprising. The main rationale for school district consolidation over the last century has been to save money by taking advantage of economies of scale. In terms of systemwide efficiency, the charter school reform has added more than 180 new administrative units to the state's list of 560 previously existing school districts. Furthermore, new or parallel oversight and administrative agencies, located primarily at state universities, cost about $180 per charter school student, and central level costs for oversight increase in most states when the state education agency is involved in assisting these new schools and taking part in oversight activities.

Charter schools face significant economy-of-scale problems. Seeking to operate numerous large schools that are often identical to each other, management companies illustrate the importance of scale to efficiency and profitability. During 2000-01, National Heritage Academies operated 22 charter schools in Michigan with an average of 448 students and the Leona Group operated 19 charter schools with an average school size of approximately 335 students per school. Edison Schools Inc. managed about 15 schools in Michigan, either as charter schools (5 charter schools averaging 926 students each) or as contract schools (i.e., schools managed under contract with school districts). As noted in Chapter 3, the average EMO-run charter school in Michigan enrolls 360 students, compared with 204 for non-EMO charter schools. As a point of comparison, the average charter school in the United States enrolled 137 students in 1998-99, and 65 percent of charter schools enrolled fewer than 200 students (RPP International, 2000)

Big charter schools, however, are not the only way to cope with the diseconomies of small size. The Michigan charter school law allows schools to set their own maximum enrollment (usually by grade level) and draw students from waiting lists in order to keep enrollment and funding at optimal levels. Charter schools also have control over their own location. Population density in urban areas allows charter schools numerous opportunities to overcome some of the problems of small scale.

Case Studies of Charter School and School District Revenues and Expenditures

In the last section we presented expenditure data on all Michigan charter schools at a fairly high level of aggregation (using the so-called *Bulletin 1014* data). In this section we attempt to drill down more deeply into charter schools' revenues and expenditures using the more detailed *Form B* data.[8] Given the complexity of the *Form B* finance data, however, it is impractical to analyze a large number of schools. Thus, this more detailed analysis is based on case studies of four fairly typical Michigan charter schools. The case study approach also makes it easier to connect revenues and expenditures to the characteristics of students attending specific charter schools. As we argued at the beginning of the chapter, this is necessary in order to make fair comparisons between charter school finances and the finances of noncharter public schools.

Description of Case Schools

Each of the four case schools was selected for a specific reason. Horizons Community High School is a public conversion charter school that started as a charter school 1995. The school is located in Wyoming, a suburb of Grand Rapids (the state's second largest metropolitan area after Detroit) and represents one of 36 Michigan charter schools sponsored by school districts or intermediate school districts. The school received revenues of $6,180 per pupil in 1999-2000 and enrolled 210 students. Because the school is sponsored by the district, all students came from Wyoming Public Schools.

Knapp Charter Academy represents a typical school operated by the state's largest management company (National Heritage Academies) and is located in Forest Hills School District, a wealthy suburban district adjacent to Grand Rapids. The school opened as a K-4 school in 1997-98 and has since expanded to the middle school grades. The school, which had total revenues of $6,713 per pupil in 1999-2000, exceeded the average for all National Heritage Academy (NHA) schools by about $250 per pupil in revenues. With an enrollment of 575 students in 1999-2000, Knapp was much larger than the average National Heritage school size of 367 students at that time (the average size of the NHA schools has been growing by just under 100 students each year as the schools add a grade each year until they reach Grade 8). The school draws most of its students from other school districts, primarily Grand Rapids.

West Michigan Academy of Environmental Science (WMAES) represents a financially troubled charter school. Opened as a K-12 independent charter school in 1995-96, the school quickly fell into debt due to mismanagement, questionable land purchases and contracts with insiders and relatives, and was required by the state to prepare a deficit reduction plan. The school contracted with Leona Group in 1998. One of the first cost saving measures the management company took was to eliminate instruction at the high school level. In 1999-2000, the school enrolled 486 students (a decline from 578 student two years before), which was larger than the Leona Group average of 347 students. That same year, the school received $6,746 per pupil in total revenue, which was less than the Leona Group average of $7,042 per pupil. The school later ended its contract with Leona Group after an acrimonious relationship and hired Choice Schools Associates to manage the school. WMAES has moved 3 times and is now located in Kenowa Hills Public School District–a small 3,500 student suburb–but provides an expansive and costly transportation program in order to bring in most of its students from Grand Rapids and a few other suburbs.

Finally, the Detroit Academy of Arts and Sciences typifies a very large management company school located in one of the nation's largest cities. Opened in 1997-98, this elementary school resembles the other four charter schools managed by Edison Schools Inc. in Michigan; however, with 842 students in 1999-2000, this school was a little larger than the Edison average of 772 students at this time. Like the NHA schools, the Edison-operated charter schools have been growing each year as the schools add new grades. By the 2000-01 school year the average Edison charter school (all elementary or lower secondary grades) had increased to 926 students per school. The school received $6,766 per pupil in total revenues in 1999-2000, compared with an average of $6,753 per pupil across all five Edison charter schools in the state.

It is noteworthy that all of the case schools except the one in Detroit are located in the Grand Rapids metropolitan area. Studying three schools in one area helped us examine the process by which charter schools draw students from a wide geographic area, not just the school district in which the building is physically located. All schools had been operating for at least three years, well past their start-up phase.

Technically, the comparisons we make are with host school districts, but since 2 of the 3 schools in metropolitan Grand Rapids area draw most of their students from Grand Rapids Public Schools (GRPS) and not the district in which they lie, we have also included comparison data for GRPS.

Charter schools often enroll students with different educational needs than their host school districts. Since several revenue sources are targeted specifically at students in high-cost programs, an important component of the financial analysis must include revenue and expenditure differences with respect to the specific enrollment characteristics of charter schools and comparison host districts. Table 4.2 describes the enrollments of the case study charter schools and comparison host districts in terms of grade level, special education and low-income population. As is evident from the table, the three charter schools in the Grand Rapids area enroll fewer low-income students than the Grand Rapids Public Schools. Both Knapp Academy and WMAES, however, enroll more low-income students than the suburban school districts in which they are physically located. The Edison school in Detroit also enrolls a lower percentage of low-income students than Detroit Public Schools. The four charter schools serve substantially fewer students with special educational needs, and the special education students they do serve typically have mild and more easily remediated disabilities.

Table 4.2 Student and School Characteristics, 1999-2000

	EMO	Number of Students	Low-Income Students	Special Education	Special Education FTE	Grades
Grand Rapids P.S.		26,799	65.3%	21.5%	13.3%	K-12
Horizons Community H.S.	None	210	0.0%	0.0%	0.0%	9-12
Wyoming P.S.		5,753	31.6%	13.0%	6.1%	K-12
Knapp Charter Academy	NHA	575	10.7%	9.5%	0.5%	K-7
Forest Hills P.S.		8,095	2.5%	12.9%	3.2%	K-12
WMAES	Leona	486	38.6%	1.7%	0.6%	K-8
Kenowa Hills P.S.		3,413	19.5%	13.2%	4.7%	K-12
Detroit Acad. of Arts & Sciences	Edison	842	48.6%	4.3%	0.0%	K-5
Detroit P.S.		169,363	67.1%	11.8%	5.8%	K-12

Revenues

Revenues for the case study schools are described in Table 4.3 and illustrated graphically in Figure 4.2.[9] Average total revenue in the charter schools for the 1999-2000 school year ranged from $6,168 per pupil at Horizons Community High School to $7,139 per pupil at the Edison charter school in Detroit. Thus, in absolute terms, Michigan charter schools are funded at significantly lower levels than their host district schools. Indeed, total revenue in the charter schools fell short of host district revenue by $1,500 to $2,000 per pupil.

A full analysis of charter school revenues and sources is beyond the scope of this chapter. Nonetheless, it is instructive to consider a few details about the sources of the revenues. For instance, it is apparent from Figure 4.2 that, among the case study schools, the proportion and total amount of state funding to charter schools exceeds state funding to host districts in all instances except in Detroit. Some of the differences between charter schools and their host districts are related to differences in the concentrations of low income, special education, and other high-effort students, which generate extra state funding.

Table 4.3 Per-Student Revenue in Selected Michigan Charter Schools, 1999-2000

	Grand Rapids P.S.	Wyoming Public Schools	Horizons Community High School	Forest Hills P.S.	Knapp Charter Acad.(NHA)	Kenowa Hills Pub. Schools	West Mich. Acad. of Env. Science (Leona)	Detroit Public Schools	Det.Acad. Arts &Sci. (Edison)
	$	$	$	$	$	$	$	$	$
State sources									
Foundation	4,716	4,584	5,962	5,448	6,175	3,764	6,170	5,540	6,414
At-risk	359	155	62	14	36	87	194	448	-
Special ed.	98	72	-	52	59	58	-	381	-
Adult	146	111	-	-	-	44	-	81	-
Vocational	6	15	-	3	-	10	-	16	-
Other grants	422	127	-	16	-	44	-	333	4
Total state	5,745	5,063	6,024	5,533	6,270	4,008	6,364	6,799	6,417
Local sources									
Property tax	863	1,167	-	1,599	63	2,228	-	425	-
Property tax-debt fund	126	693	-	1,072	-	902	-	212	-
Investments	94	159	.	228	-	145	0	133	-
Sales of food	51	107	-	179	33	183	50	15	89
Other local	157	142	-	299	54	256	51	125	105
Total local	1,291	2,269	-	3,378	149	3,713	101	911	194
Federal[10]									
Title I	312	114	-	6	16	116	137	453	248
Special ed.	148	83	-	-	-	-	55	51	-
School lunch	174	104	-	20	23	69	182	190	184
Other federal	299	222	144	134	310	170	138	296	95
Total federal	933	523	144	160	349	355	512	990	527
ISD sources	332	361	-	293	-	323	-	315	-
Total Revenue	$8,301	$8,215	$6,168	$9,364	$6,769	$8,400	$6,977	$9,015	$7,139

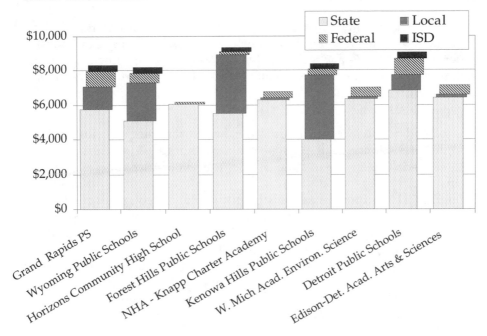

Figure 4.2 Revenue Sources in Charter Schools and Host Districts, 1999-2000

To a certain extent, host districts make up for the charter-host state funding revenue gap by relying on the proceeds of an 18-mil property tax. Thus, while local sources comprise the second largest revenue source for host districts, local sources are negligible for charter schools. Furthermore, under the state's school finance system, districts with lower property tax bases receive larger foundation grants to compensate for lower property tax revenues. In the affluent suburbs of Grand Rapids, by contrast, the districts can collect more revenues from their extensive tax base, so the state pays less to these districts in the per-student foundation grant.

Federal sources for Title I, special education, and school lunch make up the next largest revenue source for charter schools. As with state sources, the amount of federal revenue allocated to a school depends in large part on the prevalence of needy students. Ranging from about $150 per pupil at Horizons Community High School to more than $500 per pupil at WMAES and Detroit Academy of Arts and Sciences, the four case charter schools were less reliant on federal funding than Grand Rapids Public Schools ($993 per pupil) or Detroit Public Schools ($990 per pupil). By contrast, two wealthier host districts— Kenowa Hills and Forest Hills—obtained less federal revenue than the charter schools located within their boundaries. With very few poor children, these two school districts obtained almost no Title 1 funding and little federal school lunch assistance. WMAES (39 percent low-income) and Edison's Detroit Academy of

Arts and Sciences (49 percent low-income) obtained most of their federal revenue from Title 1 and the school lunch programs. Title I made up a third of federal revenue for Grand Rapids Public Schools (65 percent low-income) and half of federal revenue for Detroit Public Schools (67 percent low-income).

Expenditures

The expenditure analysis in this section begins by examining basic instructional expenditures, followed by the various components of added needs expenditures, such as special education and compensatory education. After a brief examination of instructional staff support and student support spending, various issues related to expenditures for administration and the diseconomies of small size are discussed in detail. An examination of transportation and food service expenditures reveals lower spending by charter schools than host school districts. Finally, facilities-related costs are studied.

Revenue data on the case study charter schools and their host districts (for 1999-2000) are provided in Table 4.4 and summarized graphically in Figure 4.3.[11] Just as charter school revenues are lower than those of the host districts, so are expenditures. While charter school expenditures ranged from $5,123 per pupil at WMAES to $7,107 at Edison's school in Detroit, host district spending ranged from $8,229 per pupil in Grand Rapids to $9,840 per pupil in wealthy Forest Hills. As we shall see later in this chapter, the apparent spending advantage of Detroit and Grand Rapids over charter schools evaporates after adjusting for high-cost programs for students in urban school districts.

The analysis of charter school expenditures that follows includes a fair amount of detail that some readers might wish to skip and proceed instead to the section on charter schools' cost and revenue advantages (page 62). The important point to be gleaned from this section is that charter schools—especially those run by EMOs—typically spend a smaller share of their resources on instruction (especially for students with special needs) and a higher proportion on administration than their host districts.

Basic instruction. Despite similarities in total revenue, charter school spending on basic instruction varied substantially among the four case study schools. All of the Michigan charter schools managed by National Heritage Academies and the Leona Group spent, on average, less than $2,000 per pupil on basic instruction (calculated from *Bulletin 1014*). In this respect, Knapp Charter Academy and WMAES typify the other schools managed by their parent companies. Edison's school in Detroit, spent more than $2,800 per pupil on basic instruction—approximately the same as the company average for its five

Table 4.4 Per-Student Expenditures in Selected Michigan Charter Schools, 1999-2000

	Grand Rapids Public P.S.	Wyoming Public Schools	Horizons Community High School	Forest Hills P.S.	Knapp Charter Acad.(NHA)	Kenowa Hills Pub. Schools	West Mich. Acad. of Env. Science (Leona)	Detroit Public Schools	Det.Acad. Arts &Sci. (Edison)
Instruction-Related Expenditures									
Instruction-basic	$3,219	$3,330	$3,730	$4,120	$1,860	$3,340	$1,988	$3,278	$2,905
Instruction-special education	829	691	-	638	222	528	282	1,042	127
Instruction-compensatory	294	131	-	6	-	226	3	858	-
Instruction-vocational ed.	38	59	-	21	-	41	-	200	-
Instruction-other added needs	-	-	-	-	-	0	-	0	-
Adult education	128	82	-	-	-	32	-	85	-
Instructional staff support	349	741	946	240	36	163	79	199	-
Student support services	532	474	691	579	-	488	151	172	260
Noninstructional Expenditures									
Administration	622	643	167	456	2,636	593	1,214	476	1,830
Authorizer oversight fee	-	-	-	-	180	-	180	-	180
Business office-other	188	162	47	144	-	102	156	304	-
Business office-facilities	19	-	-	131	-	-	-	9	594
Operations & maintenance	665	580	709	959	1,777	900	228	1,179	664
Transportation	370	175	-	481	-	451	640	272	-
Other	301	113	56	314	-	41	16	338	-
Community service	19	0	-	108	-	64	-	21	-
Expenditures for School Services									
Food service	305	250	-	202	56	287	187	205	465
Student activities	51	150	-	173	-	113	-	12	-
Community service	25	5	-	128	-	-	-	13	84
Debt retirement	237	779	-	1,126	-	948	-	327	-
Capital outlay (revenue)	38	89	-	11	-	35	-	89	-
Trust funds	1	-	-	-	-	1	-	-	-
Total	$8,229	$8,455	$6,348	$9,840	$6,768	$8,355	$5,123	$9,081	$7,107

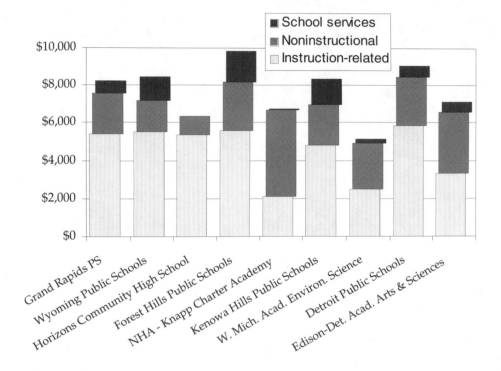

Figure 4.3 Expenditures in Charter Schools and Host Districts, 1999-2000

charter schools in Michigan. Horizons Community High School spent $3,730 per pupil on basic instruction, several hundred dollars more per pupil than its host school district.[12] Spending on basic instruction was at least $3,200 per pupil in the host school districts included in the case studies, a figure representative of the $3,369 per-student average for all host school districts in Michigan (calculated from *Bulletin 1014*).

Added needs instruction. The four case study charter schools also devoted considerably less funding to added needs instruction, a spending category that primarily includes special education and compensatory education. Grand Rapids spent at least $800 more per pupil on added needs instruction than the charter schools in its area. Detroit spent about $2,000 per pupil more on added needs instruction than Edison's Detroit Academy of Arts and Sciences.

Horizons Community High School reported no spending on special education, while Knapp Charter Academy reported spending of $222 per pupil (calculated against total membership, not just special education). WMAES claimed spending of $282 per pupil, and Edison reported $127 per pupil. In contrast to the limited charter school exposure to special education costs, Grand

Rapids spent $881 per pupil (in membership, not just special education), and Detroit spent $1,042 per pupil on special education.

Clearly, a big part of the spending differential between urban school districts—like Grand Rapids and Detroit—and charter schools comes from added costs for compensatory education. None of the case study charter schools reported compensatory education expenditures. While management companies are taking state at-risk student funding and federal Title 1 funding (see Table 4.3), the expenditure data they provide suggest that they are not providing special programs for at-risk students.[13] In contrast, Grand Rapids spent $294 per pupil on compensatory education and Detroit spent $858 per pupil.

None of the four charter schools reported expenditures for vocational education, including the charter high school. However, a small number of ISD-authorized charter schools have a distinct vocational education mission, with spending on vocational programs averaging $426 per pupil in 1997-98 compared to $156 per pupil in host school districts and less than $35 per pupil in other charter schools (Nelson, Muir, & Drown, forthcoming).

Instructional staff support. The instructional staff spending category includes libraries, audiovisual equipment, computer-assisted instruction, and staff development. The Edison school in Detroit reported no spending for instructional staff support, which is rather unusual. It is possible that Edison aggregates instructional staff support expenses into the basic instruction category. The other two management company schools spent less than $100 per pupil for instructional support services. Horizons Community High School, however, spent considerably more on instructional staff support than any of the host school districts.

Total instruction. With respect to total spending on instruction, the four case study charter schools mirror the findings in Table 4.1 for all Michigan charter schools. Basic instruction, added needs instruction(special education and compensatory education), and instructional support totaled less than $2,200 per pupil at Knapp Charter Academy and less than $2,400 per pupil at WMAES. In host school districts, basic instruction, added needs instruction, and instructional support totaled as little as $4,257 per pupil in Kenowa Hills and as much as $5,377 per pupil in Detroit. Horizons Community High School's spending on all categories of instruction was only about $200 short of its host school district.

Student support services. Providing another component of the expenditure gap between charter schools and host school districts, student services include guidance, attendance, health, psychological services, social work, and teacher consultants. In the Grand Rapids area, the three host school districts reported spending ranging from $474 per pupil to $579 per pupil. Knapp Charter Academy, on the other hand, reported no expenditures for student support services, and WMAES spent just $151 per pupil. Horizons Community High

School, however, spent more per pupil on student support services than its host school district. Detroit city schools classified only $172 per pupil as student support services. At $260 per pupil, the Edison charter school spent more than Detroit on student support services. It is likely that Detroit reports many student support service expenditures as special education or compensatory education expenditures.

Administration and support services. Strikingly, administration costs two to five times as much for management companies as expenditures for similar purposes in school districts. Administration expenses include school and general administration as well as management company fees.[14] Knapp Charter Academy, the charter school managed by National Heritage Academies, spent $2,636 per pupil on administration and "business office–other," exclusive of an estimated $180 per pupil for fees paid to its authorizer. Edison's school in Detroit spent $1,830 per pupil on administration and other business office expenses. Administration and other business office costs for WMAES, the Leona Group charter school, totaled only $1,370 per pupil. In contrast, host school district costs for administration and other business office expenses ranged from $600 per pupil in Forest Hills to $810 per pupil in Grand Rapids.

Horizons Community High School reported administrative and other business office spending of only $214 per pupil compared with $805 per pupil in Wyoming, its host school district. Clearly, Wyoming public schools continue to provide most of the administrative services to the charter school—an estimated cost of $600 per pupil. This subsidy alone accounts for two-thirds of the gap in total spending between the charter school and its host school district.

Three of the four case study schools use management companies. Administration costs may not be as high in independent charter schools. Researchers who have studied Michigan charter schools have generally concluded that management companies have higher administration expenses than independent charter schools, although Wolfram (1999) vigorously argued against this. Prince (1999) found that "mom and pop" charter schools spent less on administration and business office expenses than firm-managed schools, an "efficiency" Prince found surprising. Horn and Miron (2000) found that 29 percent of charter schools' expenditures were on administration compared with 13 percent for surrounding host districts, and that as the EMOs became more predominant in the operation of charter schools, overall spending on instruction decreased.

One reason management companies have higher administration costs is that *Form B* accounts for management fees as a "purchased service" under general administration.[15] Charter school officials also argue that these estimates of administrative costs unfairly include the authorizer oversight fee and rent or lease costs. In 1997-98, facility rental and lease costs were reported as business office costs after separating the authorizer oversight fee (2.8 percent of spending) and all business office expenditures (9.9 percent for management companies). Using these data, Nelson, Muir, and Drown (forthcoming) still found high administrative costs, equaling 17.8 percent of spending in schools run by EMOs, compared with 13.3 percent of spending for independent charter schools and 7.5 percent in host school districts.

Transportation. Michigan provides no targeted funds for transportation since the state does not require districts or charter schools to provide transportation. By not providing transportation, charter schools have an opportunity to free resources for other purposes. National Heritage Academies does not provide transportation. While it is known that Edison provides transportation for at least one other charter school it operates in Michigan, the company reported no expenditures for transportation for the Detroit Academy of Arts and Sciences. The Leona Group typically provides extensive and expensive transportation programs for the schools it operates; this is especially the case with WMAES.

Financed entirely from the foundation allowance, transportation accounted for about $230 of the per-student spending differential between charter schools (calculations in this paragraph are based on *Bulletin 1014*). Charter schools across the state averaged $58 per pupil (not just students transported), and host school districts averaged $296 per pupil. However, only a quarter of the charter schools reported any transportation expenditures. None of the 19 National Heritage schools provided transportation. Failure to provide transportation explains $481 of the spending differential between Knapp Charter Academy and Forest Hills. Similarly, Detroit public schools averaged transportation spending of $272 per pupil, while the Edison school reported no spending on transportation. Spending $640 per pupil for transportation, WMAES proved an exception among the four case study charter schools. Only four other charter schools in Michigan spent more per pupil on transportation than WMAES. The Leona Group managed four of the ten charter schools with the highest per-pupil transportation costs.

School service funds. The school service fund includes food service, athletics, and some community service. Depending on the charter school, some of the gap in total expenditures between charter schools and host school districts is attributable to school service fund expenditures.

No case study charter school reported spending on athletics, while host school district spending ranged from $12 per pupil in Detroit to $173 per pupil in Forest Hills. Edison reported community service spending of $84 per pupil. The other three case study charter schools had no community service expenditures. Host district spending on community service ranged from $5 per pupil in Wyoming to $128 per pupil in Forest Hills.

Food service accounts for some of the spending differential between charter schools and school districts, but the Edison's Detroit Academy of Arts and Sciences proved an exception, spending $465 per pupil. Among the four case study schools, Horizons Community High School reported no food service expenditures, Knapp Charter Academy reported only $56 per pupil, and WMAES spent $187 per pupil. Host school districts spent between $202 and $305 per pupil on food service.

Facilities and facility-related expenditures. Lenders, investors, and property owners often regard charter schools as risky and charge a premium or refuse to do business with them altogether. Some aspects of the small size of charter schools increase the cost of facilities and facilities acquisition. The efficient use of school facilities traditionally comes from the centralization of operations and maintenance functions at the school district level and, within schools, from the increased use of common spaces such as gyms, cafeterias, and playgrounds. Small scale, however, offers a few compensating opportunities not generally available to traditional neighborhood public schools. Charter schools can lower costs by avoiding investment in common spaces like gyms and libraries and using existing parks, playgrounds, retail cafeterias, libraries, museums and other alternatives to school facilities. The very large schools operated by companies like Edison Schools Inc. are rarely able to exploit these cost-saving opportunities. Some EMOs, such as NHA, have a financial interest—and a profit opportunity— in charter school facilities. As we shall see, this can be an effective means of generating capital.

Given the many options in the Michigan school accounting system to account for charter school spending on facilities, the only accurate measure for comparing facility costs combines expenditures for business office (facilities acquisition and purchased service cells), maintenance and operations, debt service (used only by school districts), and capital outlay.[16] Among the four case study schools, one reported no facilities expenditures and another claimed only a small amount for operations and maintenance. With a facility contributed by the school district, Horizons Community High School essentially had no facility costs. Operations and maintenance spending of $709 per pupil was a little higher than the Wyoming school district average of $580 per pupil. One could estimate the facilities subsidy as $779 per pupil, the per-student debt service payment of Wyoming Public Schools.

Edison's school in Detroit spent $594 for facilities costs under the business office function and $664 per pupil under maintenance and operations for a combined total of $1,258 per pupil. WMAES reported no facilities costs in the business office function and operations and maintenance spending of just $228 per pupil. WMAES has a history of problems in recording facilities costs.[17]

Knapp Charter Academy, managed by National Heritage Academies, reported no facilities acquisition costs, but spent $1,777 per pupil for leasing the building from J.C. Huizenga, who is also the owner of NHA. Given that Knapp Charter Academy enrolled 575 students in 1999-2000, lease payments are likely to have exceeded one million dollars annually. Estimates suggest that each facility leased by a NHA school cost between $2 million and $4 million dollars to build.[18] These figures suggest that the initial investments in the schools can be recouped within three to five years. This is possible largely by having substantially lower costs for instruction, which is accomplished with fewer students requiring special services and teachers salaries that are, on average, $15,000 less per year than the state average.[19]

Just as with the case study charter schools, the facility costs for host school districts vary sharply and illustrate the difficulty of setting a standard for comparable facility funding for charter schools. While operations and maintenance costs were rather consistent, debt service varied from less than $330 per pupil in Grand Rapids and Detroit to more than $940 per pupil in Forest Hills and Kenowa Hills. The two older cities paid off debt for most facilities years ago, while Forest Hills and Kenowa Hills relied on their ample property tax base to support such significant capital spending.

Financial Position

The ending fund balance is a common marker used to assess financial health. A negative ending fund balance, or deficit, signals financial trouble. A substantial reduction in the ending fund balance over the course of a year may indicate impending financial trouble. Measured by the change in the ending fund balance of the general fund between 1998-99 and 1999-2000, we found that the financial position improved dramatically in one case study charter school, fell in one school, and stayed about the same in two schools.

Knapp Charter Academy began 1999-2000 with a small $73 per-pupil fund balance and ended the year with $74 per pupil. In 1997-98, Knapp ended the year with a $73 fund balance. Negligible fund balances existed at all National Heritage schools. The company is not necessarily in financial trouble because National Heritage Academies contracts allow the company to keep surpluses as all or part of its management fee.[20] Similarly, Edison's three-year old Detroit Academy of Arts and Sciences began 1999-2000 with no fund balance and ended with $14 per pupil. Rather than demonstrating excellent financial control, the small fund balance suggests that Edison keeps surpluses as part of its management fee.[21]

Charter school authorizers in Michigan have encouraged financially troubled schools to contract with EMOs. Consequently, a few companies have inherited the financial problems of previously independent charter schools rather than causing the problem. In 1997-98, 40 percent of schools run by full-service companies had a negative ending fund balance (Nelson, Muir, & Drown, forthcoming). WMAES provides a good example. By the end of 1998, the school ran its deficit to $2,015 per pupil. Long-term lease obligations for facilities made up most of the deficit.[22] The school also failed to record food service and other expenditures and failed to forward employee income tax withholding to the IRS. The school hired the Leona Group to manage the school. According to the "Plan for Eliminating a Deficit Budget" filed with the state, enrollment increased, high school grades were eliminated, class size rose from 16 to 22, and para-professional positions fell from 12 to 6 positions. The general fund deficit decreased from over $2,000 per pupil at the beginning of 1999-2000 to a surplus of $600 per pupil, obtained primarily by sharp reductions in spending per pupil.[23]

The general fund balance at Horizons Community High School fell from $623 per pupil (about 10 percent of revenue) to $443 per pupil in 1999-2000. While much higher than company-run schools, the Horizons fund balance is modest compared with ISD-authorized charter schools. In 1997-98 (Nelson, Muir, & Drown, forthcoming), ISD-authorized charter schools had an average ending fund balance of $990 per pupil (14.2 percent of revenue).

The Cost Advantage of Charter Schools

In Michigan, most charter schools receive less in total per-pupil revenues than their surrounding school districts. This revenue difference, however, does not necessarily mean that charter schools have insufficient funds to accomplish the specific missions set out in their charters.

As we documented earlier in this chapter, charter schools typically receive less in terms of revenues and spend less than surrounding districts. This is usually because they provide a more limited range of services and cater to a less-costly-to-educate subset of students. On the revenue side, the schools receive less of the revenue which, under compensatory education policies, is generated by high-effort students. On the expenditure side, charter schools typically spend less than their host districts, since they typically spend comparatively little in services to special education and low-income students, transportation, food service, special education preschool programs, community outreach, and adult education.

As we pointed out in Chapter 1, the idea that more narrowly focused and coherent schools will perform better is a hallmark of theories of market choice. According to the theory, choice allows parents, teachers, students, and other stakeholders to sort themselves into communities of like-minded individuals who will be better able to focus on implementing effective learning strategies than more heterogeneous traditional school districts. Charter schools can use any one of three strategies to achieve such a focus. First, charter schools and management companies may decide to locate their schools in specific places in order to attract particular types of students or, conversely, discourage other types of students from attending. Second, schools can narrow the range of students they serve by adopting a particular market niche and marketing the school's services to only a segment of the district. Finally, legal proscriptions notwithstanding, critics have charged that charter schools do, in fact, engage in cream-skimming. These factors indicate the manner in which charter schools might partially involve themselves in the selection of students, which is contrary to the understanding that students and their families would be doing the choosing. (We defer further discussion of this issue until Chapter 5.) Whatever the cause, fair comparisons between the finances of charter and noncharter schools must take such differences in the range of services and student composition into account in order to render fair comparisons. In this section we attempt to provide such comparisons through an analysis of charter school cost and revenue (dis)advantages.

Table 4.5 identifies the cost advantages (or cost disadvantages) that the four case study schools have over their host school districts. In most cases, a "cost advantage" is the difference between charter school and host school district expenditures for

- Students in high-cost program (e.g., special education, compensatory education, vocational education, or high school education generally)
- Costs unrelated to K-12 education (e.g., adult education, community education)
- Student support services
- Discretionary support services (e.g., food service or transportation)

The cost advantage calculation is based on expenditure data in Table 4.4, and occurs when charter schools spend *less* than their host districts on these items.

By contrast, a "cost disadvantage" (appearing as a negative number in Table 4.5) occurs when charter schools spend *more* on students in high-cost programs, food service, transportation, or other support services. Charter schools could experience a cost disadvantage relative to school districts if the school enrolled a high percentage of low-income and special education students who may also depend on school-provided transportation and benefit from government-subsidized school food programs. Expenditures for student support services are also included in the cost advantage analysis because most spending in this category relates to special education, compensatory education, and guidance counseling.

The cost advantage analysis does *not* take into consideration low teacher pay, lower teacher certification standards, and reduced employee benefits as charter school cost advantages. Nor are the diseconomies of small scale and high administration costs counted as charter school "cost disadvantages." Charter schools are not considered to have a facility cost disadvantage even though Michigan provides no dedicated facilities revenue for charter schools. As demonstrated in Table 4.4 and the discussion of this table, charter school facility costs per pupil closely match school district facility costs per pupil.[24]

Table 4.5 Per-Student Revenue Adjusted for Cost Advantages of
Charter Schools

Charter School	Horizons Community High School	Knapp Charter Academy (NHA)	West Mich. Acad. of Env. Science (Leona)	Detroit Acad. of Arts & Science (Edison)
Host District	Wyoming	Grand Rapids	Grand Rapids	Detroit
Charter School Cost Advantage*				
Instruction–special education	691	607	547	915
Instruction–compensatory	131	294	291	858
Instruction–vocational	59	38	38	200
Adult education	82	128	128	85
Added cost–high school	–500	250	125	250
Student support	–217	532	381	–88
Administration and business office subsidy	591	na	na	na
Facilities subsidy	779	na	na	na
Transportation	175	370	–270	272
Food service	250	249	118	–260
Athletics	150	51	51	12
Community service	5	44	44	–50
Total Cost Advantage	$2,196	$2,563	$1,453	$2,194

* Difference between school district expenditure and charter school expenditure
based on information in Table 4.4. A charter school cost disadvantage is indicated
as a negative number.

Another assumption driving the cost advantage analysis is that high school
education costs an estimated $750 per pupil more than Grade K-8 education and
that high school students comprise one third of the students enrolled in host
school districts. Therefore, charter elementary schools have a $250 per student
cost advantage (one-third of $750 per high school student is $250), because one
third of school district students are more costly high school students. Similarly,
all host school districts also enroll students in the less expensive elementary
grades. Therefore, charter high schools have a $500 per student cost
disadvantage (two-thirds of $750 per high school student is $500), because two
thirds of school district students are inexpensive elementary students). Under
this protocol, charter elementary schools have a $750 per-pupil cost advantage
over charter high schools. Since Michigan provides no extra funding for charter
high school students, few management companies operate charter high schools.[25]

The cost advantage of charter schools ranged from $1,453 per pupil at WMAES to $2,563 per pupil at Knapp Charter Academy. In fact, Knapp and other schools operated by National Heritage Academies exploit all of the charter school cost advantages. For example, Knapp Charter Academy

- Does not provide instruction beyond Grade 8
- Spent $607 less per pupil on special education than Grand Rapids P.S.
- Spent nothing on compensatory education, vocational education, or student support services
- Spent nothing on transportation, adult education, community service, or athletics, and very little on food service

Three of the case study schools, however, did not exploit all of the hypothesized cost advantages of charter schools. With its entire student body in the expensive high school grades, Horizons Community High School had a $500 per-pupil cost disadvantage relative to its host school district. The school district, however, provided administrative subsidies and a facility.[26] WMAES spent more for transportation than Grand Rapids Public Schools, with the differential treated as a $270 per-pupil cost disadvantage for the charter school. Similarly, Edison's Detroit Academy of Arts and Sciences spent more for food service than Detroit Public Schools paid, with the differential treated as a $260 per-pupil cost disadvantage for the charter school.

The overall charter school cost advantage, however, does not translate into "profit" since charter schools receive less money in revenues to begin with. Food service programs, for example, are generally self-financed by a combination of government subsidies and meal charges. On the other hand, no extra funding exists for school district spending on transportation, which is paid for with the same general operating funds used to finance instructional expenditures. But school districts also have significant *revenue* advantages, primarily through dedicated facilities funding. Table 4.6 examines this revenue advantage by combining all sources of school district revenue (fully described in Table 4.3) and subtracting the charter school cost advantage calculated in Table 4.5. The result of this calculation is labeled as "host district comparable revenue" in Table 4.6 and represents an estimate of the revenue available to school districts for the instruction and servicing of students like those enrolled in the charter school. If host district comparable revenue is less than total charter school revenue, then the charter school has a "net revenue advantage."

Table 4.6 shows that all four charter schools had a revenue advantage. That is, the four case study charter schools had more revenue than host school districts to educate, house, and provide services for the specific types of students actually enrolled in the charter schools. Or, in mathematical terms, the cost advantage of charter schools exceeded the gap between charter school total revenue and school district total revenue in all of the four case study schools. The Knapp Charter Academy, managed by National Heritage Academies, provides the most notable example. By subtracting the $2,563 cost advantage of Knapp Academy from total revenue in Grand Rapids ($8,301 per pupil), "comparable revenue" in Grand Rapids totals only $5,738 per pupil. Knapp Charter Academy obtained total revenue of $6,769 per pupil, so the charter school revenue advantage is $1,031 per pupil. The charter school revenue advantage is much smaller in the other three case study schools: $129 per pupil at WMAES, $318 per pupil at Edison's Detroit Academy of Arts and Sciences and $149 per pupil at Horizons Community High School.

Table 4.6 Per-Student Charter School Revenue Advantage

Charter school	Horizons Community High School	Knapp Charter Academy (NHA)	West Mich. Acad. of Env. Science (Leona)	Detroit Acad. of Arts & Science (Edison)
Host district	Wyoming	Grand Rapids	Grand Rapids	Detroit
Total host district revenue	$8,215	$8,301	$8,301	$9,015
Charter school cost advantage	$2,196	$2,563	$1,453	$2,194
Host district comparable revenue	$6,019	$5,738	$6,848	$6,821
Charter school revenue *	$6,168	$6,769	$6,977	$7,139
Charter school revenue advantage **	$149	$1,031	$129	$318

* Host district revenue minus total cost advantage of charter school from Table 4.5.
** Charter school revenue minus host school district comparable revenue.

The calculations in Tables 4.5 and 4.6 are illustrative of cost and revenue advantages for charter schools. One should keep in mind that not all charter schools experience the cost advantages illustrated by the four case study schools. In fact, without the subsidized facilities and other assistance from the district, Horizons Community High School would have had a cost disadvantage. From these analyses we can conclude that charter schools that cater to upper secondary grades, provide transportation, and include at-risk students and students requiring special educational services are more likely to face cost disadvantages.

While it is often argued by advocates that charter schools are "shortchanged," the fact that over 40 for-profit EMOs established themselves in Michigan suggests differently (see Chapter 10). Indeed, it seems likely that these management companies would not be so keenly interested in operating charter schools in Michigan if they were insufficiently funded and no opportunity for profit existed.

Conclusion

This chapter explored the financial underpinning of Michigan charter schools. In keeping with the charter concept (elaborated in Chapter 1), funds follow students. As a consequence, schools that fail to attract and retain students will lose money and ultimately go out of business. Thus, this system of school finance provides the foundations of market accountability. The early sections of the chapter pointed out that the exact per-student allocation depends, to a certain extent, on student characteristics. For instance, low-income and special education students receive extra funds, which help the schools cover some of the additional costs associated with the instruction they receive. Charter schools can also take in extra funds to cover start-up expenses, such as the purchase and renovation of buildings. These funds are limited, however, are awarded on a somewhat competitive basis, and are not pegged to head count enrollments.

The state's charter school funding formula does not make sufficient adjustments according to the needs of individual schools or the services they choose to provide. For instance, there is no difference in funding between the more expensive high school grades and the less expensive elementary and middle school-grades. This likely accounts for the fact (elaborated in Chapter 5) that Michigan charter schools—especially those run by EMOs—largely avoid the high school grades. Furthermore, the funding formula provides incentives for schools to exclude students with special needs[27] and to not provide transportation. The latter results in the schools being less accessible to low income families and single parents who would find it more difficult to transport their children to and from school each day.

Turning our attention to expenditure patterns, we found that charter schools spend much more than noncharter public schools on administration—especially EMO-operated schools—and less on instruction. Over time, the percentage of spending dedicated to instruction has drifted downward. The decline occurred even as schools grew in size, matured, and passed out of the start-up phase. Using more recent data and after addressing some of the accounting issues not fully resolved in earlier studies, we reach the same basic conclusion as found in earlier studies (Horn & Miron, 2000; Prince, 1999). For management companies, administration costs two to five times as much as expenditures for similar purposes in school districts. High administration costs appear to cut into instructional spending, not the cost of facilities. Less spending on instruction reflects lower salaries for teachers, failure to provide special services, and in some cases reluctance to reduce class size, all of which might threaten the school's ability to improve student achievement. Many of these issues are discussed in latter chapters of this book.

The chapter concluded by demonstrating that in spite of the fact that charter schools both receive and expend less, they nonetheless enjoy significant cost and revenue advantages by focusing their services on less costly students. In the four case schools, the cost advantage ranged from $129 at a Leona Group school to $1,031 at the school operated by National Heritage Academies. In other words, even though traditional public schools are spending more per pupil than charter schools, they educate the same types of students found in many of the charter schools for less money.

These findings call into question claims that charter schools—and, more generally, schools that operate according to the principles of market competition—operate more efficiently than traditional public schools. Rather than offering more for less, Michigan charter schools appear to be offering less for more, after one controls for the types of services offered by the schools. We revisit the question of charter school efficiency in Chapter 11 by comparing the state's expenditures on charter schools with the educational outcomes the schools produce.

Notes

1. The first report of the national study describes charter school finance systems in 23 states and two cities. See F. H. Nelson, E. Muir, and R. Drown, *Venturesome Capital: State Charter School Finance Systems*. Washington, DC: Office of Education Research and Improvement, U.S. Department of Education, December 2000. [http://www.ed.gov/pubs/chartfin/].

2. Coincidentally, the maximum charter school payment was about the same as the state average foundation allowance. The proceeds of an 18-mil local property tax levy are subtracted from the foundation allowance, and the balance of school district funding comes from state revenue. High tax base and high-wealth school districts, usually found in suburban areas, tend to have foundation allowances exceeding the state average allowance. Most Michigan cities from which charter schools tend to draw their students had foundation allowances similar to the charter school maximum per-student payment.

3. However, school districts lose the entire foundation allowance, not just the portion covered by state aid.

4. Based on an Internal Revenue Service ruling that did not specifically disallow the practice, numerous charter schools have successfully obtained tax-exempt financing to purchase or build facilities. Due to the greater risk, interest rates are higher than those paid by districts, and other costs of borrowing are substantially higher.

5. Michigan provides about $350 per pupil (averaged across all students in the state) directly to ISDs for special education. ISDs are also allowed to levy a property tax. Charter schools should be more integrated into the ISD structure, but progress has been slow.

6. For traditional public school districts, the general fund excludes debt retirement and some capital outlay. The general fund does not include food service spending for either charter schools or school districts.

7. See Arsen, Plank, & Sykes (1999), Horn & Miron (1999), Khouri et al. (1999), Prince (1999), and Wolfram (1999).

8. Information on *Form B* (the financial report school districts and charter schools file with the state) and *Bulletin 1014* (which summarizes information from *Form B*), is available at [http://www.state.mi.us/mde/]. The case study analyses in this chapter rely on the *Form B* version of the Michigan uniform financial reporting system. Most researchers use *Bulletin 1014*, which contains only three broad categories of per-student revenue (local, state, and federal) and seven broad categories of expenditures. Reporting only general fund revenue and expenditures, *Bulletin 1014* does not include capital outlay, debt retirement, or the school service funds (primarily food service and athletics) that can be found in the *Form B* data.

9. The revenue data shown in Table 4.3 and illustrated in Figure 4.2 include both unrestricted and restricted funds. The latter includes support for food service, debt, and capital outlay.

10. In addition to federal charter school start-up assistance, other federal programs could include immigrant education, bilingual education, vocational education, drug-free schools, GOALS 2000, Eisenhower professional development, and Title VI innovative education. Knapp Charter Academy and Detroit Academy obtained federal start-up continuation grants of about $40,000 each in 1999. Most charter schools operated by National Heritage Academies obtained less than $100 per pupil for all forms of federal revenue. In 1999, 61 operational charter schools obtained federal start-up funding of approximately $40,000 each, regardless of size. Preoperational start-up funding, averaging $94,000 per school, went to 25 proposed schools.

11. The expenditure data in Table 4.4 combine restricted, unrestricted, operating, and nonoperating funds.

12. In 1997-98, average spending on basic education among ISD-authorized schools exceeded $3,500 per pupil (more than 50 percent of spending). See Nelson, Muir, and Drown (forthcoming).

13. The case study schools are probably representative of management company schools in Michigan. In 1997-98, only 12 of 102 charter schools reported any spending on compensatory education (Nelson, Muir, & Drown, forthcoming). Full-service management companies spent less than $10 per pupil. Independent charter schools averaged $133 per pupil. ISD-authorized charter schools spent an average of $88 per pupil on compensatory education.

14. *Form B* classifies school administration as a component of instructional support. In Table 4.4, school administration and general administration were combined.

15. In 1997-98, all purchased services in the general administration function totaled 6.5 percent of spending for full-service company schools and 12.2 percent for schools associated with limited-service companies (Nelson, Muir, & Drown, forthcoming). Purchased services for general administration came to only 3.8 percent of spending in independent schools, 4.4 percent in ISD-authorized schools, and only 0.4 percent in host school districts.

16. Charter schools record facilities costs on *Form B* in several different ways. They can establish a separate capital projects fund to record the costs for buildings, land, and equipment. Some charter schools record facilities acquisition and improvement as operations and maintenance in the general fund, which is the preferred method for recording rent for a building rather than a capital lease. The business office variable on *Form B* is also used by charter schools to report facilities cost. Rent is sometimes recorded as a business office expense. (The facilities acquisition cell of the business office function should be used for actual purchases of facilities, while the purchased service cell should be used for rent or leases of facilities.) Khouri et al. (1999) found that 89 percent of charter schools said they leased their facilities in 1998-99.

17. The 1996-97 audit listed debt service requirements of $479,903 for 1999-2000—over $1,000 per pupil based on actual 1999-2000 enrollment. Facilities issues are at the core of WMAES's past financial problems. According to the "Plan for Eliminating a Deficit Budget" filed with the state, in 1995-96, the school did not expense $300,000 in capital improvements and in 1996-97 did not expense another $180,000 in capital improvements. According to the 1996-97 independent financial audit, WMAES contracted to pay $2.9 million for improved land. The Academy paid another $475,000 for further improvements to the land. All leases and contracts were made with members of WMAES's board of directors.

18. Estimates suggest that J.C. Huizenga, the owner of NHA paid close to $4 million for each of its first schools (Naudi, 2001). Other estimates suggest that the first 21 NHA schools cost on average $1.9 million to build (Reinstadler, 1999). As we described in our first evaluation of Michigan charter schools (Horn & Miron, 1999), the design and construction of the NHA school buildings provide an innovative example from which traditional public schools could learn. The post-and-frame buildings cost substantially less to build and future adaptations will not be costly since there are few interior weight-bearing walls.

19. Representatives from National Heritage Academies have informed us that they do not profit or benefit from the heavy investments in facilities since NHA leases the schools from another company. This other company, however, is also owned by J.C. Huizenga and shares office space with NHA.

20. A multistate review of 20 contracts with 8 private firms and 2 nonprofit providers released by the Charter School Friends National Network (Lin & Hassel, 1999) revealed that no contractor charged a simple fixed fee. Some contracts simply allowed management companies to keep the surplus. Other contractors charged a percentage of revenues or expenditures, usually in the 7

percent to 12 percent range. The contracts with National Heritage Academies that we have reviewed all stipulate that NHA's fees will be based on the per-pupil expenditures and that NHA will receive 98 percent of each charter school's net per-pupil expenditure.

21. In 1997-98, according to the National Charter School Finance Study (Nelson, Muir, & Drown, forthcoming) all full-service company schools averaged a small negative fund balance (–$65 per pupil). In contrast, ending fund balances in independent charter schools averaged $990 (14.2 percent of expenditures).

22. The school did not have to borrow to finance most of this deficit. All of the lease payments for the four subsequent years of the lease were recorded as liabilities, but the payments are not due until future years.

23. *Form B* data are not audited, and the $600 surplus figure may change. The 1996-97 audit listed $479,903 in debt retirement that is not included on the 1999-2000 *Form B*. No significant facilities expenditures were reported on the 1999-2000 *Form B*.

24. Two other assumptions are important to the analysis. First, Knapp Charter Academy and WMAES are matched to Grand Rapids rather than the school district in which they are physically located. The match is based on the assumption that the schools enroll more students from Grand Rapids Public Schools than any other school district. Grand Rapids enrolls 27,000 students, providing a significant supply of potential charter school students. WMAES, in particular, spends more than $600 per pupil (not just students transported) on transportation and is physically located in a wealthy suburban school district of just 3,500 students.

25. Neither school districts nor charter schools generate funding based on grade level. Most charter schools, particularly those operated by EMOs, cater to low-cost elementary students. On the other hand, four out of five students in the average ISD-authorized charter school are middle or high school students. In charter school states where high school students generate extra funding (e.g., Arizona: 10 percent to 40 percent more, Florida: 14 percent more, and Minnesota: 24 percent more), the charter schools served about the same proportion of middle and high school students as did the surrounding traditional public school districts.

26. The administrative subsidy is estimated as the difference between charter school and school district costs for administration and running a business office. The facility subsidy is estimated as the amount the school district pays for debt retirement.

27. There is a funding lag in special education payments, and charter schools, as well as noncharter public schools, are seldom refunded the full costs of the special education services they provide.

5

Choice and Access

An important element of the theory of school choice is that families will sort into schools according to their agreement with the school's educational philosophy and mission (see Chapter 1). This narrowing or coherence in charter schools' missions, choice proponents claim, allows schools to spend less time managing internal conflicts and more time pursuing agreed-upon strategies to advance student learning. Further, proponents argue that choice can help alleviate the racial and economic segregation so prevalent in the public education system. Indeed, by breaking the link between where students live and the schools they attend, school choice might allow poor and minority students to attend schools previously inaccessible to them. A few studies or policy pieces that support this include Finn, Manno, and Vanourek (2000) and RPP International (2000).

Critics charge, to the contrary, that school choice actually reinforces segregation on the basis of income, race, ethnicity, and other invidious categories (Arsen, Plank, & Sykes, 1999; Cobb & Glass, 1999; Horn & Miron, 2000). While some charge that such sorting comes about as a result of cream-skimming by charter schools, it is also possible that social sorting is the result of where charter schools choose to locate and the particular niches to which they market themselves.

In this chapter we assess evidence for the proposition that charter schools lead to social sorting by examining data on the social characteristics of the students and families who choose to attend them. As we shall see, the data present cause for concern, as Michigan charter schools enroll students with demographic characteristics rather different from those in surrounding areas. Unfortunately, available data do not allow us to determine the extent to which such sorting is due to self-selection by families versus selectivity by the schools.

Along with addressing equity questions related to social sorting, a careful examination of student and family characteristics is also important in evaluating charter school outcomes. Legions of studies have found strong statistical relationships between income, race, family structure, and other background characteristics, and variations in student achievement (see, e.g., Coleman et al., 1966; Grissmer et al., 2000; Hanushek, 1997). Thus, establishing the demographic profile of Michigan charter school students is essential if we are to fairly assess test scores and other educational outcomes.

The chapter begins by analyzing the grade levels covered by charter schools. Next, we examine a number of student and family characteristics commonly found in studies explaining variations in student outcomes. These include race/ethnicity, family income, parents' education level, and family structure (e.g., single-parent status). We also include analyses of students' educational aspirations, the amount of time parents spend volunteering in charter schools, previous school attended, and reasons for enrolling in a charter school. These factors, while discussed less frequently in debates over educational policy, help us understand the less obvious attitudinal factors that can influence student performance. The chapter also contains a discussion of special education in Michigan charter schools as well as results from parents and students regarding reasons they chose a charter school.

Distribution by Grade

The financial analysis in Chapter 4 suggested that many Michigan charter schools seek to control costs by focusing on less-costly elementary and middle grade students and by avoiding students in the high school grades. This conclusion is clearly borne out in Figure 5.1. Indeed, only 13 percent of charter students are enrolled in secondary schools, compared with 67 percent who are enrolled in lower elementary grades (K-5), and 20 percent in middle schools (Grades 6-8). Over time, the trend has been toward fewer schools serving high school populations.

This, not coincidentally, corresponds with the growth in the proportion of schools managed by EMOs which, for financial reasons, have largely avoided these relatively costly students (see Chapter 4). National Heritage Academies, for instance, has decided not to provide secondary schools at all. Their model is to start their schools with only Grades K-4 and then to add a grade each year up to Grade 8. In this way, NHA schools can feed their new classes (e.g., fill classes in newly added grades with students from their lower grades) and after the initial year limit new enrollments to largely incoming kindergarten students. Since parents choosing charter schools at the middle school or high school level are more likely to turn to charter schools because their child has unique or

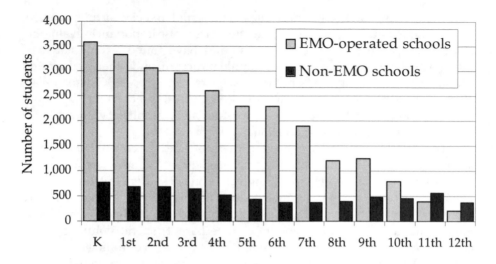

Figure 5.1 Distribution of Students by Grade Level for Charter Schools With
or Without EMOs, 1998-99

special needs not being met in their traditional public school (including
disciplinary problems), it seems likely that NHA would prefer to enroll
kindergartners, who are less likely to require these expensive services.[1]

The Leona Group, which operates 20 charter schools across the state, has
also learned about the cost savings in avoiding instruction at the secondary
grades. In one K-12 charter school, they eliminated Grades 9 through 12 months
after taking over the school. In other schools that had previously focused
exclusively on secondary instruction, the Leona Group added grades at lower
grade levels, thereby shifting enrollments to the less costly lower grades.

Limiting student intake to kindergarten might also render the impact on
the local district less apparent, since the children have never enrolled in the local
schools. Our case studies of schools districts (see Chapter 7 as well as Horn &
Miron, 2000) found several districts that gradually reported fewer and fewer
students leaving the traditional public schools, even while the charter school
enrollments grew. This apparent contradiction is explained by the fact that an
increasing proportion of students were entering charter schools as kindergartners.

Racial/Ethnic Composition of the Charter Schools

Discussions of race are almost always controversial in education and elsewhere.
Charter school proponents often claim that the schools cater to a larger
proportion of minority and low-income students. For instance, the Michigan

Association of Public School Academies (MAPSA), the lobby group advocating for charter schools in Michigan, claims that the charter schools are exemplary in catering to minorities (MAPSA, 2000). A large, federally sponsored study of charter schools (RPP International, 2000) also noted that Michigan's was an example of a state whose charter schools are catering to minorities. Using these studies' methodology on the most recent data confirms these earlier results: 40 percent of charter school students are white compared to 75 percent statewide.

The picture painted by the data, however, depends to a large extent upon the comparison groups one uses to benchmark the findings. The findings in both the MAPSA and RPP International studies compare ethnicity data from the largely urban charter schools with overall state averages, rather than the average of the host districts in which charter schools lie. Quite simply, charter schools in urban areas are, with some exceptions, more likely to draw from a pool of minority and low-income students. As a consequence, comparisons with the entire state stack the deck in charter schools' favor.

We contend that a much better comparison group is the districts in which the charter schools are located, since it restricts charter-noncharter comparisons to more similar pools of potential charter school students. This method paints a rather different picture, with host districts enrolling roughly equal proportions of white students (40 percent for charter schools and 37 percent for host districts; see Figure 5.2). Thus, while these figures do not provide evidence of social sorting, neither do they support the earlier studies' claims that Michigan charter schools serve a higher proportion of nonwhite students than noncharter public schools. Table 5.1 provides a more detailed breakdown of racial and ethnic groups in charter schools. Here we can see that African Americans comprised just over 54 percent of charter school enrollments, while white students comprised 40 percent of the enrollments. These aggregate figures, however, mask substantial variations in the proportions of minorities enrolled in charter schools over time and well as large differences that exist across charter schools.[2]

The differences in the proportions of whites and minorities across schools is rather unsettling. As for school-to-school variations, in 1998-99 approximately 20 percent of Michigan charter

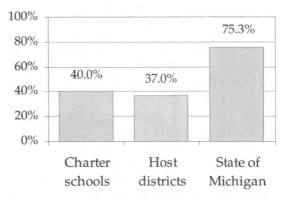

Figure 5.2 Proportion of White Students in Charter Schools, Host Districts, and State of Michigan, 1998-99

schools had no white students enrolled, and another 15 percent enrolled fewer than 4 percent white students. Likewise, about 5 percent of the schools had no minorities and another 9.5 percent had fewer than 4 percent minority students.

The fact that a charter school has few minorities or only minority students is not sufficient evidence to suggest that segregation is taking place. In order to estimate this we need to compare each charter school with its host district. When doing this we found that 14 percent of the charter schools had at least 20 percentage points more minority students than their respective host districts. For example, a few of the schools operated by Charter School Administrative Services have no white students enrolled even though they are situated in districts where more than 80 percent of the students are white. On the other extreme, we found that 11 percent of the charter schools had at least 20 percentage points more white students that their host districts. For example, only four percent of the students in Detroit Public Schools are white, yet two charter schools that lie within the district borders enrolled more than 90 percent white students. Another charter school was located within a district that until recently was under a federal desegregation order. Only eight percent of the students in the district were white, yet 73 percent of the charter school students were white. These examples cast doubt upon charter schools' viability as a force for reducing further segregation.

Table 5.1 Charter School Enrollments by Ethnic/Racial Group (1999-2000)

	Native Am./ Alaskan Native	Asian or Pac.Islands	African American	His-panic	White	Total
Number	516	310	24,988	1,790	18,545	46,149
Percent	1.1%	0.7%	54.1%	3.9%	40.2%	100%

Perhaps the most interesting school-to-school variations involve EMOs (see Figure 5.3). While the overall proportion of nonwhite students in EMO schools is similar to that of their host districts (39 percent), we find that schools established by Helicon & Associates, which are in small towns and suburban areas, enroll slightly fewer minorities than their host districts. More strikingly, National Heritage Academies, which establishes schools in largely suburban areas, enrolls nearly 80 percent white students, compared to 60 percent in respective host districts. The remaining four EMOs locate their schools largely in urban areas with few white students. Yet three of these EMOs enroll noticeably fewer minorities than the surrounding districts. The reverse is true for Charter School Administrative Services, whose schools enroll fewer than 1 percent white students, compared to 11 percent in their respective host districts.[3]

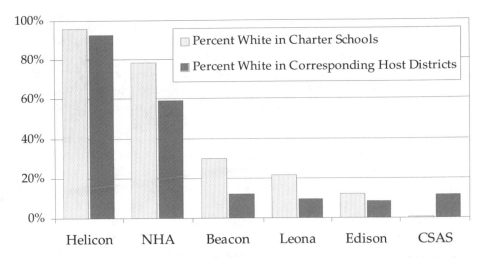

Figure 5.3 Proportion of White Students Enrolled in EMO Charter Schools
Compared With Their Host Districts (1998-99)

   While it does not constitute a racial or ethnic group, we also compared charter and noncharter school students by gender. Here we found remarkably even proportions, with 50.5 percent male 49.5 female during the 1999-2000 school year. It is interesting to point out, however, that there was considerable variance among schools. In some schools, the proportion of females was as high as 81 percent, while in one charter school there were no female students at all. Some schools, it should be pointed out, have missions that target students of one gender or the other.

Income, Family Structure, and Other Characteristics

Race is far from the only relevant factor in a discussion of student and family characteristics. In this section we discuss family income, parents' education level, students' educational aspirations, household structure, and parent volunteerism.

Family Income

The best commonly available indicator of family income is the proportion of students in a given school who qualify for free or reduced lunches (FRL). Unfortunately, data on eligibility for federal lunch programs in charter schools are severely limited because the program is mandatory only for districts offering all grades, K-12. Since only 5 percent of Michigan charter schools offer all grade levels, few are required to participate in the program. And relatively few have chosen to participate. Only 13 schools participated in the FRL program during the 1996-97 school year (Michigan Department of Education, 1999a) which is equivalent to 17 percent of the charter schools. For the 2000-01 school year 98 charter schools—a little more than half of the schools—participated in this program. Many charter school principals we interviewed cited the complexity of federal paperwork and the lag between application and actual funding as reasons for not participating in the program.[4]

As with data on race and ethnicity, the conclusions one should draw from the FRL data depend largely upon the choice of benchmarks. The federally sponsored national charter school study (RPP International, 2000) suggests that Michigan's charter schools are catering to more low-income students than the public schools (39.3 percent in charter schools vs. 28.7 percent for all public schools in the state). Once again, however, the picture is different when we compare charter schools with their host districts. Here, we find that the proportion of charter school students qualifying for FRL is virtually indistinguishable from their host districts (see Figure 5.4).

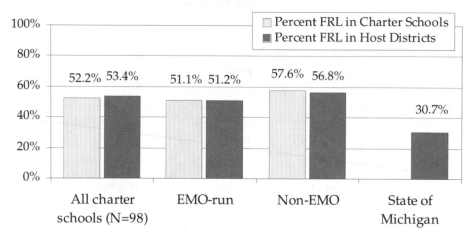

Figure 5.4   Proportion of Students Qualifying for Free or Reduced-Price
             Lunch (2000-01)
Note: The data were weighted according to school enrollment.

It is important to point out that there is considerable variation across the charter schools as well as across the sending districts. Some charter schools enroll considerably lower proportions of FRL students. Overall, 25 percent of the charter schools have FRL concentrations that are at least 20 percentage points lower than their host districts. One school, for instance, reports enrolling 8 percent FRL students, compared to 65 percent in its host district. Other schools enroll considerably higher proportions of FRL students than their host districts.

In total 14 percent of the charter schools had FRL concentrations that were at least 20 percentage points higher than their respective host district. For example, one school reported 78 percent FRL enrollment, compared to just 18 percent in its host district.

There are also interesting, if small, differences among EMO and non-EMO schools. Overall, charter schools operated by EMOs report a lower proportion of students qualifying for FRL, reflecting in part the fact that EMOs are more likely to establish schools in districts where there are fewer low-income families. Once again, there is considerable variations across EMOs (see Figure 5.5). Schools operated by the Leona Group, Advantage, and Mosaica have the highest levels of students qualifying for FRL relative to their host districts. Only two EMOs have noticeably lower proportions of students qualifying for FRL: Edison Schools Inc. and National Heritage Academies. While Edison claims that it serves the poorest and most disadvantaged schools in a given district, these data on FRL say otherwise.

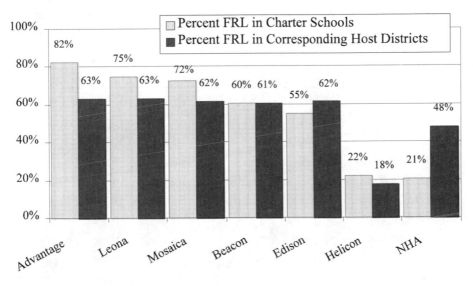

Figure 5.5 Proportion of Students Qualifying for FRL in Charter Schools and Their Corresponding Host District, by EMO (2000-01)

Given the weaknesses in the school lunch data discussed above, we sought to supplement the income analysis with responses to an item on our parent survey about household income. Unfortunately, we were unable to administer the survey to respondents in noncharter schools, preventing systematic charter-host district comparisons.

In 1998, surveys with items referring to household income were administered to a sample of parents in 51 charter schools.[5] The annual family income reported by the sampled parents indicated that 29.4 percent had annual family incomes of less than $30,000 and 54.4 percent had family incomes that were greater than $40,000. Table 5.2 illustrates the range of family incomes for Michigan charter schools, as well as for a range of comparison and subgroups.

In the absence of charter-host district comparisons, we are able to draw comparisons to charter schools in other states. As Table 5.2 indicates, Michigan charter school families had slightly higher family incomes than charter school families in the composite comparison group,[6] which includes charter schools in Connecticut, Illinois, and Pennsylvania. The EMO-operated schools served families with slightly higher family incomes than the non-EMO–operated schools. Indeed, 34 percent of respondents from non-EMO charter schools reported annual family incomes of $30,000 or less, compared to 28 percent for EMO-operated schools. This tendency to enroll children from higher income families is particularly true for charter schools operated by National Heritage Academies, with only 13 percent of respondents reporting annual incomes of $30,000 or less. (NHA is often singled out in this book because it is the largest EMO operating in Michigan.)

Table 5.2 Average Annual Family Income for Charter School Families

	Michigan Charter Schools (N=1,040)	Composite Comparison Group (N=611)	EMO- Operated Schools (N=742)	Non- EMO Schools (N=298)	National Heritage Academies (N=188)
Less than $10,000	4.6%	5.2%	4.2%	5.6%	1.1%
$10,000-$19,999	10.7%	11.8%	8.2%	16.8%	3.4%
$20,000-$29,999	14.1%	15.3%	15.2%	11.5%	8.4%
$30,000-$39,999	16.2%	13.7%	15.7%	17.5%	20.8%
$40,000-$59,999	31.4%	28.8%	32.9%	27.6%	42.7%
$60,000-$99,999	17.0%	19.7%	17.5%	15.7%	19.7%
$100,000 or more	6.0%	5.4%	6.3%	5.2%	3.9%
Less than $30,000	29.4%	32.3%	27.6%	33.9%	12.9%
$40,000 or more	54.4%	53.9%	56.7%	48.5%	66.3%

Parents' Education Level

We turn now to a number of other indicators of student and family characteristics. Like the survey data on family income, these indicators do not allow for comparisons between charter and noncharter schools. Nevertheless, they help paint a more complete picture of the types of students and families choosing to attend Michigan charter schools and provide important context for interpreting data on academic and other outcomes. The data do allow us to make comparisons among charter schools in Michigan (e.g., EMO vs. non-EMO schools) and with charter schools in a handful of other states.

The level of parents' education is often found to influence student achievement, even after one controls for race and income. The level of formal education of the sampled parents varied considerably: Slightly less than 3 percent indicated that they had not completed high school, 25.6 percent of the parents ended their formal schooling after graduating from high school, 38.3 percent completed less than four years of college, 15.5 percent obtained a bachelor's degree, 6.3 percent had a BA plus some graduate courses, and 11.4 percent completed a graduate or professional degree. EMO-operated schools appear to cater to families with slightly higher levels of education attainment than non-EMO schools, and the parents of children in National Heritage Academies had the highest levels of formal education. Overall, Michigan charter school parents are similar to charter school parents in other states surveyed. Table 5.3 summarizes these findings.

Table 5.3 Highest Level of Parents' Formal Education

	Michigan Charter Schools	*Composite Comparison Group*	*EMO-Operated Schools*	*Non-EMO Schools*	*National Heritage Academies*
Did not complete high school	2.9%	5.3%	2.7%	3.4%	1.7%
Completed high school	25.6%	27.3%	25.3%	26.4%	28.1%
Less than four years of college	38.3%	35.2%	37.6%	40.1%	35.4%
College graduate	15.5%	16.4%	16.0%	14.4%	19.1%
Graduate courses, no degree	6.3%	7.1%	5.8%	7.5%	5.1%
Graduate/professional degree	11.4%	8.8%	12.6%	8.2%	10.7%
Total % With College Degree	33.2%	32.3%	34.4%	30.1%	34.9%

Highest Level of Education Charter School Students Plan to Complete

Surveys were also administered to charter school students in 1998.[7] These were limited to students in Grades 5-12. In the surveys, students were asked about the highest level of education they planned to complete. Generally, we would expect students with greater family resources and social capital to have higher educational aspirations. Thus, educational aspirations may provide further clues about social sorting in charter schools. Just under 5 percent of the sampled students expected to stop their schooling after high school, while 9.5 percent planned to complete a two-year degree, 30.4 percent planned to complete a four-year degree, and approximately 26 percent planned to go on to graduate school, which was explained to the students to include training after the bachelor's degree that included a master's, doctoral, or professional degree (see Table 5.4). Not surprisingly, nearly 30 percent of the students were still not sure about their future school/training plans beyond high school.

Comparisons between Michigan charter schools and those in the composite comparison group are made problematic by the relatively high proportion of students answering *Not sure yet*, which is perhaps not surprising given that a high proportion of Michigan charter school students are in the elementary grades. We do, however, find some interesting differences among Michigan charter school students. Students enrolled in EMO-operated schools tend to have slightly higher educational aspirations than those in other charter schools. Indeed, while nearly 28 percent of students in EMO schools plan to pursue a graduate or professional degree, less than 22 percent of students in non-EMO schools plan to do so. On the other end of the spectrum, fewer students in EMO-run charter schools plan to terminate their education with high school.

Table 5.4 Highest Level of Formal Education That Students Expect to Complete

	Michigan Charter Schools (N=1,880)	Composite Comparison Group (N=2,182)	EMO-Operated Schools (N=1,284)	Non-EMO Schools (N=596)	National Heritage Academies (N=299)
Complete high school	4.9%	6.7%	4.1%	6.6%	2.3%
Two-year college	9.5%	8.9%	8.1%	12.6%	8.1%
Four-year college	30.4%	29.4%	29.4%	32.4%	34.6%
Graduate/professional degree	25.9%	36.7%	27.8%	21.6%	26.8%
Not sure yet	29.3%	18.2%	30.5%	26.7%	28.2%

Household Types

Previous research has found that students from single-parent homes are at a disadvantage in terms of academic performance. Almost 82 percent of the parents surveyed indicated that their children were in two-parent homes, while 17.5 percent were in single-parent homes and 0.7 percent lived in other types of households (e.g., student living with other relatives or residing in state facility). Table 5.5 illustrates the self-reported data on household type, plus data for other comparison groups.

Table 5.5 Household Types for Students Attending Charter School

	Michigan Charter Schools	*Composite Comparison Group*	*EMO-Operated Schools*	*Non-EMO Schools*	*National Heritage Academies*
Two parents/guardians	81.8%	69.9%	86.2%	70.9%	92.5%
Single parent/guardian	17.5%	29.3%	13.6%	27.4%	7.5%
Other	0.7%	0.8%	0.3%	1.7%	0.0%

It is apparent from the table that Michigan charter schools attract more traditional two-parent families than the composite comparison group.[8] Equally notable is the fact that EMO-operated schools attract more two-parent families than do the non-EMO schools. This finding is especially strong for schools operated by National Heritage Academies.

Amount of Time Volunteering at Charter Schools

Not all educationally significant background variables can be described in terms of demographic attributes, however. It is possible that even where charter schools attract low-income, nonwhite, single-parent students, they tend to select children in this group who come from families who place a high value on education. In analyzing responses to the parent surveys, it was interesting to find that 64 percent of the parents reported that they did not volunteer at all or only to a very limited degree (i.e., less than three hours per month). A much smaller proportion of the parents reported volunteering quite extensively. Specifically, almost 15 percent of the parents volunteered between four and six hours per month, 6.3 percent volunteered between seven and nine hours per month, 4.3 percent volunteered between 10 and 12 hours, and 10.3 percent volunteered more than 12 hours per month.

Only 23 percent of the sampled Michigan parents believed that voluntary work was required at their charter school, although from interviews it is clear that the schools expect greater support and volunteer work from parents. This figure was much lower than in other states. For example, 46 percent of the parents in the composite comparison group believed that volunteering at the school was required. We also found that parents whose children attend EMO schools volunteered more than parents at non-EMO schools. In total, nearly 65 percent of the sampled Michigan parents reported that they did not volunteer at school at all, or to a very limited degree (i.e., less than 3 hours per month).

Previous School Attended

In 1998, when we surveyed charter school students, approximately 56 percent of the students reported that they had been enrolled in their charter school for one year or less. Almost 29 percent of the sampled students had been enrolled for two years, and just over 15 percent of the students indicated that they had been enrolled for three or more years.

As Figure 5.6 illustrates, approximately 70 percent of the sampled students in the Michigan charter schools had previously attended public schools. Of the remaining 30 percent, 15 attended either a private or a parochial school, 5.6 percent were home schooled, and 9 percent did not attend school (i.e., they were entering kindergarten and had not previously attended school).[9]

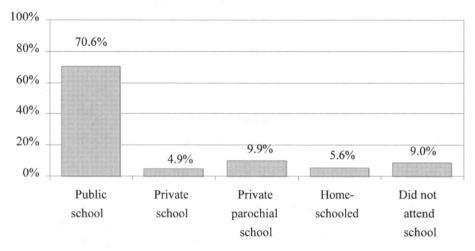

Figure 5.6 Previous School Attended by Charter School Students: Responses From Sampled Parents

Among the schools in our sample, there was considerable variation in the types of schools from which the charter schools were attracting their students. While several charter schools had no students that previously attended a private/parochial school, a few schools had more than half of their students coming from non-public–school backgrounds.

When comparing Michigan with other states, we found that Michigan charter schools attract more students from private or parochial schools than the composite comparison group. Among the Michigan charter schools, we found that the EMO-operated schools attracted more students from private or parochial schools than non-EMO schools. Particularly noteworthy is that 25.5 percent of the students at schools operated by National Heritage Academies came from private or parochial schools (6.1 percent from private and 19.4 percent from parochial private schools).

The large differences in the school types from which charter schools attract students speak to the mix of public and private interests these schools serve. While some schools or groups of schools attract students from a variety of school forms, some schools obviously recruit more extensively from families that have previously enrolled their children in private or parochial schools. This suggests that Michigan charter schools are providing new public school options to a significant number of families that were already exercising nonpublic school options before the advent of charter schools.

Special Education—or the Lack of It—in Michigan Charter Schools

Special education is one of the most complicated and controversial areas that schools and policymakers need to address. Critics charge that charter schools either avoid enrolling special education students or "counsel them out" once they are enrolled. Charter school operators, for their part, point out that even a single student with a severe disability could bankrupt a small charter school. In this section of the chapter we take up this vexing issue.

Significant improvements have been made in the instruction of students with special needs within the public school sphere over the last few decades. A large body of complex rules and regulations covering the area of special education has evolved, many of which require legal expertise to interpret. Charter schools are bound by most of the same special education rules and regulations as regular public schools. Several factors suggest that charter schools will face great difficulties when it comes to special education. First, many staff members and school leaders are new or have relatively little experience in this area. Second, many of the charter schools—because they are new—do not have procedures and routines in place to screen and provide services to students with special needs. Third, charter schools are already devoting a smaller proportion of their budgets to instruction than are regular public schools (see Chapter 4 on charter school finance), so students who require extra support are harder to accommodate. Finally, there is a shortage of certified special education teachers. In part because of their lower teacher salaries, it is likely that charter schools have a harder time recruiting and retaining these scarce teachers.

In the remainder of this section, we provide an overview of relevant federal and state laws and regulations regarding the provision of special education in public schools. We then provide an overview of the organization, funding, and monitoring of special education in Michigan, followed by data on the number and percentage of students with various disabling conditions. Finally, we draw comparisons between EMO and non-EMO schools.

Federal and State Legislative and Regulatory Requirements

Specific federal legislation establishing the educational rights of students with disabilities and federal funding for special education programs originated with the Education of All Handicapped Children Act (1975). The 1997 amendments and reauthorization of that act, referred to as the Individuals with Disabilities Education Act (IDEA), provides states with guidelines and financial incentives for providing appropriate educational services to students in publicly funded schools.[10] In addition, legislation such as Section 504 of the Rehabilitation Act of 1973 and Title II of the Americans with Disabilities Act enumerates specific penalties for not providing appropriate services for students identified as having a disability. States may not seek exemption from these federal special education or civil rights laws or regulations (Ahearn, 1999; Lange, 1997). Although all state charter school laws require charter schools to comply with federal and state special education regulations, there are typically not any clear guidelines for charter school compliance with special education and other federal disability rights requirements. Special education, undoubtedly the most regulated area of public education, is often not addressed in detail in state charter school laws (Dale, 1999).

Under Michigan law, charter schools—like all public schools—are responsible for providing special education services. Likewise, all public schools are expected to provide a full range of services so that students with disabilities can be placed in the least restrictive environment that still allows them to function effectively.[11] The intermediate school districts play an important role in providing, coordinating, and channeling special education funding for school districts and charter schools. However, considerable uncertainty exists in the application to charter schools of special education funding, admission policies, and compliance monitoring.

Finance. As discussed in some detail in Chapter 4, all local education agencies in Michigan receive state foundation funding based on the number of students enrolled. Per-pupil special education funding is determined using a formula that includes the number of hours per day (full-time equivalents) that a student receives services and the category of the identified disability and/or the type of program providing services. In addition to the per-pupil foundation grant, districts complete a final cost report at the end of the school year for payment of unreimbursed costs for special education services. As highlighted in Chapter 4, the districts do not receive sufficient special education funds from federal and state sources, so they must cover the shortfall by using general operating funds.

Admission policies and compliance monitoring. State regulations regarding admission and inclusion of students with disabilities are based on federal regulations outlined in the Individuals with Disabilities Education Act (IDEA) of 1997. Since charter schools are considered local education agencies in Michigan, they must provide the same safeguards to ensure that students are not discriminated against or denied admission based on ability.

IDEA requires that states provide specific plans for monitoring school compliance with rules and regulations pertaining to programs for students with disabilities. As of the fall of 2001, the Michigan Department of Education Office of Special Education is revising state monitoring procedures and schedules to comply with the requirements included in the reauthorization of IDEA and to include charter schools in all aspects of compliance monitoring.

Students Receiving Special Educational Services and the Nature of Their Disabilities

The percentage of enrolled students receiving special education services in charter schools is considerably lower than that reported by traditional public schools. Table 5.6 provides a comparison between average state of Michigan enrollments and Michigan charter school enrollments by disability group. The total share of students with disabilities in Michigan public schools was 12.3 percent 1998-99. In the same year, charter schools in Michigan, enrolled only a small proportion (3.7 percent) of students with disabilities.[12]

There are a number of possible explanations for the lower proportion of students with disabilities in the charter schools. Charter schools may avoid enrolling students with special needs due to higher costs for special education, the requirement for specialized and certified staff, and/or the complex nature of these services. Also, parents are made aware by charter school representatives that charter schools have limited resources (human and financial). Interviews with parents suggest that in many cases parents are under the impression that charter schools practice inclusion only, rather than providing a range of services (from most- to least-restrictive) depending on the needs of individual children.

In some instances, charter school staff may be unaware that children with mild disabilities are enrolled in their schools. We know from our field work that some parents choose a charter school for their child with special needs because they want their child mainstreamed completely and not labeled. Therefore, when they enroll their child in the charter school, they do not inform school officials that their child has/had a disability or an individualized education plan. Some charter schools have insisted that this is a common occurrence, both for children with special educational needs, as well as for children with behavioral or disciplinary problems (Horn & Miron, 2000).

The bottom two rows of in Table 5.6 include the percentage of all students with disabilities by category. From these data we can see that not only do charter schools have a lower overall percentage of students with special education needs (see comparisons in top three rows), but that students with disabilities in charter schools tend to have disabilities that are milder in nature and that are more easily remediated. In fact, charter schools had no children

Table 5.6 Percentage of Enrolled Students With Disabilities by Category

	Learning Disabilities (LD)	Speech & Language Impaired (SLI)	Mentally Impaired (MI) *	Emotionally Impaired (EI)	Physically & Otherwise Health Im-paired (POHI)	Autistic Impaired (AI)	Severely Multiply Impaired (SXI)	Hearing Impaired (HI)	Visually Impaired (VI)	Total**
USA 1997-98	5.60%	2.28%	1.15%	0.92%	0.54%	0.08%	0.20%	0.14%	0.05%	10.90%
State of Michigan 1998-99	5.27%	3.00%	1.49%	1.08%	0.79%	0.22%	0.22%	0.20%	0.06%	12.33%
Michigan Charters 1998-99	1.52%	1.37%	0.24%	0.32%	0.20%	0.02%	0.0%	0.05%	0.02%	3.74%
Distribution of all students with disabilities by category										
State of Michigan	42.7%	24.3%	12.1%	8.8%	6.4%	1.8%	1.8%	1.6%	0.5%	100%
Michigan Charters	40.6%	36.8%	6.6%	8.5%	5.4%	0.4%	0.0%	1.3%	0.4%	100%

Notes: * Mental Impairments (MI) includes educable (EMI), trainable (TMI), and severely (SMI).

** Totals do not include children ages 0-5 who qualify for preprimary special education services. This accounts for 0.02 percent in the traditional public schools and 0 percent for the charter schools. Also, we did not include Macomb Academy in our figures since this charter school serves only special education students. Had we included the students from this school, the charter school total would have increased to 3.9 percent.

with multiple disabilities and almost none with autism, visual impairments, or hearing impairments. Unfortunately, the data do not allow us to determine to what extent these patterns are due to parent self-selection versus screening by charter school officials. Whatever the cause, special education enrollment patterns in charter schools should raise concerns among policymakers.

Most of the children with disabilities in charter schools fall into two categories: speech and language impairments and learning disabilities. Nevertheless, the proportion of students in these typically high-incidence categories is still surprisingly low compared with the traditional public schools. There are at least two possible reasons for charter schools to report high proportions of students with speech and language impairments and learning disabilities. First, both disabilities are usually identified during elementary grades, with SLI reaching peak identification by second grade. Charter schools in Michigan largely cater to Grades K-6. Second, programming for both disabilities can be accomplished in fairly cost-effective manners within the regular education classrooms with the support of speech and language teachers and special education teacher consultants. Speech and language teachers can legally be responsible for caseloads of up to 60 students, while teacher consultants can be responsible for up to 25 students. These caseload numbers are considerably larger than the 15 students legally allowable for most other disability categories. In addition, students with SLI or LD rarely require costly related services that school districts may have to provide students with other types of disabilities.

Education Management Organizations and Special Education

Special education teachers and some parents of students with disabilities have "loudly" left charter schools operated by education management companies (EMOs) (see Evaluation Center, 2000). At least one teacher has taken up a law suit against National Heritage Academies, and several families have threatened to do so.

From a policy point of view, the relevant question is: Are these simply isolated incidents, or indicative of more general problems? Here, the data yield a mixture of conclusions. Our findings indicate that EMO-operated charter schools actually had a slightly higher proportion of students with disabilities than schools with no EMO (3.8 percent compared with 3.3 percent). Nevertheless, non-EMO schools were more likely to have students with disabling conditions that required more resources and years of service to address. For example, forty percent of the special education students in the EMO-run charters had speech and language impairments—the easiest and least costly disabilities to accommodate—compared with 21 percent in the non-EMO charter schools. The reverse is true for students with more severe disabilities, who are enrolled in greater proportions in non-EMO schools than EMO schools (Horn & Miron, 2000).

Further Thoughts on Special Education

While the findings reported in this section suggest that not all is well with special education in the charter schools, it is important to recognize that regular public schools also are not able to fully satisfy parents who have students with special needs. In fact, a large number of the parents we surveyed indicated that one important reason for choosing charter schools was the inability of their previous school to accommodate the child's special needs (see Table 5.7).

While charter schools are expected to do more for less, in many cases the inclusion of students with disabilities appears to be beyond what some of these schools are able to manage. We have seen, however, that some charter schools are clearly up to the challenge. Livingston Developmental Academy and Macomb Academy are two such charter schools. Livingston Developmental Academy, although not established primarily to serve students with special needs, provides specialized instructional techniques that have proven successful with certain types of learning problems. Macomb Academy, on the other hand, was established specifically to work with students with mental impairments.

Beyond Demographics: Reasons for Choosing Charter Schools

Up to this point, we have examined a number of factors that could be expected to influence student achievement and other educational outcomes. These have included familiar indicators such as race, poverty, and family structure, and less familiar indicators such as educational aspirations and parent volunteerism. We turn now to a discussion of the reasons parents and families choose charter schools. Like data on student and family demographics, this information allows us to further explore whether families who choose charter schools are different in educationally significant ways from other families and, thus, whether charter schools enjoy any kind advantage by virtue of the students they enroll.

As we shall see, the reasons reported by parents for choosing a charter school are often different from reasons given by students, in part because the parent sample covers students in all grades (K-12) while the student sample covers only Grades 5-12. While it was interesting to consider the student's perceived reasons, it was clear from the survey data as well as from interviews with students that the choice of schools was really a parental decision. In fact, the students reported that the most important reason they enrolled in a charter school was that their parents thought the school was best for them.

Parents' Reasons for Choosing Their Charter School

Table 5.7 contains the rank-ordered reasons for choosing a charter school provided by our sample of 1,040 parents in 1998. The parents were asked to rate each factor on a 1 to 5 scale (1=*Not Important* to 5=*Very Important*) according to how important it was in choosing their charter school.

As one can see from the results in Table 5.7, some parents chose a charter school because of what they did not like at their local traditional public school, while others chose a charter school because of what was being promised.[13] A number of state and national charter school studies suggest that the reasons parents choose a charter school are indicative of what actually exists at the charter school. An example of such an inference might be the following: parents say they choose due to the high quality of instruction; therefore, charter schools have a high quality of instruction. It is important, however, to distinguish between reasons for choosing and what actually exists at the charter school, especially since most of the parents chose their charter school before it was even open and would have had limited information about the actual quality of instruction that would be offered.

In order to differentiate between what parents expected and what the school actually provides, a portion of the parent questionnaire was designed to have parents contrast their initial expectations with what they currently perceived or were experiencing at the charter school. Here we found statistically significant differences between what parents initially expected and what they were currently experiencing. This indicates that while parents chose for a particular set of reasons, these expectations were not being met. Chapter 9, which addresses customer satisfaction, looks at these data in greater detail.[14]

Parents in the composite comparison group were more likely to report that lack of special services at the previous school was an important reason for choosing than parents in Michigan charter schools. Likewise, parents at EMO-operated schools were less likely to see lack of special services at previous schools as an important reason for choosing a charter school.

Parents in EMO-run schools indicated that their preference for a private school was a more important reason for choosing a charter school than did the parents in non-EMO schools. One other interesting difference was evident in the importance of recommendations or referrals from their previous school. The parents in EMO schools were less likely to note referrals from previous schools as important than were parents in the non-EMO schools.

Table 5.7 Parents' Reasons for Choosing Their Charter School, Rank Ordered by Mean Scores

	Not Important 1	2	3	4	Very Important 5	Michigan Charter Schools M (SD)	Composite Comparison Group M (SD)	EMO M (SD)	Non-EMO M (SD)	NHA M (SD)
Good teachers and high-quality instruction	1.6%	2.0%	7.6%	19.3%	69.5%	4.53(0.84)	4.56(0.83)	4.55(0.85)	4.48(0.82)	4.70(0.68)
I prefer the emphasis and educational philosophy of this school	1.6%	1.8%	9.3%	26.8%	60.5%	4.43(0.85)	4.34(0.94)	4.48(0.83)	4.31(0.91)	4.67(0.66)
Safety for my child	4.8%	4.2%	14.0%	17.6%	59.4%	4.23(1.13)	4.44(1.04)	4.24(1.14)	4.19(1.12)	4.44(1.01)
Academic reputation (high standards) of this school	4.1%	4.3%	16.9%	27.8%	46.9%	4.09(1.08)	4.37(0.92)	4.15(1.07)	3.95(1.09)	4.51(0.81)
Promises made by charter school's spokespersons	9.5%	8.3%	21.9%	29.1%	31.1%	3.64(1.26)	4.11(1.14)	3.77(1.21)	3.32(1.32)	3.73(1.18)
My interest in an educational reform effort	10.9%	10.6%	27.6%	27.8%	23.1%	3.42(1.25)	3.83(1.25)	3.47(1.23)	3.30(1.30)	3.68(1.12)
My child wanted to attend this school	18.0%	11.1%	24.5%	17.6%	38.8%	3.28(1.44)	3.49(1.44)	3.16(1.42)	3.58(1.46)	2.68(1.30)
I was unhappy with the curriculum and instruction at previous school	25.2%	7.9%	16.7%	15.8%	34.4%	3.26(1.60)	3.26(1.60)	3.26(1.60)	3.26(1.60)	3.24(1.58)
My child has special needs that were not met at previous school	35.9%	9.4%	14.6%	13.4%	26.7%	2.86(1.65)	3.09(1.66)	2.67(1.63)	3.31(1.61)	2.53(1.57)
Convenient location	31.0%	19.5%	27.9%	11.0%	10.7%	2.51(1.32)	2.94(1.54)	2.51(1.28)	2.51(1.40)	2.91(1.25)
I prefer a private school but could not afford one	40.9%	12.5%	20.5%	11.5%	14.6%	2.46(1.47)	2.98(1.63)	2.56(1.47)	2.24(1.46)	2.75(1.44)
My child was performing poorly at previous school	45.8%	9.5%	16.5%	9.2%	19.1%	2.46(1.58)	2.75(1.63)	2.28(1.50)	2.92(1.67)	2.20(1.42)
Recommendations of teacher/official at my child's previous school	63.1%	9.4%	15.6%	6.0%	5.8%	1.82(1.23)	2.49(1.60)	1.70(1.12)	2.11(1.42)	1.66(1.04)

Note: All items are on a 5-point Likert scale with 1 = *Not Important* and 5 = *Very Important*.
Items are rank ordered according to strength of satisfaction with Michigan charter schools.

Students' Reasons for Choosing Their Charter School

The majority of student respondents indicated that their parents' preference was the primary reason for choosing the charter school. Nearly 50 percent of the students rated as "Very Important" that their parents thought the charter school would be better for them. Following this was an item dealing with the perceived safety at the charter school. The full set of results on students' reasons for choosing their charter school can be found in the appendices of Horn and Miron (1999). Our analysis of the reasons that students gave for choosing a charter school revealed large differences between students in charter high schools and students in lower grades. The reasons for choosing charter high schools were more often due to difficulties the students were experiencing in their previous schools. Smaller school size was also a more important factor for high school students than for students at the lower levels.

The results suggest that students in EMO-operated schools were less likely than students in non-EMO schools to choose a charter school due to poor performance in their previous school or because they did not receive sufficient individual attention from teachers in their previous school. Convenient location was also another factor in which the EMO and non-EMO schools differed. Students in EMO-operated schools were less likely to cite convenient location as an important factor. This is likely related to the fact that the EMO-operated schools often do not provide transportation to and from schools.

In summary, we can see that the primary reasons parents chose charter schools were centered around the perceived quality of instruction and the particular philosophy or curricular profile of the school. Safety and—to a lesser extent—dissatisfaction with previous schools were other factors that influenced the decision to choose a charter school. Students reported that the decision to attend a charter school was largely made by their parents. However, they noted concerns about teacher quality at previous school and the belief that teachers would be better at the charter school as reasons for attending charter schools.

Conclusion

An important element of the theory of school choice is that families will sort into schools according to their agreement with the schools' educational philosophy and mission. This, it is believed, will yield schools with a mission coherence that allows them to focus more of their energies on implementing effective educational interventions and less on refereeing philosophical conflicts. However, as public schools, charter schools may not select students on the basis of ability, philosophical conviction, race, or income. Critics often charge that, such strictures notwithstanding, this process of sorting leads to segregation (or resegregation) on race, income, and other invidious categories. Or, such sorting might grow from an attempt to cut costs, as was suggested in Chapter 4.

In this chapter we have found some evidence that Michigan charter schools have contributed to social sorting among students. First and foremost, charter schools have largely avoided educating the more-expensive-to-educate students in the high school grades. There is less evidence of sorting in terms of family income, although student characteristics in schools operated by specific EMOs clearly differed from their respective host districts, both in ethnicity and proportion of students qualifying for free and reduced lunch. The picture painted by these comparisons is considerably less sanguine than the one provided by previous studies (which relied on comparisons to state averages).

Once we look school by school, there is evidence that a large portion of charter schools are contributing to sorting by race. Indeed, we found that many charter schools enrolled a significantly smaller proportion of minority students than surrounding noncharter schools, and that others enrolled significantly higher proportions of these students.

Analysis of data on special education raises more serious concerns about sorting, both in terms of the overall proportion of special education students and the severity of disabilities represented in the charter schools. We also examined data on parents' education, family structure, and volunteerism. Here, though, we lacked the data necessary to make systematic comparisons between charter and noncharter schools.

It is important to note that the data presented in this chapter point to concerns about social sorting arising from charter schools but do *not* allow us to diagnose the reasons behind such sorting. While critics have charged that charter schools engage in intentional cream-skimming, the enrollment data presented in this chapter do not allow us to assess the extent to which enrollment patterns arise from self-selection by families versus selectivity by the charter schools themselves. It is also worth considering that charter schools' enrollment patterns are likely driven in part by location decisions. Quite simply, charter schools that choose to locate in inner cities are more likely to end up enrolling higher proportions of nonwhite, low-income students than schools that locate in the suburbs. Finally, schools' decisions about which market niches to fill are also likely to drive enrollment patterns. Further research is needed to assess the reasons behind social sorting in and around Michigan charter schools.

Further research will not, however, help resolve some of the larger policy questions related to sorting in charter schools. As stated at the outset of the chapter (and in Chapter 1), sorting is a core component of the idea of school choice, as families select schools that most closely match their educational preferences. But what if families' educational preferences are correlated with their race and income? For instance, schools featuring Afro-centric curricula are more likely to attract African American families, schools offering Latinocentered curricula more likely to attract Latinos, and so on. The question for policy makers is whether such social sorting, even if driven by the pursuit of educational preferences, is acceptable in public schools.

Notes

1. In our parent surveys there is a weak positive relationship between grade level and agreement with the statement, "My child has special needs that were not met at the previous school" (rho = 0.25, p < 0.01). Appendix E in Horn & Miron (2000) provides enrollment profiles for the major EMOs. From these profiles it is apparent that National Heritage Academies and Edison Schools Inc. most closely restrict their enrollments to the lower elementary grades.

2. The proportion of nonwhite students has varied considerably over the years, especially between 1996 and 1998 when a large number of suburban charter schools were added. During interviews, some community representatives referred to "ethnic cleansing" in a few charter schools. We examined two of these alleged cases during our fieldwork in 1998. While we did see drops of 5 to 7 percent in the concentration of minorities between school years we could not link these drops to a change in school policy and largely could not substantiate these claims. However, it appeared that drops in the proportion of minorities were more prevalent in schools with high attrition rates.

3. Cobb & Glass (1999) found that charter schools in Arizona had fewer minorities than their host districts and that half of the charter schools exhibited evidence of substantial ethnic separation. In the states included in the composite comparison group, we found that the proportion of minorities was substantially higher than the state average, yet comparable to the school districts in which the charter schools are established.

4. Some particularly interesting findings about FRL participation include the following:

- Seventy-five of 130 EMO-run schools 75 of 130 schools reported FRL data, compared with 23 of 31 non-EMO schools.
- Large charter schools are more likely to participate in the FRL program than small schools.
- All NHA schools now have FRL data. A few years ago none of their schools appear to have participated.
- About a third of Beacon schools participate in the program, and two of the three Edison schools participated in the program and reported data
- Approximately one-quarter of the schools operated by Leona Group, Mosaica, and Helicon and Associates did not participate in the FRL program.
- No schools linked with Educare, Choice School Associates, Schoolhouse Services and Staffing, Smart Schools, or Synergy Training Solutions participated in the program. Most surprising is that no schools operated by

Charter School Administrative Services participated in or had data on FRL, since their schools are located in areas where the proportion of families qualifying for FRL is very high.

Schools that wish to participate in the program can arrange to contract out lunch services so that the school is not burdened with having a kitchen and cafeteria. At National Heritage Academies, for example, the school saves on kitchen staff and the need to have and maintain a cafeteria by having cold lunches delivered to the school. All the students eat lunch in their classrooms.

5. Surveys were administered to a sample of parents and guardians at 51 charter schools in 1998. The Parent Charter School Survey was administered to different groups of parents at two points in time, the first time during January and February 1998 and the second in May 1998. A total of 1,040 completed parent surveys were returned, which corresponds with a 61 percent response rate.

6. The composite comparison group (CCG) included schools from Connecticut, Pennsylvania, and Illinois that were in at least their second year when surveyed in order to match the average age of the Michigan charter schools. We also employed a weighting scheme in order to compensate for the unequal distribution of schools across the three states. The weight w compares the number of cases actually sampled from each state with the number of cases that would have been sampled were the sample to have drawn equally from each state. This adjustment alleviates the problem introduced by the fact that one state has more cases than other states and thus would overwhelm an unweighted composite index. Formally, the weight is given by the following expression:

$$w = \frac{n_{equal}}{n_i}$$

where n_{equal} is the number of cases that would have been drawn had the sample been drawn equally from each of the states, and n_i is the number of cases actually sampled from a given state i, where i is an index variable representing states. The number of cases sampled, assuming we could have taken an equal draw from each state, is given by

$$n_{equal} = \frac{\sum_i n_i}{3}$$

where n_i is the number of cases sampled in a given state i. The denominator (3) represents the number of states in the sample.

7. The aim of the student sampling was to select at least three classes (Grades 5-12) or at least 40 students at each school. A total of 1,880 student surveys were collected from the schools. The response rate, which was calculated on the number of students who completed the surveys in the sampled classes, was 92.8 percent.

8. Given that divorce rates tend to increase with the age of the families' children, this comparison was made problematic by the fact that a larger share of Michigan charter school students are in the elementary grades than is the case with the comparison group states. For this reason we re-analyzed the data for only families with children in Grades K-6 and found that the large differences between Michigan charter schools and the CCG were largely unchanged.

9. It is common that after the first year of charter school operation, the largest group of new students is at the entry grade level for a particular school.

10. The IDEA designates specific categories of disabilities eligible for special education services, although the names of these disabilities vary somewhat from state to state. More detailed descriptions of the disabilities categories and the identifying labels used in Michigan are provided in Horn and Miron (2000).

11. While all public schools are required to have a plan to provide a full continuum of services, charter schools typically provide only inclusive classes and minimal pull-out options. This is one area that appears to need further attention from charter schools

12. Because the special education enrollment figures across districts were rather similar and because the prevalence of disabilities is generally quite uniform we have used the state averages for comparison purposes rather than an aggregate of host districts.

13. According to the National Study of Charter Schools (RPP International, 1998), parents choose charter schools because they either are dissatisfied with the public schools and/or are attracted to charters. The predominant areas of parental dissatisfaction with public schools are (i) low academic expectations, (ii) poor instructional practices, (iii) environment and culture, (iv) safety, and (v) sense that parents are not welcome at school. The top six reasons parents were attracted to charter schools were: (i) nurturing environment, (ii) safe environment, (iii) value system, (iv) quality of academic program, (v) high standards for achievement, and (vi) small class size.

14. Data on initial expectations contrasted with current experience, as well as a discussion of these data, can also be found in Horn & Miron (1999).

6

Teachers' Characteristics and Working Conditions

Charter schools are schools of choice for teachers as well as families. As we saw in Chapter 1, the charter school concept suggests that choice leads educational actors to sort themselves according to educational philosophy. Agreement on educational philosophy by school staff and parents, in turn, might allow schools to spend more time focusing on instruction and less time managing internal conflicts. Facilitating school choice for teachers might also promote a shared professional culture and higher levels of professional autonomy, which the literature suggests leads ultimately to improved levels of student achievement (Lee & Smith, 1996). Moreover, charter proponents often argue that by providing a better match between teachers' educational preferences and schools, charter schools will encourage teachers to innovate.

However, as with choice among families, choice for teachers might also have a darker side. Critics have argued that the aforementioned sorting leads to charter schools that are populated with teachers with inferior training and experience.

This chapter examines the issue of demographic sorting with discussions of teachers' background characteristics (including role, grade levels taught, gender, race, and age) and their professional credentials (including certification, experience, and formal education). Next, the chapter attempts to assess the extent to which charter school teachers in Michigan are sorting themselves into schools on the basis of educational philosophy through an examination of the reasons teachers seek employment in the schools. Finally, the chapter attempts to assess the extent to which charter schools are fertile ground for innovation through an examination of teacher working conditions, including autonomy, professional opportunities, salary, and turnover.

Teacher Demographics

We begin with a brief overview of charter school teachers' demographic characteristics. This will help us to assess the extent to which the charter reform is leading teachers to sort themselves (or to be sorted) into schools on the basis of race, ethnicity, and other such categories. There are three main sources of data for the findings reported in this section. One is the teacher surveys we administered in 1998.[1] Another is data from the Michigan Department of Education. The third is secondary documents describing teacher qualifications at the state and national levels. The survey data were collected in 1998 as part of a state-mandated evaluation.

The task of interpreting survey (and other) data is facilitated by examining comparison groups on comparable indicators, which provide some sense of what is typical. As with the race and income data presented in the previous chapter, the logical comparison group is matched host districts. Unfortunately, administering survey instruments to traditional public schools was beyond the scope of this particular project. Moreover, the fact that we had survey data for only one year in Michigan makes longitudinal comparisons impossible. To partially address these limitations, we constructed a "composite comparison group" comprised of teachers and staff in three other states that completed the same surveys (Connecticut, Illinois, and Pennsylvania).[2] We also made comparisons with charter school data from the federally sponsored studies of charter schools conducted by RPP International (2000).

Role and Proportion of Staff Devoted to Instruction

Among the 728 teachers and staff responding in Michigan charter schools during 1998, 68.5 percent indicated they were teachers and 12.6 percent were teaching assistants. Approximately 4 percent indicated they were principals or school directors, and 14.8 percent indicated they had some other title or position. We received no surveys from student teachers during data collection.

The distribution of school staff by role is rather similar to data for traditional public schools (National Center for Education Statistics, 2000), although the charter schools had slightly more teaching assistants and considerably fewer "other" staff. The fact that our charter school sample had fewer "other" staff is partially due to the fact that our sample excluded clerical and cleaning staff.

Distribution of Teachers and Staff by Grade Level

The teachers and staff were asked to indicate which grade they worked with most. The distribution of teachers reflected the enrollment patterns for students. In other words, most teachers (65 percent) worked at the elementary level, while 22 percent worked at the middle school level, and only 13 percent worked at the secondary level. As for the composite comparison group, only 38 percent of teachers and staff indicated they worked in elementary schools, while 19 percent taught at the middle school level and 43 percent in high school. The enrollment patterns in the composite comparison group clearly differed from Michigan charter schools.

Gender and Race/Ethnicity

Like other public schools, females comprised the majority (80 percent) of teachers and staff in charter schools. Among the school directors/principals, 70 percent were female and 30 percent male. The proportion of female staff in Michigan charter schools was higher than in the composite comparison group. This may be explained in part by the fact that Michigan charter schools are more heavily concentrated at the elementary level, where females typically comprise a larger proportion of school staff.

From the data we collected with surveys, we determined that 86.1 percent of teachers/staff were white, 7.9 percent African American, 1.3 percent Hispanic, 0.8 percent Asian or Pacific Islander, and 3.9 percent Native American. As Table 6.1 shows, the proportion of minorities working in Michigan charter schools is lower than that in the composite comparison group (CCG) schools.

Table 6.1 Distribution of Charter School Teachers/Staff by Ethnicity

	Michigan Charter Schools (N=728)	Composite Comparison Group (N=937)	EMO (N=478)	Non-EMO (N=250)	National Heritage Academies (N=132)
White	86.1%	56.6%	92.8%	73.0%	95.4%
Black	7.9%	31.0%	5.3%	12.9%	2.3%
Hispanic	1.3%	10.0%	0.6%	2.5%	0.8%
Asian	0.8%	1.5%	0.9%	0.8%	1.5%
Native American	3.9%	0.9%	0.4%	10.8%	0.0%

The Michigan data are also broken down according to whether or not the schools are operated by EMOs. The EMO-operated schools employed fewer minorities (7.2 percent) than the schools not operated by EMOs (27 percent). In the schools operated by National Heritage Academies, the largest EMO operating in Michigan, fewer than 5 percent of the staff were minorities. (As before, NHA is singled out because it is the largest EMO operating in Michigan.)

Age

The age distribution among Michigan charter school teachers indicates that they are younger than charter school teachers in other states and substantially younger than their counterparts in traditional public schools. Among classroom teachers, 46.2 percent were under 30 years old, 24.7 percent were in their 30s, 22.1 percent were in their 40s, and 7 percent were 50 or older. Table 6.2 illustrates the age distribution of charter school classroom teachers compared with the composite comparison group (CCG) and a national distribution. Both Michigan charter school teachers and teachers in the CCG were younger than the national average for public school teachers.

Table 6.2 Age Distribution of Charter School Classroom Teachers* Compared With Composite Comparison Group and National Distribution

	Michigan Charter Schools	Composite Comparison Group	EMO	Non-EMO	National Heritage Academies	National Public School Teachers**
Younger than 30	46.2%	37.7%	51.6%	33.6%	67.7%	11.0%
30-49	46.8%	46.2%	42.5%	56.8%	30.4%	64.2%
Older than 49	7.0%	16.1%	5.9%	9.6%	2.0%	24.8%

* Includes only staff who identify themselves as classroom teachers.
** Source of national data is *State Profiles of Public Elementary and Secondary Education, 1996-97.* U.S. Department of Education (NCES, 2000).

The data were also broken out for EMO and non-EMO schools. Here we found that EMO-operated schools had noticeably younger teaching staffs, with classroom teachers at National Heritage Academies younger still (see Table 6.2). Since younger teachers generally command lower salaries than older teachers, the relative youth of Michigan charter school teachers might the reflect the type of cost-control strategies discussed in Chapter 4.

In summary, we have found in this section that charter school teachers in Michigan are less racially and ethnically diverse and younger than charter school teachers in other states. In the next section we investigate whether the relative youth of Michigan charter school teachers is related to their levels of experience, certification status, and other qualifications for teaching.

Certification and Qualification of Teachers

Along with their youth, we find that Michigan charter school teachers are less experienced and have less formal education than their counterparts in traditional public schools. We begin by discussing formal certification.

Certification of Teachers

Of the 486 staff who indicated they were classroom teachers in 1998, 7.2 percent reported they were not certified to teach in Michigan. Of those not certified, 1.9 percent were certified to teach in another state, 3.5 percent were working toward certification, and 1.9 percent were neither certified nor working to obtain certification (see Table 6.3). These findings are of particular interest, since by law all classroom teachers in Michigan—charter and noncharter alike—must be certified; although exceptions granted to traditional public schools are also valid for charter schools. State data on teacher certification, while vague and incomplete, suggest that charter schools in Michigan do not differ greatly from traditional public schools in terms of the proportion of their staff having valid certification.[3]

Table 6.3 Distribution of Current Certification Status of Classroom Teachers*

	Michigan Charter Schools	Composite Comparison Group	EMO	Non-EMO	National Heritage Academies
Certified to teach in this state	92.8%	76.9%	94.1%	89.7%	96.0%
Certified to teach in another state	1.9%	2.4%	2.1%	1.4%	2.0%
Working to obtain certification	3.5%	16.8%	3.0%	4.8%	2.0%
Not certified and not working to obtain certification	1.9%	3.8%	0.9%	4.1%	0.0%

* Includes only staff who identify themselves as classroom teachers.

Teacher certification requirements in charter schools vary by state. The data in Table 6.3 indicate that certification rates in Michigan are much higher than in the composite comparison group, which is comprised of charter school teachers in Connecticut, Illinois, and Pennsylvania. While Michigan regulations require 100 percent of charter school teachers to be certified, the regulations for the three states in the composite comparison group are less stringent.[4]

In addition to having a valid teaching certificate, teachers are also required by law to teach only subjects in which they are certified. For example, a physical education instructor has to be certified like any other teacher, but physical education teachers are certified to teach only physical education and not physics or social studies. Most charter school teachers indicated they were teaching a subject area in which they were certified (see Table 6.4). Michigan charter schools had a higher percentage (94.4 percent) of teachers who were teaching in a subject area in which they were certified than those in the composite comparison group (79.4 percent). In part, this may be due to the fact that most Michigan charter schools are elementary schools, whereas only 32.1 percent of charter schools in the composite comparison group are elementary schools. Certified elementary teachers can teach all core subjects, while secondary level teachers are certified to teach only the subjects in which they had a major.

Table 6.4 Distribution of Teachers According to Whether or Not They Have Certification for the Subjects They Teach*

Certification for the subjects taught	Michigan Charter Schools	Composite Comparison Group	EMO	Non-EMO	National Heritage Academies
Yes	94.4%	79.4%	94.7%	93.7%	96.0%
No	2.3%	11.5%	2.1%	2.8%	1.0%
Not Applicable	3.3%	9.1%	3.2%	3.5%	3.0%

* Includes only staff who identify themselves as classroom teachers.

Formal Education

In terms of formal education, charter school teachers in the composite comparison group (CCG) appear to be more qualified than Michigan charter school teachers (see Table 6.5). Among the 480 classroom teachers we surveyed in Michigan charter schools, 82.7 percent had a B.A. as their highest college degree, 14.2 percent had an M.A., 2.5 percent had a five- or six-year certificate, and 0.6 percent had a Ph.D or Ed.D.

Table 6.5 Highest Formal Academic Degree for Classroom Teachers*

	Michigan Charter Schools	Composite Comparison Group	EMO	Non-EMO	National Heritage Academies	Michigan Public School Teachers**
Bachelor's	82.7%	61.2%	84.6%	78.3%	90.8%	46.6%
Master's	14.2%	33.9%	12.8%	17.5%	6.1%	48.1%
5- or 6-year Certificate	2.5%	2.6%	2.1%	3.5%	3.1%	4.7%
Doctorate	0.6%	2.2%	0.6%	0.7%	0.0%	0.6%

* The charter school results include only staff who identified themselves as classroom teachers.
** Source of data for Michigan is *State Profiles of Public Elementary and Secondary Education, 1996-97*. U.S. Department of Education (NCES, 2000)

Classroom teachers in the state's traditional public schools tend to have more formal training than the charter school teachers, with nearly three times more of them receiving master's degrees. Among the surveyed charter school teachers, 42.7 percent were working toward another degree, with 85.6 percent of those working toward an M.A. The national figures are rather similar to those for the state of Michigan, except that the national average has slightly more teachers with Bachelor's degrees and slightly fewer with graduate level degrees.

Years of Experience

Survey data indicate that the typical Michigan charter school teacher has approximately six years of total teaching experience, most of which came in traditional public schools. This is approximately the same as the average amount of teaching experience among charter school teachers in the composite comparison group (CCG). However, Michigan's charter school teachers have less experience than teachers in the state's traditional public schools. Indeed, only 7.4 percent of the noncharter public school teachers have less than three years of teaching experience, while 21.5 percent have between three and nine years of experience, 29.4 percent have between 10 and 20 years of experience, and 41.9 percent have more than 20 years of teaching experience (NCES, 2000).

Table 6.6 Years of Teachers' Experience in Various School Types for Charter School Classroom Teachers*

Years of Experience	Michigan Charter Schools Mean (SD)	Composite Comparison Group Mean (SD)	EMO Mean (SD)	Non-EMO Mean (SD)	National Heritage Academies Mean (SD)
Private school	0.7 (2.0)	0.8 (2.2)	0.7 (2.1)	0.8 (1.9)	0.7 (2.1)
Parochial school	0.6 (2.1)	0.3 (1.2)	0.8 (2.4)	0.2 (0.9)	1.2 (3.1)
Charter school	1.8 (0.9)	1.7 (0.7)	1.7 (0.8)	2.1 (1.0)	1.4 (0.6)
Public school	2.8 (4.7)	3.2 (5.4)	2.5 (4.3)	3.6 (2.2)	1.1 (1.7)
Total years of experience**	6.0 (5.9)	5.9 (6.0)	5.7 (5.8)	6.7 (6.2)	4.5 (4.6)
Years at current school***	1.8 (0.9)	1.7 (0.7)	1.7 (0.8)	2.1 (1.0)	1.4 (0.6)

* Includes only staff who identified themselves as classroom teachers.
** Total years of experience as an educator in the school types listed in the table
*** The Michigan data were collected in 1998 when the majority of the schools were in their second or third year of operation. Likewise, schools in the composite comparison groups were selected because they were in their second or third year of operation.

Teachers in EMO-operated schools generally have fewer years of experience and have been employed for fewer years at their current school than teachers in non-EMO schools. As with other analyses of EMO-operated schools, schools operated by National Heritage Academies stand out because, among Michigan charter schools, the teachers they employ have the least number of years of teaching experience and the fewest years employed at their current school.

Reasons to Seek Employment at a Charter School

The teacher surveys listed a number of possible reasons why teachers and staff might seek employment at a charter school. The staff were asked to rate each reason on a five-point scale according to how important each reason was in influencing their decision to seek employment at the charter school. Table 6.7 includes the results from Michigan charter school teachers and staff and compares them with charter school teachers in other states, as well as with subgroups of the Michigan schools. The items are rank-ordered from the most to least important factors for choosing to seek employment at a charter school.

One intrinsic and one extrinsic factor were among the most important reasons for seeking employment in charter schools: the opportunity to work with like-minded educators and small class sizes. Other important factors that influenced classroom teachers to join a charter school were committed parents, academic reputation, interest in an educational reform effort, school safety, more emphasis on academics, and promises made by charter school spokespersons. The two least important factors were difficulty in finding other positions and convenient location.

Many factors that influenced decisions to seek employment at charter schools were related to a better working environment; for example, working with small classes, committed parents, school safety, and high academic standards. Table 6.7 presents the frequency of responses for each item across the various comparison groups. Some interesting differences exist between comparison groups, but they are rather small.

Some charter school advocates and even some researchers have equated reasons for choosing a charter school with what actually exists at the school (Finn et al., 2000). For example, they assume that because "academic reputation/high standards" were important reasons for seeking employment, charter schools must, therefore, have a good academic reputation and high standards. In reality, the schools were quite new when the surveyed teachers sought employment, and there was likely insufficient information on which to base such judgments. In our surveys, we examined the initial expectations of charter school teachers and parents and contrasted these with what was currently

Table 6.7 Reasons for Seeking Employment at a Charter School, Classroom Teachers Only

	Not important 1	2	3	4	Very important 5	Michigan Charter Schools Mean (SD)	Composite Comparison Group Mean (SD)	EMO Mean (SD)	Non-EMO Mean (SD)	NHA Mean (SD)
Opportunity to work with like-minded educators	3.7%	3.3%	14.9%	36.2%	41.9%	4.09 (1.01)	4.19 (0.91)	4.14 (1.01)	3.99 (1.03)	4.39 (0.84)
This school has small class sizes	4.5%	3.9%	16.5%	32.9%	42.2%	4.04 (1.07)	4.06 (1.01)	4.11 (1.05)	3.88 (1.12)	4.28 (0.80)
Parents are committed	6.4%	7.6%	23.0%	31.9%	31.1%	3.74 (1.16)	3.51 (1.22)	4.00 (1.03)	3.13 (1.23)	4.36 (0.69)
Academic reputation (high standards) of this school	8.7%	7.2%	24.5%	29.0%	30.7%	3.66 (1.23)	3.57 (1.17)	3.82 (1.20)	3.28 (1.21)	4.42 (0.75)
My interest in being involved in an educational reform effort	7.1%	9.8%	20.5%	37.1%	25.5%	3.64 (1.17)	4.04 (1.00)	3.70 (1.14)	3.51 (1.22)	3.94 (0.85)
Safety at school	6.9%	8.9%	26.4%	30.1%	27.7%	3.63 (1.17)	3.79 (1.17)	3.71 (1.14)	3.44 (1.24)	4.01 (0.87)
More emphasis on academics as opposed to extracurricular activities	6.0%	9.1%	27.7%	34.1%	23.1%	3.59 (1.12)	3.42 (1.11)	3.76 (1.07)	3.20 (1.14)	4.12 (0.79)
Promises made by charter school's spokespersons	16.1%	13.9%	26.1%	28.8%	15.1%	3.13 (1.29)	3.53 (1.22)	3.28 (1.25)	2.77 (1.31)	3.27 (1.18)
Difficult to find other positions	25.1%	16.3%	25.1%	16.7%	16.9%	2.84 (1.41)	2.39 (1.40)	2.93 (1.39)	2.65 (1.44)	2.82 (1.33)
Convenient location	26.9%	16.1%	28.2%	17.6%	11.2%	2.70 (1.33)	2.93 (1.37)	2.72 (1.32)	2.66 (1.37)	2.80 (1.29)

Note: The items are rank ordered (by mean scores) from most to least important reasons for seeking employment.

being experienced in the schools. The results of this analysis indicated that there was a statistically significant difference between what was expected and what was found/experienced in the charter schools. We shall examine this issue more extensively in Chapter 9.

Working Conditions and Levels of Satisfaction

In this section, we examine overall levels of satisfaction with working conditions and describe differences between groups of schools. Among the working conditions we discuss are (i) school facilities and available resources, (ii) professional autonomy and influence in decisions at the school, (iii) salary and benefits, and (iv) other areas.

The atmosphere of a school likely influences a teacher's job satisfaction. Factors such as facilities, autonomy, and salary are important to teachers. Both site visits and results from teacher surveys indicated that the quality of facilities varied widely, as did teachers' level of satisfaction with facilities and available resources. Teacher satisfaction with these issues is also relevant to the topic of innovation in charter schools. Indeed, literature on innovation in organizations suggests that people innovate when they have sufficient resources, appropriate incentives, and professional autonomy (see, e.g., Mintrom, 2000).

School Facilities and Available Resources

The quality of facilities varied extensively among the charter schools. Therefore, it was not surprising to see a split in the responses from teachers and staff concerning the quality of their school's facilities. Approximately 46 percent of the staff were satisfied or very satisfied with the school buildings and facilities (see Table 6.8). On a related item, 43 percent of the teachers and staff agreed or strongly agreed that the physical facilities were good, while the rest were either not satisfied with the facilities or were uncertain.

The survey results indicated the schools also vary widely in the availability of resources. Just over 38 percent of teachers and staff indicated they believed their school had sufficient financial resources. On a related item, nearly 43 percent of the teachers and staff indicated they were satisfied with the resources available for instruction. Nevertheless, in a few schools, the teachers expressed strong concerns about the lack of textbooks. Site visits and interviews confirmed this.

The Michigan charter schools' teachers/staff perceptions of facilities and resources for instruction are compared with the composite comparison group in Table 6.8. This comparison indicates that Michigan charter schools' teachers/staff are more satisfied with their buildings and facilities and general resources than teachers and staff in the composite comparison group. This is somewhat surprising given that our evaluations in the states that comprise the composite comparison groups suggest that these states have more start-up resources and state funding than the Michigan schools (see Horn & Miron, 2000; Miron & Nelson, 2000; and Nelson & Miron, 2001). On the other hand, the Michigan schools are likely to have more resources available for facilities and instructional materials since they cater to "low-cost" students, while the charter schools in the composite comparison group are more likely to serve at-risk students, students at the secondary level, and students that require special education services. In terms of satisfaction with instructional materials, Michigan charter school teachers/staff had levels of satisfaction that were similar to their counterparts in the composite comparison group.

Table 6.8   Satisfaction With School Facilities and Available Resources, All Teachers and Staff

School buildings and facilities	Michigan Charter Schools (N=728)	Composite Comparison Group (N=937)
Very satisfied or satisfied	46.5%	37.6%
Uncertain	26.1%	27.1%
Very dissatisfied or dissatisfied	27.4%	35.3%
This school has good physical facilities		
Strongly agree or agree	43.1%	32.0%
Uncertain	24.2%	27.7%
Strongly disagree or disagree	32.7%	40.2%
This school has sufficient financial resources		
Strongly agree or agree	38.1%	31.7%
Uncertain	24.0%	24.1%
Strongly disagree or disagree	37.9%	44.3%
Resources available for instruction		
Very satisfied or satisfied	42.8%	44.8%
Uncertain	29.1%	28.1%
Very dissatisfied or dissatisfied	28.0%	27.1%

Teacher Autonomy and Influence in Decisions at School

The charter school survey asked teachers/staff to reflect on their initial expectations and compare these with their current experiences in their schools. The survey asked teachers/staff whether their schools are "supporting innovative practices" and whether the teachers/staff are "autonomous and creative in their classrooms." Initially, charter school teachers/staff had high expectations that their school would support innovative practices (78 percent); but after working in the schools for at least a half year, only 65 percent thought this was true. Initially, 81 percent of the teachers/staff expected autonomy and creativity to be evident in their classrooms; but only 71 percent indicated that they found this to be true.

As was the case with teacher autonomy and perceived support for innovations, a majority of teachers also expected initially that they would be able to influence the steering and direction of the school (74 percent); a little more than half the teachers (54 percent) found this to be true after working in the school.

On the whole, data collected by the evaluation team indicated considerable differences among schools in terms of professional autonomy for teachers. In some schools, the demand on teachers to develop new curriculum materials allowed them considerable autonomy but also caused many to become frustrated given the enormity of the task. In part, this is why we saw a number of schools resort to "canned curriculums" rather than develop new curricular materials that were in line with the school's profile.

Teachers in EMO-operated charter schools had slightly higher expectations for autonomy than did teachers in other charter schools. After working in the schools, however, teachers in EMO-operated schools were less optimistic about autonomy than their non-EMO counterparts (Nelson & Miron, 2001). A number of the full service EMOs have rather rigid curriculums and teachers are expected to follow these closely. National Heritage Academies, for instance, emphasizes a "teacher-centered" instruction, while Advantage Schools Inc. (now taken over by Mosaica) uses direct instruction that follows closely scripted instructional materials. In schools operated by these two companies, the curricular materials are prepared in advance; and teachers have little leeway in terms of the timing or method of delivering the curricular materials. This is also the case for Edison Schools Inc. and a few other EMOs.

Professional Development Opportunities for Teachers

From interviews of school principals/directors, we found that the professional development of teachers in most charter schools was primarily received through in-service days, seminars, conferences, and workshops. For many of the schools, this is the only form of professional development, while others also provide in-service training before the school year starts. Some teachers reported that they attend weekly meetings with the administration to determine what the staff need to change or develop. Nevertheless, several principals/directors indicated that the work load in charter schools was greater than in traditional schools, which led to difficulty in scheduling time for training. To remedy this problem, some schools tried to train teachers on the job as opposed to sending them to conferences or related professional development activities. A few principals stated that there was no professional development available thus far or that professional development opportunities were provided on an as-needed basis. Horn and Miron (1999) discuss further the self-reported professional development activities in Michigan charter schools.

The survey results indicate that while teachers initially had high expectations for professional opportunities, these expectations were rarely realized in practice. Initially, 65.4 percent of the teachers believed there would be new professional opportunities; yet only 49 percent believed this to be the case after working in their school for at least a half year. This difference between initial expectations and current experience was similar to what we found for the composite comparison group, and both differences were statistically significant.

Other Aspects of Teacher Satisfaction

In this section, we examine teacher satisfaction with working conditions and overall operation and performance of their school. In Chapter 9, we will look more closely at levels of satisfaction as we explore its relationship to other measures of school performance.

Table 6.9 provides a ranking of mean scores on items related to work environment from the charter school survey. This ranking indicates that teachers/staff are most satisfied with the overall leadership/governance of their school and least satisfied with instructional materials. This is not to say that teachers are, on average, very satisfied with any of the working condition factors. The highest mean scores were below 4.0 (on a 5-point scale), and most were in the 3.0 to 4.0 range. This indicates a somewhat neutral level of satisfaction on most of these items and may reflect a "wait and see" attitude, considering the length of time these schools have been open. Similar results were obtained from a school climate survey administered to largely the same schools.

In general, the teachers/staff are clearly satisfied with their schools, although there were great discrepancies between what they initially expected and what they were experiencing after working in the schools for at least half a year. As with the items discussed above, the surveys used a number of identical items to examine and compare the charter school staffs' "initial expectations" as opposed to "current experience."[5] These particular items will also be discussed in Chapter 9. On 14 out of 14 items, what the teachers/staff were reporting as "current experience" was significantly less positive than their "initial expectations" ($p < .05$).[6] The biggest discrepancies between initial

Table 6.9 Levels of Teacher and Staff Satisfaction With Working Conditions

	Not very satisfied			Very satisfied		Michigan Charter Schools	Composite Comparison Group	EMO	Non-EMO	NHA
	1	2	3	4	5	Mean (SD)	Mean (SD)	Mean (SD)	Mean (SD)	Mean (SD)
Administrative leadership of school	6.8%	11.2%	18.6%	25.4%	38.0%	3.77 (1.26)	3.67 (1.23)	3.83 (1.22)	3.64 (1.31)	4.43 (0.73)
Evaluation or assessment of your performance	6.8%	7.1%	21.3%	38.6%	26.2%	3.70 (1.13)	3.70 (1.11)	3.74 (1.16)	3.62 (1.08)	4.24 (0.80)
Availability of computers and other technology	8.1%	15.4%	18.7%	26.4%	31.3%	3.57 (1.29)	3.64 (1.29)	3.28 (1.30)	4.13 (1.08)	3.52 (1.01)
School governance	7.2%	9.9%	28.3%	31.7%	22.9%	3.53 (1.16)	3.42 (1.21)	3.55 (1.14)	3.50 (1.20)	4.07 (0.78)
School buildings and facilities	7.9%	19.5%	26.1%	23.6%	22.9%	3.34 (1.24)	3.06 (1.28)	3.33 (1.20)	3.36 (1.32)	4.02 (0.97)
Fringe benefits	11.6%	15.4%	26.0%	26.6%	20.3%	3.29 (1.27)	3.32 (1.19)	3.24 (1.25)	3.38 (1.31)	3.74 (1.00)
Salary level	6.3%	17.3%	37.1%	27.2%	12.1%	3.22 (1.07)	3.02 (1.17)	3.20 (1.03)	3.25 (1.14)	3.36 (0.97)
Resources available for instruction	9.6%	18.4%	29.1%	29.1%	13.7%	3.19 (1.17)	3.29 (1.22)	2.99 (1.14)	3.56 (1.15)	3.15 (1.07)

Note: The items are rank ordered (by mean scores) from highest to lowest levels of satisfaction.

expectations and current experience in Michigan charter schools include the following, which are rank-ordered from largest to smallest mean difference:

1. The school will have/has effective leadership and administration.

2. Students will receive sufficient individual attention.

3. Teachers will be/are able to influence the steering and direction of the school.

4. Students will be/are eager and motivated to learn.

5. There will be/is good communication between the school and parents.

6. There will be/are new professional opportunities for teachers.

7. Support services will be/are available to students.

Differences in expectations and experiences on items does not necessarily imply overall dissatisfaction with these aspects of their school. Given the feedback we received from teachers and staff, it seems that in many instances teachers simply expected too much. Since many of the teachers are also very young and inexperienced, their expectations may be higher than normal. Unfortunately, we do not have comparable data from regular public schools.

Teachers' Salaries and Benefits

Only 46 percent of the charter schools reported data on teacher salaries for 2000-01. This figure is very low and raises questions about the schools' openness to external review and, more generally, to accountability requirements associated with the charter school concept. The average teacher salary for those charter schools reporting data was $34,183. The range in average teacher salaries by school went from a minimum of $16,614 to a maximum of $55,623. The higher salaries were at ISD or district charter schools. Schools operated by Edison also reported high salary figures, although there are questions about the accuracy of their reported data for two schools.[7] The average teacher salary for the host districts was $49,725.[8]

Disparities in salary between the charter schools and host districts can be extremely large. Seven charter schools had salaries that were similar to or higher than their respective host districts. Two of these schools had salaries that were more than $6,000 larger than the host district's. At the other extreme, the teachers in five charter schools had average salaries that were $30,000 or more lower than their counterparts in the host districts. The largest difference in average teachers salaries between a charter school and its host district was $40,155.

Over time, it appears that the difference in salaries has decreased slightly. In 1995-96 the average difference was $17,339, in 1996-97 it was $16,832, and in 2000-01 it was $14,452. Unfortunately, fewer and fewer schools are reporting these data, so the changes in these figures may be due to missing data. In terms of overall expenditures, the charter schools clearly have an advantage over their host districts, with substantially lower salaries and lower costs for benefits.

Three factors might explain why average charter school salaries are substantially lower than average salaries for teachers in traditional public schools. The first is that, according to interview data from school principals, it was common to have pay scales for teachers with similar qualifications that were 10-20 lower than the surrounding districts. The second reason is that teachers—on average—in traditional public schools have higher qualifications and more years of experience than teachers in charter schools. The third possible reason is that charter schools cater mostly to lower elementary grades, while host districts cater to Grades K-12. Salaries tend to be lower for teachers at the elementary level compared with the secondary level. A number of charter school principals reported that their teachers could qualify for bonuses, which may or may not be included in average salary data reported to the state.

While charter school teachers make considerably less than their public school counterparts, not all are dissatisfied with their salary, with just under 40 percent reporting they were satisfied or very satisfied (see Table 6.9). It is worth noting that a number of schools reported that they could not afford higher salaries because they needed to divert operational funds into capital investments related to the renovation and development of facilities.

Teacher Retention

One factor that limits charter schools' human capital resources is the relatively high rates of attrition among teachers and staff. It is important to point out that not all attrition is problematic. As previously discussed, charter schools should be attracting teachers and parents with similar goals and philosophy. If teachers/staff do not have a strong commitment to the school's mission, they may choose to leave or they may be asked to leave, while those who agree with and follow the mission remain.

In Michigan it was difficult to obtain good data on attrition or retention. It was clear from interviews and site visits that high rates of attrition in many charter schools have negatively affected the ability to develop the schools and implement a curriculum that matches their missions. The attrition rates varied extensively across the schools. In a few cases, we observed that nearly 100 percent of the teachers changed at least two years in a row. Studies from other states that consider teacher retention or attrition indicate that this is a particular problem area for charter schools. In Pennsylvania, Miron and Nelson (2000) found that approximately 60 percent of teachers remained in the schools during the second and third year of that reform. A study completed by the Ohio

Legislative Office of Education Oversight (2001) reported that 55 percent of charter school teachers employed in Ohio charter schools continued to work at the same charter school past the first year. This was compared with a 78 percent retention rate for teachers employed by corresponding city school districts.

As an indicator of potential future attrition, our surveys asked teachers whether they felt secure about their futures at the schools and plan to return the following year. While 40.9 percent of staff in Michigan charter schools indicated they were not insecure about their future at their particular school, 34.5 percent of the teachers and staff indicated that they were insecure. It is unclear whether this insecurity is due to uncertainty about the charter school reform or due to uncertainty about the future of their particular school and its ability to live up to its mission. Among those teachers not planning to return the next year, a female teacher expressed that she would not be returning due to "frustration with lack of supplies and professional support—mostly the lack of professional support and guidance." There was a difference between the percentage of Michigan charter school staff (87.8 percent) and the comparison group (80 percent) who stated they planned to return to their position the following year (see Table 6.10 for detail).

An examination of factors that may cause teacher attrition is important to school districts. The Michigan charter school teachers/staff who indicated that they did not plan to return the next year differed from other teachers in that they had lower levels of satisfaction in terms of governance, leadership, salary, and benefits. These differences were statistically significant.

Table 6.10 Teachers' Perception of Their Job Security and Expected Retention Rates for Michigan Charter School Teachers/Staff Compared With Composite Comparison Group

	Michigan Charter Schools	Composite Comparison Group
Teachers are insecure about their future at this school		
Strongly agree or agree	34.5%	34.4%
Uncertain	24.6%	21.9%
Strongly disagree or disagree	40.9%	43.8%
Teachers plan to work at this school next year		
Yes	87.8%	80.0%
No	12.2%	20.0%

Conclusion

We began this chapter with the charter concept, which holds that teachers' choice of schools will generate communities of like-minded professionals united behind a common set of purposes. Our findings suggest that teachers are, in fact, choosing charter schools for the intended reasons. Indeed, the "opportunity to work with like-minded educators" was the most highly rated reason, indicating that at least some "good" sorting is taking place. However, there is also evidence that choice and sorting are leaving charter schools with teachers that are less ethnically diverse, younger, more poorly compensated, and less educated than charter schools in other states and noncharter public schools. Michigan charter schools appear adequate, though, in terms of certification (per the legal requirement).

However, even if shared professional cultures are being established in some schools, high levels of teacher attrition will likely make it difficult to maintain this over time. Among the predictors and cited reasons for attrition, the following can be noted: concerns about working conditions, conflicts in the schools, poor salaries, extensive noninstructional duties, and the fact that most teachers found that their expectations were not being met. Finally, it should be pointed out that Michigan charter school teachers do not appear to be receiving the autonomy and new professional opportunities they expected.

Qualified and committed teachers are an essential component in the charter school reform, especially since many of the schools aim to develop and use unique curricular materials delivered with unique or innovative instructional approaches. As we have seen in this chapter, the teachers employed by Michigan charter schools have less formal education and fewer years of teaching experience than their counterparts in traditional public schools. By itself, this tells us little about the teachers' ability to innovate. Young teachers are perhaps more likely to break out of the molds occupied by their more experienced colleagues. Having said that, new teachers, like new professionals in any field, must have time to get their bearings. Perhaps it is a bit too optimistic to assume that newly minted teachers will be able to master their craft sufficiently to act as innovators.

Just as classroom teachers are likely an important component of charter school success, they might also be one of the key factors explaining why some charter school reforms are failing. Some states have provided provisions and incentives in their charter school law to assure that qualified teachers are attracted and retained in charter schools. No such measures have been enacted in Michigan aside from the requirement that all charter school classroom teachers have a teaching certificate.

Notes

1. In order to better understand the nature and reliability of the survey data, it is necessary to describe the sampling design and methods used to collect and analyze the data. As part of a large state-mandated evaluation, we surveyed teachers and staff in 51 of the 106 operating charter schools in 1998. This included all of Michigan except for schools in Detroit and surrounding counties, which were covered by another evaluation team from Public Sector Consultants (Khouri et al., 1999). All classroom teachers, other instructional staff, and key administrators were sampled. A total of 728 out of 812 teachers and staff returned completed surveys (equivalent to an 89.7 percent response rate). The item response rate for each question was typically 96 percent or higher. More detailed information about the survey sample and results can be found in Horn & Miron (1999).

2. A description of the composite comparison group and the manner in which we calculated and weighted the data from the states in the comparison group were provided in endnote #6 in Chapter 5.

3. During site visits to charter schools, we were informed by parents and school personnel that classes in their schools were being led by noncertified staff on a regular basis. Some schools hid the practice by having students of two classes listed as enrolled in one certified teacher's class. This might amount to as many as 30-40 students. The students often sat in different rooms and had different instructors. In at least two of the schools in question, these classes were led by uncertified school administrators. It was not clear whether the authorizers were aware of these deficiencies. We could not determine how common or widespread these deficiencies were.

4. In Connecticut, at least 50 percent of the teachers employed in a charter school must be certified at the time of hiring, while the remaining 50 percent can obtain temporary certificates if they complete required tests and are judged eligible for the state's Alternative Route of Certification. Illinois does not specify a percentage of certified teachers required in their charter schools but does stipulate that noncertified teachers must meet alternative criteria. In Pennsylvania, regulations require that 75 percent of the charter school staff must be certified.

5. See Horn & Miron (1999) for more details about these survey items and complete results from the Michigan schools.

6. The Wilcoxon signed rank test was used to compare the paired distributions of responses.

7. Two of Edison's charter schools reported average teacher salaries above $50,000, while the average at their other schools was only $36,900. The two schools with high salaries also reported an average of more than 28 pupils per teacher, while the other schools reported an average of 21 pupils per teacher.

8. This figure ($49,725) includes only host districts of those 76 charter schools that reported data on teacher salary. Host districts were counted only once when calculating an average salary for this group. The average teacher salary for all in-state host districts that have charter schools within their boundaries was $48,594.

7

Innovation and Impact

Talking with parents at a new charter school located in a mid-sized town, we learned that the local district had recently surveyed all the families that had left to enroll in the charter school. Apparently, the district wanted to know why they had chosen to leave. The survey results revealed that a common complaint was that the district schools had not provided sufficient adult supervision on the playgrounds. In response to this, the district superintendent requested that all schools see to it that there were school personnel or parent volunteers on the playgrounds immediately before and after school as well as during lunch and recess. One charter school parent told us that she had four children go through the public schools and that she and other parents had complained about the lack of adult supervision for nearly a decade: "It was only after the charter school opened that the district began to listen and act."

This account illustrates an important component of the charter concept that we have not yet addressed in this book. The benefits of charter schools, according to their proponents, will not be confined to the students who choose to enroll in them. Rather, charter schools are also supposed to serve as laboratories of innovation that will create exemplary practices worthy of emulation by noncharter schools. The competitive pressures created by the schools, moreover, will provide an incentive for noncharter schools to innovate themselves. Charter schools, on this account, will provide broad public benefits to charter and noncharter students alike.

Charter opponents agree that charter schools will have an impact on noncharter schools. However, they claim that the impact will be mostly negative. Rather than laboratories of innovation, opponents claim that charter schools will drain resources from needy and deserving public schools by "skimming the cream" from the public school population, a claim that is given at least some credence by the findings reported in Chapter 5. Critics also suggest that the movement of students into and out of charter schools creates an intolerable level of instability and uncertainty for public school administrators.

This chapter seeks to assess the impacts—both positive and negative—of Michigan charter schools on noncharter public and private schools. We begin by examining the impact on surrounding public school districts. Here we consider some of the critics' claims about charter schools' impact on enrollments and funding, as well as their effect on administration and educational practices. Following this, we take a brief look at the impact of charter schools on private and parochial schools. Finally, we take up proponents' claims that charter schools will serve as public education's R&D sector by assessing the extent to which charter schools have impacted educational practice in noncharter schools.

The findings reported in this chapter are based on in-depth case studies of public and private schools in or near four large urban areas[1]: Grand Rapids, Holland, Kalamazoo, and Lansing. Where appropriate, we also draw upon other studies on Michigan charter schools. Research for the case studies was conducted in the Spring and Summer of 2000. We collected and reviewed documentation and data from districts, charter schools, and private schools, as well as media accounts. We also conducted interviews with representatives from the charter schools, private schools, traditional public schools, and management companies that operated schools in the case study districts. It is important to bear in mind that our conclusions are limited by the fact that they are based on research in just four districts. More information on the methodology as well as detailed results from the case studies, can be found in an earlier technical report (Evaluation Center, 2000).

Impact on Surrounding School Districts

Charter schools might have a variety of impacts on surrounding noncharter public schools. In the following sections we focus on fiscal, administrative, and compositional impacts. We also briefly consider charter schools' impacts on surrounding non-public schools.

Fiscal Impacts

Charter schools' fiscal impacts on noncharter public schools is a central component of the debate over the desirability of charter laws. It is not surprising, therefore, that the issue has attracted the attention of a large number of scholars, practitioners, and other observers. Two of the strongest of these studies have found that charter schools do, in fact, have significant fiscal impacts on noncharter public schools and that the impact is often negative. Rofes (1998) conducted in-depth interviews in 25 districts across the country and found that nearly half reported strong or moderate financial impacts from charter schools. Similarly, a recent study sponsored by the U.S. Department of Education (RPP International, 2001) found that more than half of the 49 districts they studied reported that charter schools had negatively affected their fiscal condition.[2]

Our findings in the four Michigan case studies confirm that charter schools can have a substantial enrollment impact on surrounding district schools. Grand Rapids Public Schools (GRPS), for instance, lost between 150 and 300 students to charter schools between the 1997-98 and 1999-2000 academic years. Similarly, during the 1996-97 school year Holland Public Schools showed a net enrollment loss due to charter schools of approximately 200 students. According to district officials, this amounted to a loss of approximately $2 million in revenues, resulting in what they characterized as substantial cuts in programs and staff. Officials in Lansing report that between 1,500 and 2,000 students have transferred to charter schools. This, combined with a sharp decline in the local birth rate, has led to significant losses in students and, ultimately, the consolidation of four elementary schools. Similarly, officials in Kalamazoo Public Schools say that the district lost $3 million during the 1999-2000 academic year and $2.5 million during the 2000-01 academic year because of enrollment in charter schools. This reportedly led to a number of staff cuts in elementary school libraries.

District officials commonly emphasized, however, that simply counting the number of students transferring from district to charter schools probably understates the enrollment impact of charter schools. This is because these numbers exclude students who enroll in charter schools for kindergarten. Since districts never obtain records on these students, it is difficult to know how many would have enrolled in district schools but for the existence of charter schools. For instance, the first year a charter school is in operation it recruits students for a range of grades. In subsequent years, elementary level charter schools (which includes most charter schools in Michigan) tend to recruit kindergartners, while admitting fewer students in the upper grades to fill spots left by students that chose to leave. As a consequence, surrounding district schools are likely to record a decline in the number of their *existing* students moving to the charter schools after the first year they are open.

Furthermore, it is likely that charter schools' fiscal impact depends upon both the number of students drawn away from district schools and the *patterns* of such losses. In theory, a 20 percent reduction in enrollment should produce both a reduction in revenues *and* a reduction in the demand for services. However, some district officials observe that unless students are recruited in neat "blocks," there are certain fixed costs that superintendents cannot reduce without negatively affecting the district. For instance, a Spanish teacher will cost the district the same amount in salary, benefits, and other expenses whether the teacher has 10 or 25 students. Until demand for Spanish drops below some critical point, the district probably cannot let the teacher go.

A study by the Mackinac Center for Public Policy (Ladner & Brouillette, 2000) examined impact of charter schools in a number of Detroit area districts, including Dearborn, Inkster, Highland Park, and Flat Rock. At least one district official interviewed by these researchers reports that the fiscal impact of charter schools is "a wash" given that enrollment losses mean reductions in expenditures. It is unclear from the report whether this school is typical of those in the Detroit area. Nonetheless, the quotation illustrates that the *net* fiscal impact of charter schools on surrounding districts must account for both the fiscal drain that charter schools create in school districts and the reduction in demands on district budgets that accompanies it. However, we have been unable to estimate this net impact and we are not aware of any rigorous studies that have done so.

Administrative and Operational Impacts

The impact of student movement between charter and noncharter schools is not only fiscal but also administrative and managerial. Markets are often characterized by frequent movements of customers from one service provider to another. As with producers in any market, school districts are faced with the challenge of planning for changes in the size and composition of their customer base.

A recent U.S. Department of Education study found that district schools have responded to the administrative uncertainty created by competition in at least two ways. First, many schools report that they have become more customer-friendly since the advent of competition from local charter schools. Second, many schools report employing improved systems for tracking student movement between district and charter schools in order to enhance their ability to forecast and plan for student movement.[3]

Our case studies of Michigan school districts found similar changes in the administration and operation of public schools. The most common change in school operations is enhanced efforts to communicate with parents and the community. Many of these efforts come in the form of marketing. Lansing Public Schools, for instance, purchased ads in newspapers and on television, and have created a Web site to help attract and retain families in district schools. In other cases, parent communication comes in the form of newsletters, picnics, activity nights, and so on. Another district reported spending $65,000 during one year for marketing.

District officials in the case study districts also report more personalized attempts to communicate with parents, such as a greater willingness on the part of teachers to meet with parents to talk about their children's performance in school. As with the studies cited above, we found that the Michigan case study districts are also stepping up their efforts to track student movement between charter and noncharter schools. Some of the districts, for instance, have surveyed and interviewed parents whose children have either left for or returned from a charter school.

District officials report, however, that their attempts to plan for student movement between charter and noncharter schools are often frustrated by what they view as charter schools' strategic manipulation of the fact that state payments to schools are based on enrollment on the fourth Friday after the school year starts. Several of the officials interviewed charged that some charter schools begin counseling students to return to district schools just after the official count, allowing the charter schools to keep the monies appropriated for those students, but relieving them of the burden of educating them.

Another obstacle to effective planning by districts comes when families "double enroll" in both a charter and a noncharter school, deferring their final enrollment decision until just before the beginning of the school year. Many decide to stay in the host district but find that their child's paperwork has already been sent to a charter school that requested it. This not only increases paperwork burdens that accompany any student transfer, but also taxes districts' ability to plan effectively for classroom space, the ordering of materials, transportation, special education, and personnel. Because budgets are developed and approved long before the "official" count day, local public schools are unable to develop budgets that reflect real needs for the following school year. As an added complication, traditional public schools must accept all students who return from charter schools at any time of the year, and they must consider and plan for the possibility that a charter school will close and that the district will have to absorb large numbers of students.

The administrative uncertainty facing districts is only likely to increase over the years. Since most Michigan charter schools are pre-high school (86 percent of all charter school students are enrolled in Grades K-8), there is potential for a major enrollment and resource impact in the next four to eight years, when a large number of charter school students will be returning to the traditional public schools for high school instruction. High school instruction, as we noted in Chapter 4, is considerably more expensive than instruction at the elementary and middle school levels.

Impacts on the Social Composition of Schools by Race, Class, and Ability

A common criticism of school choice plans—including charter schools—is that they will lead to social sorting and even greater segregation based on race, family income, and ability. Chapter 5 contains extensive data that illustrate that student populations in charter schools are less diverse than comparable noncharter public schools in terms of ethnicity, family income, and presence of students with special educational needs. However, such sorting also has an impact on the districts from which charter schools draw their students. In this section we supplement Chapter 5's macro-level analysis with an analysis of how social sorting is impacting some specific school districts in Michigan. Generally, we find that surrounding schools are also becoming less diverse, since neighboring charter schools are enrolling high proportions of single minority groups or no minorities at all.

Data from Grand Rapids Public Schools indicated that 287 students left GRPS for charter schools, while 143 returned during the 1999-2000 academic year. When we looked at the background characteristics of students moving, we found that while whites made up more than half of the departing students, they comprised only 36 percent of returning students. Conversely, while 36 percent of departing students were black, this group comprised over half of returning students. Unfortunately, the data do not allow us to determine the reasons behind these differences. Whatever the reasons, these data suggest a process by which white students are migrating to charter schools, leaving an ever higher concentration of black students in district schools. These findings seem corroborated by trends in district enrollment. While the proportion of black students attending GRPS increased slightly (i.e., 1.5 percent) between the 1996-97 and 1998-99 academic years, the proportion of white students decreased by 4.1 percent.

In a number of districts, it was reported that students returning to the local school district are often in need of special education services or have records of disciplinary problems. One district official reported that 48 special education students returned to the local public schools from charter schools shortly after the fourth Friday counts during one year alone. Further, it has been reported that students with severe special education problems or unique educational/custodial needs are "counseled away" from charter schools during the recruitment and enrollment periods. At first, we questioned the validity of the claims made by district officials and some parents that charter schools were counseling out students with special education needs. Later, after we analyzed the enrollment data and found that only 3.7 percent of the students in charter schools were receiving special education services compared with 12.5 percent in traditional public schools, we became inclined to believe them.

Impacts on Non-Public Schools

Our research design was not explicitly designed to gauge charter schools' impact on private and parochial schools. However, it became apparent during the course of our field research that charter schools are having an impact on private and parochial schools as well as on traditional public schools.

National Heritage Academies (NHA), which is the largest private operator of charter schools in the state, has a program and profile that are attractive to middle-class Christian families (Chapter 10 has more details about this EMO). A 1999 *Wall Street Journal* article (Golden, 1999) highlighted the tension that existed between NHA and the Christian school associations in West Michigan. The Christian schools were reportedly losing substantial numbers of students to the cost-free NHA charter schools. We interviewed representatives of the Grand Rapids Christian School Association a year after this article appeared. They indicated that NHA was then taking steps to avoid recruiting from their schools, such as removing names of families already enrolled in Christian schools from its direct mailing lists.

The Christian school associations in both Grand Rapids and Holland noted that most students left during the first year the neighboring NHA schools opened. Since then, the number of students moving to NHA schools has slowed considerably and the number of students returning from charter schools has increased over time. This does not include students entering kindergarten at the NHA schools, many of whom otherwise would have been enrolled in a Christian school. Officials at Holland Christian Schools noted that they now have much smaller than average elementary-level classes. They did expect, however, that since NHA does not provide high school instruction, they would get many of these students back after Grade 8.

From our parent surveys in 1998, we determined that 25.5 percent of the NHA families had previously attended a private school, with 19.4 percent coming from private parochial schools. In many ways this is not surprising, since charter schools might be viewed as a cheaper substitute for parents wishing to move their children away from traditional public school systems. Grand Rapids Christian School Association, which surveys departing parents, indicated that 99 percent of families leaving for charter schools cited cost as the most important reason.

Like the traditional public schools, there is evidence that non-public schools are changing their operational practices somewhat in response to competition from charter schools. The Grand Rapids Christian School Association, for instance, reports that it has stepped up its marketing activities and has sought to develop better lines of communication with parents. As an official from Holland Christian Schools Association put it, "Charter schools have made education a more competitive arena."

Impacts on Educational Practice

The administrative impacts discussed above are mixed, while net fiscal impacts are more difficult to assess. According to charter proponents, any negative impacts are justified if charter schools induce districts to improve their educational practices sufficiently. Competition in markets, after all, is never without costs. Firms spend time and resources on marketing and other efforts to get a leg up on their competitors. According to market theory, however, such costs are justified by improvements in overall quality and efficiency. We consider now whether these impacts have been accompanied by changes and improvements in educational practice.

The Troublesome Concept of Innovation

Much of the discussion about charter schools' educational impacts is couched in terms of "innovation." As noted earlier, the charter concept suggests that charter schools will serve as public education's R&D sector, generating innovative practices that can then be adopted by other schools. Charter schools, it is thought, are well situated to produce innovations because the autonomy created by waivers from many existing school regulations will afford them schools a more capacious opportunity space than other schools. Along with opportunity, competition and choice are thought to provide charter schools with the motivation to innovate.

Unfortunately, attempts to assess the level of innovation diffusion from charter to noncharter schools are hampered by an astonishing lack of agreement on the meaning of the term "innovation." On its face, the concept of innovation is quite straightforward. The root of the word derives from the Latin *novus*, which means new. An innovative educational practice, therefore, is any such practice that is new. However, a little thought reveals that the concept is fraught with ambiguities. Indeed, how new must the practice be to be considered innovative? Must it be truly unique or may it build on other practices? Perhaps innovations can consist in combining existing program elements in new ways, or in finding new ways to implement and deliver existing program elements.[4]

As we have struggled with the meaning of the term innovation, we have come to believe that one must address three questions when determining whether a school or educational practice is innovative. Different answers to these questions, in turn, lead to different definitions of innovation.

- Is the practice *effective* in generating its intended outcomes?
- What is the *unit of analysis* used in describing the practice?
- What is the *context of comparison* for the practice?

Below, we will consider and discuss each question.

Effectiveness. In ordinary language, it would be odd to call a practice innovative if it were ineffective in bringing about its goal or intended outcome. In other words, a fundamental condition for innovativeness is that it "works" in some sense. Yet, much of the debate over whether charter schools and charter school practices are innovative focuses on the novelty of various educational processes, without clear reference to outcomes. In part, this is understandable, since we often lack clear and scientifically grounded causal knowledge about the relationship between educational processes and outcomes. However, the innovation debate's focus on the novelty of processes is curious given that the charter concept also emphazes accountability for outcomes, rather than inputs and processes. Given that the current innovation debate is largely over process, and since it is well beyond the scope of this book to explore evidence for the effectiveness of specific charter school teaching practices, we too cast our discussion primarily in terms of educational processes.

Unit of analysis. The second question asks which aspects of a charter school's educational program are relevant in assessing innovation. Perhaps the most demanding criterion for innovation is that charter schools generate wholly new program ideas or "elements." For the purpose of our state evaluations, we have usually grouped innovations into three areas: (i) curriculum, (ii) instruction, and (iii) operation and governance. An example of a program element might be a new reading curriculum, a new assessment technique, or a new lecturing technique. However, a less stringent definition is that an innovative school, while not devising a new element, combines existing program elements in a way not done previously. Here, there is an analogy between innovation among educators and innovation among chefs. An innovative chef is one who devises new recipes or ways of combining ingredients. Few would insist that innovation in the kitchen requires inventing new ingredients. Rather, the innovation comes in how preexisting ingredients are combined.[5]

Scope/context of comparison. All assessments of innovation involve (often implicit) comparisons between the school in question and other schools. If an innovation is something new, then the question here is: "New in what context?" Indeed, an educational practice might be new in a given school district, but widely used elsewhere. Thus, under the most stringent (and perhaps unrealistic) definition, a practice is innovative only if it is has never been tried before—anywhere. Clearly, few charter schools—if any—are innovative when compared against all other schools. As the scope of comparison becomes smaller, the requirements for innovation become less stringent. Some have argued, for instance, that a charter school practice is innovative if it involves something not currently offered by noncharter public schools in the area.[6]

Combining the last two criteria yields four types of innovation, shown in Figure 7.1. The four categories range in stringency from Type I (least stringent) to Type IV (most stringent).[7] Type IV innovation is perhaps best described as the R&D view of innovation, since it requires that charter schools develop new elements (not just combinations of elements) that have never been tried before. While proving such a statement is difficult, it seems unlikely that any charter schools have been innovative under this tough standard. Type III innovation is somewhat less strict since, although it requires that the practice be completely new, it requires only that the school combines existing elements in a new way. Finally, under Types I and II, the comparison group moves from the nation as a whole to the local educational marketplace, with Type I involving new combinations of preexisting elements and Type II wholly new elements. Types I and II, therefore, might also be viewed in terms of "product differentiation," since they involve creating new or unique (though not entirely novel) choices for local consumers of education.

The previous discussion underscores the fact that questions about the innovativeness of charter schools cannot be resolved by research and data alone. Rather, important conceptual issues remain unresolved, since behind the definitions lie different visions of what charter schools are for. Behind Types III and IV innovation lies a view of charter schools as primarily laboratories for educational experimentation. Behind Types I and II innovation lies the notion that charter schools exist primarily to provide choice to education consumers. Charter school practices are more likely to seem innovative under the Types I and II definitions than under the others. Thus, it is perhaps not surprising that charter proponents tend to push for the former definitions while charter opponents push for the latter.

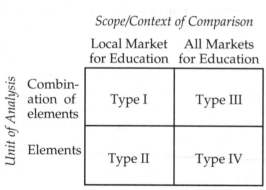

Figure 7.1 Four Types of Innovation

Innovation in Michigan Charter Schools

While rigorous analyses are made difficult by the conceptual ambiguities surrounding innovation, we are unaware of any Michigan charter schools that are producing substantial Type III or Type IV innovations. Moreover, it is likely that few charter schools—or perhaps noncharter schools—nationwide are producing such innovations. That is, few are generating practices or combinations of practices that are new in a larger national context. Thus, charter schools have largely failed to serve as an R&D sector in the same sense that a drug company might produce a wholly new treatment for cancer. This does not, however, rule out the possibility of Type I or Type II innovations.

One, albeit imperfect, way to identify innovations is simply to ask the charter schools. In our earlier state evaluations we summed up *self-reported* innovations from the charter schools (Horn & Miron, 1999, 2000; Reynolds, 2000). In the area of curriculum and instruction, the most commonly mentioned practices are listed below:

- Internships in the community or community service activities
- Coenrollment of high school students in community college courses
- Multigrade classrooms
- Development of individual learning plans for all students
- Small class size and use of teaching assistants and volunteers in classrooms
- Direct instruction
- Cooperative learning
- Montessori methods
- Before- and after-school programs
- Team teaching

A number of the self-reported innovations pertained to school organization and governance, which are largely restatements of the key components of the charter school concept. These include having their own school board and the fact that teachers are all at-will employees without tenure. Other common self-reported innovations were

- Modular/block scheduling
- Alternative scheduling of school day and school year
- Contracting out of management and services to EMOs
- Transportation provided by parents
- Bonuses for teachers to supplement low salaries
- Uniforms
- Involvement of parents

Our studies, however, were limited by the fact that we could not gain access to data on practices in traditional public schools, which made it impossible to make systematic comparisons with existing educational practices. As discussed above, most, if not all, definitions of charter school innovation involve comparisons between charter schools and other schools. A study by Mintrom (2000) was able to make such comparisons.

Mintrom simultaneously examined two dimensions of innovation. First, he stipulated that innovation consists of charter school practices that are not currently prevalent among matched noncharter schools. He identified such practices by surveying administrators in both charter and noncharter schools and then comparing the types of practices each group reported using. Second, Mintrom used charter and noncharter administrators as a "jury of peers," asking them to rate how innovative they considered the practices identified in the first round. Combining these two dimensions, Mintrom devised an index of innovativeness.

Mintrom's conclusions are not encouraging for charter proponents. Michigan charter schools, according to this study, are innovative only in a minimal sense, since many of the practices they employ were already quite prevalent in noncharter public schools. Earlier studies by Horn and Miron (1999) and Reynolds (2000) came to similar conclusions. The one area where Mintrom found some clear evidence of innovation is in organization and governance. To a large extent, these innovations are built into the very structure of the charter concept, which is largely a new way to organize schooling.

In many respects, the largely negative findings on charter school innovation are perhaps not surprising. Models of innovation in the academic literature stress a number of key factors that are often lacking in charter schools. One such factor is a clear motivation to innovate. Many charter proponents have argued that the need to attract and retain parents in an open education market would provide charter schools with the motivation to innovate. However, it is apparent from our case studies that a large number of parents are seeking not innovation but a back-to-basics approach to education. This desire explains, in large measure, the pervasiveness of management companies such as National Heritage Academies, whose programs are predicated on a desire to return to a more traditional form of education. Under such circumstances, the desire for innovation in charter schools conflicts with the system of market accountability under which the schools operate. Moreover, the Michigan charter school law—like most others—is quite vague on the meaning of "innovation" in charter schools, making the statutory exhortation that charter schools innovate difficult to interpret and facilitate.

Another key factor in models of innovation is resources, both fiscal and human. While Chapter 4 argues that many charter schools actually receive more money than other schools serving similar populations, it is perhaps expecting too much for start-up organizations to channel large amounts of time and money into developing new educational practices. These difficulties are probably exacerbated by the fact that charter school teachers in Michigan are quite young and that there is high turnover among them (see Chapter 6). Indeed, the literature on innovation finds that it is more often the large, well-endowed organizations and firms that produce innovations (Rogers, 1995). This conflicts with the common view that small, nimble charter schools will serve as incubators of new practices.

Having said this, it is clear that some Michigan charter schools are employing unique and even new educational practices. Moreover, it is clear that some of the schools are providing choices that were not previously available in many communities. However, this is not happening on a large scale.

The Diffusion of Charter School Innovations and Practices

Even if charter schools are not particularly effective in generating new educational practices, their value might lie in their ability to spur districts to adopt practices that, while perhaps not new to education, better serve particular student populations. Indeed, there is evidence that charter schools are doing just that. A U.S. Department of Education-sponsored study (RPP International, 2001) found that nearly one-half of the 49 districts studied reported implementing at least one new educational program in response to charter schools. These included all-day or extended-day kindergarten, reintroduction of arts and music, before- and after-school programs, creation of specialty schools, and new approaches to scheduling and organizing instruction (i.e., multigrade classrooms).

The evidence from our Michigan case studies is similar. While most district officials believe they were doing innovative things before charter schools came onto the scene, they acknowledge that the existence of charter schools in their communities has induced them to be even more vigilant about seeking out practices that better meet their students' needs and in reflecting upon their own missions. Among the examples from our case districts, the following can be noted:

- Two districts were implementing and/or promoting district choice programs such as magnet schools or intradistrict choice.

- One district developed what it called a preventative approach in seeking to keep its families from moving to charter schools; this included consideration of enhanced technology programs.

- Another district instituted smaller class sizes and was planning to experiment with new programs, such as the adoption of a new discipline policy, for all district schools.

Representatives from charter schools tended to exaggerate the impact they were having, while district officials tended to discount the influence of charter schools on decisions they were making regarding new programs and practices. In reviewing all the data we have collected on the topic, it is clear that the presence of charter schools was coinciding with noticeable changes in some surrounding noncharter schools. In part, this change is due to the competition presented by charter schools and, in part, some of these changes were in response to other structural changes and mandates from the state that were influencing all schools.

The diffusion of ideas from charter to noncharter schools, however, might be a hollow victory if it fails to leverage improvements in student performance. After all, the charter concept holds that the true test of school quality lies in outcomes, not in the choice of educational processes.

Two recent studies assessed the impact of charter schools on district students' test scores on the Michigan Assessment of Educational Progress (MEAP) tests. Eberts and Hollenbeck (2001) found that fifth-grade students in districts that host charter schools score approximately 1.5 percent higher on the writing portion of the MEAP, controlling for student, school, and district characteristics. However, the effect is either minuscule or nonexistent for fifth-grade science, fourth-grade math, and fourth-grade reading. Moreover, there is evidence that the size of the impact has decreased over time.

One potential problem with Eberts and Hollenbeck's estimates of the charter effect is that the causal arrows between charter and noncharter schools might run in both directions. That is, whether or not there is a charter school in a given district might depend, in part, on test scores in that district. If charter schools tend to locate in low-scoring districts, then this might artificially depress Eberts and Hollenbeck's estimates of the charter impact.[8] An earlier study by Bettinger (1999) attempted to account for this reciprocal causality using a statistical technique known as instrumental variables.[9] The results of the instrumental variable model suggest that the charter impact is negative, but statistically insignificant. The findings of both studies are at odds with research by Hoxby (2000) that suggests that competition among traditional public schools enhances test scores.

When interpreting these findings it is important to bear in mind that there are considerable obstacles to the diffusion of educational practices from charter to noncharter schools. Diffusion of practices can come about either through a *collegial* process of collaboration or a *competitive* process (Miron & Nelson, 2000). In the collegial model, charter and noncharter school officials share ideas in a spirit of give and take. However, it is clear that there are few venues in which such exchanges take place, a fact that is no doubt explained in part by the atmosphere of competition and mistrust that often prevails between charter and noncharter school staff. The competitive model requires no such explicit collaboration. However, it does require that charter schools represent a credible threat to enrollments in noncharter schools. While high concentrations of charter schools in some communities make this threat real, charter school enrollment in the state remains very low in most areas (see also Arsen et al., 1999).

The proprietary nature of most EMO curricula also reduces the likelihood that any innovations developed by these schools might be adopted by other schools. Teacher contracts with EMOs often stipulate that any new practices or inventions created by their employees belong to the company. This practice, of course, is not uncommon in the private sector. However, it conflicts with the charter school law's goal of encouraging the transfer of educational practices among schools (see Chapter 10).

Finally, it is important to bear in mind that traditional public schools are often resistant to the very idea of charter schools, to say nothing of any educational practices that emerge from them. Diffusion requires both an originator of an idea and someone who is willing to adopt it. In a phrase, it takes two hands to clap.

Conclusion

Charter proponents argue that the public value of charter schools lies not only in their ability to improve their own students' performance and prospects, but also those of students who remain in traditional public and private schools. In this chapter we have sought to assess a variety of charter school impacts on noncharter public and private schools.

Based on case studies of four charter-rich districts, we began our examination with charter schools' fiscal impacts. Such impacts are difficult to assess objectively, because such an analysis involves separating the impact of charter schools from the complex web of other forces affecting public schools. With this in mind, we did find evidence that charter schools are having at least modest impacts on district enrollments. The overall fiscal impact of such departures is no doubt attenuated somewhat by the fact that districts are no longer responsible for educating departing students. However, it is difficult to assess the net fiscal impact of the drain from charter schools. Indeed, whether a district can realize savings from dropping enrollments likely depends in part on the pattern of departures. In many cases, districts are unable or unwilling to cut certain fixed costs associated with education.

There is also some evidence that charter schools are changing the way districts relate to parents and families. Each district we studied reported increased marketing activities and enhanced efforts to communicate with families and articulate their educational missions. Competition from charter schools also appears to have spurred districts to offer new services, such as before- and after-school programs, all-day kindergarten classes, and instruction in foreign languages. Many district officials complain that the need to engage in marketing diverts resources away from educational activities, thus underscoring one of the indirect fiscal impacts of charter schools. Whether the costs of competition are justified depends on whether the need to compete makes schools spend their other resources more wisely and efficiently.

As for social impacts, there is evidence that charter schools are leading to greater segregation by race, family income levels, and ability—not only in charter schools but in surrounding communities. Thus, the analysis provides evidence from a few case districts of the larger demographic trends discussed in Chapter 5.

Finally, we found that there is at least modest evidence that charter schools in Michigan have changed educational processes in noncharter schools, including adoption of new programs, enhanced concern for mission, and so on. However, it is less clear that these practices are as innovative as charter proponents had hoped. One obstacle to studying innovation in charter schools lies in the difficulty of developing a widely accepted, clear operational definition of innovation. Using a reasonable definition, Mintrom (2000) found that most of the practices being exported from charter to noncharter schools are not very innovative, inasmuch as most of them are already in use in noncharter public schools. The evidence of charter school impact on student performance in district schools is even weaker, with two rigorous studies unable to find any widespread or significant impact. In any case, it is clear that charter schools in Michigan have not served as the hotbeds of innovation and systemic impact that proponents had hoped they would.

Notes

1. Large school districts tend to keep better records of student mobility, including interviews or surveys of families that have children who are entering or exiting a district school.

2. Readers should bear in mind that these two studies relied on different samples of noncharter public schools.

3. Another study of charter impact sent a team of parents into charter and noncharter schools in the District of Columbia to assess their customer orientation (Teske et al., 2000). These authors found that charter schools were more responsive and open to the parent-visitors than noncharter schools in the district.

4. The difficulty of resolving these issues has led some authors to retreat to almost wholly subjective definitions of innovation. Rogers (1995), for instance, defines innovation as "an idea, practice, or object that is perceived as new by an individual or other unit of adoption." In a nutshell, this definition holds that something is innovative if those adopting it think it is. Without denying the subjectivity in identifying innovations, it seems to us that a more objective (or at least intersubjective) definition is needed if we are to have a constructive policy debate about whether charter schools are, in fact, innovative.

5. Closely related to this is the notion of innovation in implementation. Here, innovation comes in finding new ways to deliver preexisting educational packages or interventions.

6. Pennsylvania's Charter Appeals Board has canonized this definition in administrative case law by defining an innovation as any practice used by a charter school not currently in use by the school's host district. See Miron & Nelson (2000) for a more detailed discussion.

7. Naturally, these two dimensions are, in reality, continuous rather than discrete. We have presented them as simple dichotomies for ease in exposition.

8. Glomm, Harris, & Lo (2000) found some evidence that Michigan charter schools tend to locate in lower-scoring districts. However, this effect is quite weak and sensitive to specification of the statistical model.

9. Here, the analyst finds a variable that is correlated with the suspected causal variable (in this case, the existence of charter schools in a district) but that is not correlated with the outcome variable (in this case, district MEAP scores). The instrumental variable Bettinger chose was proximity to a state university that grants charters. Using this as a predictor of the number of charter schools provides an indicator of charter location that is not contaminated by the dual causality mentioned above. Bettinger pointed out, however, that the instrumental variable "breaks down" over time, as universities began chartering schools farther away from their campuses.

8

Student Achievement

Proponents of charter schools often predict that the autonomy-accountability bargain on which the schools are based will lead to improvements in student learning. Indeed, for many stakeholders, test score results are the single most important measure of charter school quality.

In this chapter we assess the impact that charter schools in Michigan and elsewhere are having on student achievement by comparing achievement gains in charter schools with gains in comparable noncharter schools. The chapter begins by painting a picture of what we know about charter schools' impact on achievement nationally and how findings from Michigan fit into this broader picture. We then go on to present in greater detail findings from our own work on Michigan charter schools. While our work is, to date, the most comprehensive assessment of charter schools' impact on achievement in Michigan, a handful of other researchers have presented more in-depth examinations of achievement at certain grades. Thus, the chapter also includes findings from these studies.

Michigan in National Context[1]

In spite of the central role that achievement plays in the charter concept, surprisingly few studies or evaluations have analyzed student achievement in charter schools. Citing both the relative newness and small size of charter schools, many researchers have avoided the question of achievement altogether. More recently, and with the maturing of the movement, a few studies have taken up the question of charter schools' impact on student learning and achievement. Our review of the literature turned up only 15 statewide studies[2] that provide acceptable assessments of the value that charter schools are adding to their students' achievement levels,[3] drawing upon data from just eight states. Thus, the most striking finding relates to how little we know about charter schools' impact on student achievement.

Table 8.1 summarizes findings from the studies using a 5-point rating scale that ranges from –2 (negative impact) to 0 (no impact) to +2 (positive impact). Overall, the studies provide a mixed picture. Studies of charter schools in Arizona and Colorado present evidence that the schools are having a positive impact on student achievement, while studies of the District of Columbia and Michigan provide evidence that the charter effect is negative.

Table 8.1 Summary of Studies on Charter Schools' Impact on Student Achievement

State	Number of Studies	Average Quality Rating*	Average Impact Rating**
Arizona	2	3.5	1.4
Colorado	5	1.0	1.5
Connecticut	1	3.0	1.0
District of Columbia	1	1.5	–2.0
Georgia	1	1.0	1.0
Michigan	3	2.7	–1.7
Pennsylvania	1	1.5	0.0
Texas	1	4.0	1.0
Overall	15	2.1	0.2***

* The quality rating is scaled from 1 to 4, with 4 indicating the highest quality studies. See Miron and Nelson (2001) for details.
** The impact rating is scaled as follows: *2=positive impact; 1=mixed to positive impact; 0=mixed impact; –1=mixed to negative impact; –2=negative impact.*
*** The overall average impact rating (bottom right in the table) includes weights for study quality. See Miron and Nelson (2001) for details on the weighting procedures.
Source: Authors' calculations.

As the third column in Table 8.1 suggests, there is considerable variation in the quality of the 15 studies we reviewed. The positive findings in the Colorado studies, for instance, are tempered by the fact that most provide only single-year snapshots of achievement. Similarly, the positive findings in the Arizona studies, particularly one by researchers at the Goldwater Institute, are given credence by their high relative quality.[4] Interestingly, there appears to be little or no relationship between the studies' findings and their quality. In other words, there is no evidence that the strongest studies tend to produce positive findings, the weakest studies negative findings, and so on.

Of particular relevance to us are the findings from Michigan. All three studies of charter school achievement find that the schools have a negative impact. Moreover, all three studies are of comparatively high quality. We turn now to a more detailed examination of the evidence from Michigan.

Assessing Charter School Impacts in Michigan

To date, four studies have attempted to assess Michigan charter schools' impact on student achievement.[5] The most comprehensive study was included in the last of our evaluation reports, *An Evaluation of the Michigan Charter School Initiative: Performance, Accountability, and Impact* (Horn & Miron, 2000). This study examined results from the Michigan Educational Assessment Program (MEAP) from the 1995-96 to the 1999-2000 academic years. The study covered all grades and subjects, with the exception of the Grade 11 examinations, which were excluded due to difficulties in finding suitable comparison groups. The other studies largely comport with our own findings. Because of this, and because our findings are easier to present to a nontechnical audience, we restrict our discussion to our own findings. Appendix B provides a brief overview of other studies of student achievement in Michigan charter schools.

As researchers, educators, and policymakers across the country are realizing, schools are best held accountable for the "value" they add to their students' learning. This involves a comparison between where the students were academically when they came to the school with where they are after a certain amount of time at the school. Simply listing raw charter school scores from top to bottom, such as is common practice in newspapers, tells us more about which types of students choosing to attend charter schools than about how much value the schools add.

Researchers typically use two techniques to estimate value added. Some studies look at a slice of test scores at a single point in time and use various statistical techniques to control for differences in socioeconomic status, parents' education, and other background factors known to be correlated with student achievement. In layman's terms, statistical controls work by comparing each school with similar schools, as measured by the background factors. Generally, that portion of the variation in test scores that is not explained by the background factors is thought to be the value added by the schools. Other studies assess value added by tracking students over time (see, e.g., Sanders & Horn, 1993). Here researchers estimate the valued added by comparing the "pretest" score, which measures the achievement level the student brought to the school, with the "posttest" score. Unlike cross-sectional studies, students in these designs each serve as their own comparison group. The larger the pre/post difference, the more value the school is thought to have added to the student. In either case, the goal is essentially to observe the unobservable: How would students in charter schools have fared if they had remained in traditional public schools?[6]

Our own research on the achievement impacts of Michigan charter schools employed a hybrid approach that draws upon the strengths of *both* the cross-sectional and temporal analysis strategies. First, we tracked changes in test scores in each charter school, noting whether scores were growing, declining, or remaining stable. Simply observing trends, however, would not allow us to distinguish growth (or decline) due to noncharter impacts from other sources of growth (or decline). Therefore, we compared each charter school's achievement trend with that of its host district. Host districts, while not perfect comparison groups (see below), provide a reasonably similar group of students against which to judge charter school achievement trends.

For each grade level and subject area test we computed charter schools' relative gains. The relative gains analysis compares changes in each charter school's pass rates (i.e., percent of students meeting state standards) on the Michigan Educational Assessment Program (MEAP) test against that of its host district.[7] In examining the trends, we were interested not so much in the charter school trends themselves, but in how they compared with the host district trends. This analysis, then, asks how the change in charter schools' scores compared with the change in host districts' scores.

Let us illustrate the relative gains approach by way of an example. Figure 8.1 graphs artificial data on MEAP pass rates. We emphasize that these data are artificial and for the purposes of illustration; no inferences should be drawn from them.

In the example, we see that the charter school trend (denoted by the solid line) goes down slightly between the first and second year, followed by a fairly sharp decline. If we were to consider only this trend, we would conclude that charter schools have a negative impact on student achievement. The more important issue, however, is how the charter school trend compares with that of its matched host district. Indeed, it is possible that the decline in charter school pass rates is part of a larger set of forces affecting charter and noncharter schools alike. In the example, we find that while both the charter and host district trends are negative, the pass rate in the charter school is falling *faster* than the pass rate in the host district. Thus, we must conclude that the charter school is having a negative net impact on student achievement.

The graph, while suggestive, is a rather imprecise way to compare charter and host district trends. First, it is often difficult to "eyeball" differences in the charter school and host district trend lines. Second, new charter schools are constantly opening and a few are closing, which creates the challenge of examining trend lines of different lengths.

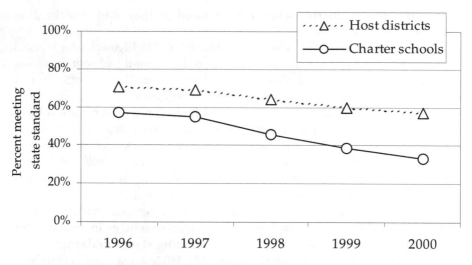

Figure 8.1 Illustration of Relative Gains Method

We address the second problem by calculating the "average annual change" in charter and host district MEAP scores. Averaging allows us to compare two-year trends with three- and four-year trends. Naturally, we will want to give more weight to information from longer trends. To address the first problem (that of eyeballing differences in trends), we simply subtract the host district average annual gain from each charter school's average annual gain. Thus, a *positive* value indicates that a charter school has outgained its host district while a *negative* value indicates that the school has *been* outgained. This *relative gains* value will be our primary measure of charter school impact in the analyses that follow.

While this approach is far superior to simply comparing the rankings of charter and noncharter schools, it still suffers from a number of limitations imposed by the state's testing regime. First, we know from the analysis in Chapter 5 that while, in the aggregate, charter schools are similar to host districts, there are important differences in the concentration of special education students and—in some cases—the proportion of students qualifying for the free and reduced-priced lunch program. Researchers often control for such differences statistically (if not through random assignment) by obtaining data for each student and/or school on such measures as free and reduced-price lunch status. The results of these analyses generally suggest that SES might account for as much as three fourths of the performance variation between schools. As discussed in Chapter 5, nearly half of the charter schools do not participate in the free and reduced-priced lunch program, leaving us unable to include rigorous controls for demographic characteristics.[8]

Second, the fact that the MEAP is not administered every year means that we cannot track individual students'—or even cohorts of students'—progress over time. Instead, we can only trace "consecutive cohorts." That is, we must compare this year's fifth graders with last year's, this year's seventh graders with last year's, and so on. As a consequence, we cannot rule out the possibility that the trends we observe are the result of changes over time in the types of students choosing to attend charter schools instead of, or in addition to, the "charter effect."[9] This, indeed, is a very serious limitation. However, in the absence of improvements in the state's testing policies, we must make approximations based on existing data, imperfect as it is.

A Summary of the Findings

Having described how we analyzed the achievement data, we turn now to a summary of findings from this analysis. Before stating the bottom line, however, we begin with a number of important observations that will help readers understand our findings.

The first observation is that the trends in MEAP pass rates in many Michigan charter schools are very haphazard. Figure 8.2 plots pass rates for the Grade 5 MEAP test for six fairly typical schools.[10] As the graph shows, it is not unusual for a school's pass rate to change by 20 percentage points or more from one year to the next. These schools, moreover, are merely typical—many schools show considerably more year-to-year variation. Of particular interest is the fact that the year-to-year trends are often inconsistent, going up one year, down the next, and perhaps up again in the third year. As a consequence, researchers, policymakers, and citizens should be very cautious in making generalizations based on just a few years of data about any particular school.[11]

Another challenge to those seeking generalizations about Michigan charter schools is that there is tremendous variation in how charter schools' gains match up against their host districts. As discussed above, our primary measure of charter school impact is the relative gain, or each charter school's average annual gain (loss) minus its host district's average annual gain (loss). Figure 8.3 illustrates this school-to-school variation in the Grade 4 reading portion of the MEAP. Most charter schools' average annual gains were similar to those of their host districts; on the graph, these are the cases represented by the tall bar above and near the zero point on the horizontal axis. However, the graph also shows that a considerable proportion of charter schools' average annual gains were as much as 20 percentage points above or below that of their host districts. A small proportion of the schools led or trailed their host districts by as much as 40 percentage points.

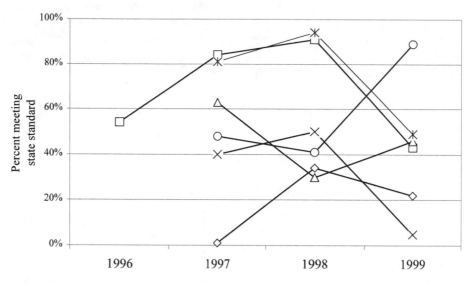

Figure 8.2 Typical Temporal Variation in MEAP Pass Rates, Writing 5

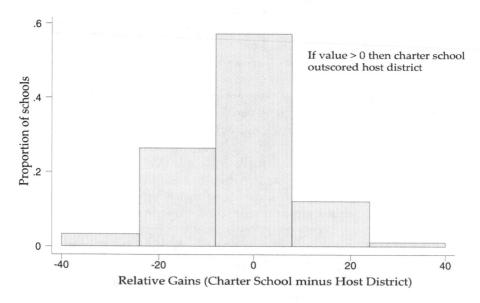

Figure 8.3 Variation in Relative Gain Scores, Reading 4

Finally, it is worth pointing out that schools that have a positive (or negative) impact in one subject or grade level often have no impact (or an opposite impact) in other subjects and grade levels. For instance, examination of correlations among the relative gain scores indicates that there is almost no discernible relationship between charter schools' impact on Grade 5 science scores and those in Grade 8 science. A full presentation of correlations among the scores is presented in Appendix B, Table B.1.

Bearing these points in mind, we move now to some generalizations. The generalizations are based on averages of the relative gain scores, but with a couple of twists. First, we give more weight to schools with more students tested than to those with just a handful of students taking the tests. While the successes and failures of small schools are certainly important, from a statewide policy perspective, it is important not to overgeneralize from small cases—or to undergeneralize from large ones. Second, we give more weight to schools reporting more years of data. Given the often dramatic year-to-year variation in schools' test scores, we should be much more confident in characterizing trends with four and five years of data than trends with just two or three years of data.[12]

The findings are summarized in Figure 8.4. A quick glance at the figure shows that with the exception of fourth-grade math, all of the bars are below the horizontal line at zero. Once again, a negative score implies that, on average, charter schools' annual gains (losses) were less (more) than those of their host districts. We turn next to a subject-by-subject examination of the findings. More detailed results are provided in Appendix B.

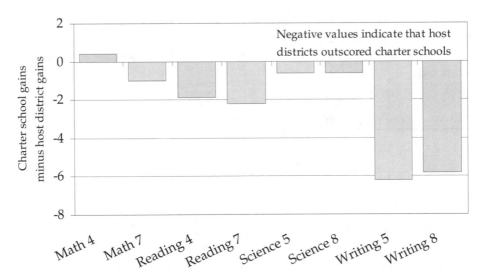

Figure 8.4 Average Relative Gain Scores

Beginning with the math scores, once again we find that Grade 4 math is the only subject and grade level on which charter schools' average annual gains outpaced those of their host district. The relative gain score was 0.4 percent, which means that the average charter school pass rate on this particular portion of the MEAP was approximately a half percentage point higher than the host district's.[13] This, of course, is a very small advantage and is noteworthy only because it is the only positive finding for charter schools. The findings for Grade 7 math are negative, but only slightly so. Indeed, charter schools' average annual change in pass rate was one percentage point lower than those of their host districts—once again, a small difference.

The charter-host district differences were somewhat larger for the reading portions of the MEAP. Here, the average charter school was outgained by its host district by 1.9 percentage points on the Grade 4 assessment and 2.2 points on the Grade 7 assessment. The differences on the science portions of the MEAP, like the math portion, were small; charter schools' were outpaced by their host districts by 0.6 percentage points in both the Grade 5 and Grade 8 assessments. By far the largest discrepancies between charter schools and their host districts came in the writing portions of the MEAP. Here, the average charter school was outgained by 6.2 percentage points on the Grade 5 assessment and 5.8 percentage points on the Grade 8 assessment.

Interestingly, schools that opened earlier in the Michigan charter school movement have generally posted stronger relative gain scores (relative to their host districts) in math and reading than those that opened later. The pattern does not appear to hold for science and writing scores, however. Table 8.2 shows these patterns. One possible explanation for the differences between the newer and older schools is that as time goes by more schools are able to climb the "learning curve" and figure out how to produce better academic outcomes. Another relates to the trend over time toward more EMO-operated schools. We turn next to an analysis of student achievement in EMO versus non-EMO schools.

Table 8.2 Differences in Charter School Impact Between New and Old Schools

Number of years open	*Average Relative Gain**		
	Math & Reading	*Science & Writing*	*All Subjects Combined*
2	−3.5	−0.4	−1.9
3	−2.2	−5.4	−3.8
4	−1.2	−1.2	0.7
5	−0.9	n.a.	n.a.

* Scores are averaged across subjects and grades.

EMOs and Student Achievement

As noted earlier in the book, Michigan's charter school experiment is perhaps most notable for the prominent role that private management companies have played. Indeed, the most recent estimates suggest that approximately three fourths of all Michigan schools are managed—either wholly or in part—by an education management company.

Proponents of privatization argue that public services can often be delivered more efficiently by for-profit firms, with government providing only direction and oversight. In Osborne and Gaebler's now-famous words, governments are to "steer" but not "row" (Osborne & Gaebler, 1992). According to the argument, when government opens up the delivery of education and other public services to private firms, competitive pressures compel them to focus on bottom line efficiency. On this view, government agencies usually focus not on outcomes but on budget maximization and bureaucratic survival. Finally, critics charge that government agencies can face political constraints that force them to operate inefficiently and even irrationally (Wolf, 1988).

To test the idea that privately owned and operated firms will do a better job of running charter schools, we compared the relative gain scores of privately managed schools with those non-EMO schools. As before, the relative gain scores compare charter schools' average annual gains with those of their host districts. Here, the values shown in the graph are EMO-managed schools' relative gains minus those of non-EMO schools. Thus, negative values indicate that non-EMO schools outperformed (i.e., had higher relative gains than) EMO schools.

As Figure 8.5 shows, charter schools managed by EMOs did worse than other charter schools in all subjects and grades, with the exception of Grade 7 math. The EMO deficiency is particularly great in Grade 4 math and Grade 5 writing, where the average EMO-managed school was outgained by more than 5 percentage points by the average non-EMO school. These findings are confirmed by Eberts and Hollenbeck's (2001) analysis, which was based on individual-level test scores and included a number of relatively powerful statistical controls.

Figure 8.6 provides comparisons among some of the EMOs that operate 5 or more charter schools. To simplify the analysis, we drew comparisons only on the Grades 4 and 5 portions of the MEAP. From the graph it is apparent that although EMO-managed schools, as a group, did worse than other charter schools, there are notable variations among management companies. While schools managed by each of the selected companies were outgained by their host districts, schools managed by National Heritage Academies did best, having been outscored by just over one percentage point, and Leona Group schools did worst, having been outscored by more than four percentage points.

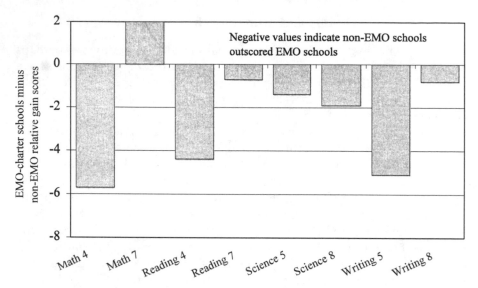

Figure 8.5 Comparison of EMO and Non-EMO Charter Schools in Terms of
Average Relative Gains

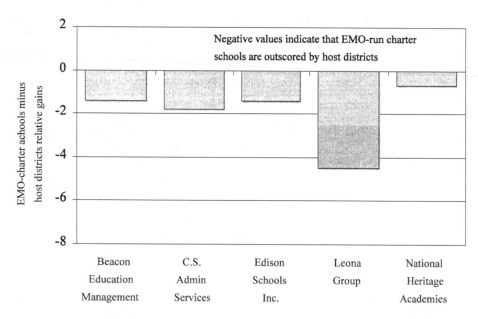

Figure 8.6   Comparisons Among Selected EMOs: Grades 4 and 5 Average
Relative Gains

Conclusion

This chapter sought to assess the value Michigan charter schools have added to their students' achievement levels by comparing them with ostensibly similar students in their host districts. We found considerable variation among charter schools, with some clearly outgaining their host districts and others lagging far behind. In the aggregate, however, our findings cast doubt on proponents' claims that Michigan charter schools will leverage gains in student achievement. With the exception of Grade 4 math, MEAP pass rates in the typical charter school grew less (or fell faster) than those in their host districts. Finally, we found that, while there are some variations among companies, as a group charter schools managed by for-profit EMOs gained less (or fell faster) than other charter schools. This casts at least some doubt on privatization advocates' claims that introducing competitive pressures into educational management will lead to improvements in performance.

Like most attempts to assess achievement impacts, however, we must end by reminding the reader that our findings our limited by weaknesses in the data. These limitations include missing data on free and reduced-price lunch status and the fact that the MEAP system does not allow researchers to track single cohorts of students over time. Talk of data limitations may make eyes glaze over and perhaps bring to mind the old adage that "if figures lie, then only liars figure." However, these limitations will make for uncertain answers to questions about student outcomes until better data become available.

Notes

1. Material in this section is drawn from Miron & Nelson (2001).

2. Citations to the studies are as follows: Antonucci (1997), Bettinger (1999), Colorado Department of Education (1997, 1998, 1999, 2000, 2001), Eberts & Hollenbeck (2001), Gronberg & Jansen (2001), Henig et al. (1999, 2001), Horn & Miron (1999, 2000), Miron & Nelson (2000), Mulholland (1999), and Solmon, Paark & Garcia (2001).

3. See Miron & Nelson (2001) for the criteria used to select these studies.

4. Even the strongest studies of student achievement in charter schools, however, are subject to important limitations. See Nelson & Hollenbeck (2001) for a critical review of the Goldwater Institute study.

5. A study by Public Sector Consultants, Inc. of Michigan charter schools is excluded because it examined data only from charter schools in the Detroit metropolitan area.

6. In slightly more technical terms, the evaluator must be able to demonstrate that the program was both a *sufficient* and *necessary* condition of the observed changes in behavior. To say that the program was sufficient is to say that the introduction of the program was empirically associated with the change in behavior. Demonstrating that the program was a necessary condition is more difficult, since it requires that the change in behavior would not have occurred but for the introduction of the program.

7. For the purposes of an impact evaluation, we need a measure that is, as much as possible, comparable across schools (both charter and noncharter) and over time. To our knowledge, the Michigan Educational Assessment Program (MEAP), though not perfect, best meets these criteria. The MEAP is the only test that all Michigan schools—charter and noncharter—are required to administer. The MEAP is a criterion-referenced testing program based on specific criteria set by Michigan educators. Criteria for each test are based on what students should have learned up to the grade in which the test is administered. Because the same versions of the test are administered to all students, it is comparable across schools in any given year. We are more cautious about using MEAP scores to make comparisons over time, given that many tests are changed over time in an effort to refine and improve them. The *MEAP Handbook* (Michigan Department of Education, 1999b), for its part, encourages the use of MEAP scores to make comparisons over time within a given grade level but cautions against making comparisons across grade levels.

The MEAP system tests students in math, reading, science, and writing. Math and reading tests are administered in Grades 4, 7, and 11. Science and writing tests are administered in Grades 5, 8, and 11. Using data provided by the Michigan Department of Education (MDE), we constructed a database of MEAP scores that spans from the 1995-1996 academic year to the 1998-1999 academic year. While MDE data sets report the number and percentage of students falling into each of several performance categories, for simplicity in exposition we restricted most of our analyses to the percentage of students earning a passing grade on these tests.

8. We have, however, developed a blunt and imperfect technique for controlling for student background. Up until the most recent year, new charter schools have increasingly located in suburban areas. To take advantage of this, we have broken the data out according to cohorts by first year of operation. In short, we take first year of operation as an imperfect proxy for student demographic background. Generally, breaking the data out by cohort changes our conclusions very little. Thus, we have not presented that analysis here.

9. Another issue related to the use of consecutive cohorts is that students tested in later years are likely to have had longer exposure to their charter school. That is, in the early days of the Michigan charter school movement, when most schools were new, a fourth grader would have had no more than a year or two of charter experience. As the movement reached its fifth year, it is possible that many of the fourth graders tested would have attended the charter school since kindergarten.

Thus, the proportion of the variation in scores explained by the charter effect should have increased over time. Unfortunately, data limitations leave no systematic way to test this hypothesis.

10. Schools were selected by calculating the standard deviation of MEAP pass rates for each school. The standard deviations of the schools plotted in the graph are within a few points of the mean standard deviation for all schools reporting scores on the Grade 5 writing assessment. However, the Grade 5 writing assessment, on average, shows greater temporal variation than other portions of the MEAP.

11. Kane & Staiger (2001) have provided, to our knowledge, the most rigorous analysis of the instability of time series of school test scores. Using data from North Carolina, 28 percent of the variance in Grade 5 reading scores is due to sampling variations, while 10 percent is due to other "non-persistent" factors.

One factor that often explains why some schools' time trends are less consistent than others is the number of students tested. Quite simply, when just a few students take a test in any given year, a particularly strong or poor showing by any one of them can significantly raise or lower the school's aggregate scores. In the Michigan assessment data, we find a small to modest negative relationship between charter school enrollment and year-to-year variations (as measured by the standard deviation) in that same school's test scores. We have omitted Grade 11 scores because of the small number of charter schools teaching at that level.

Subject	Grade 4	Grade 5	Grade 7	Grade 8
Math	−0.17		−0.35	
Reading	−0.44		−0.39	
Science		0.07		−0.40
Writing		−0.30		−0.10

12. More specifically, the weight for the number of students tested is the number of test takers averaged across each year for which data are reported. The "number of years" weight is simply the number of years in which a given school reported data on the relevant portion of the MEAP. We combined information from the two weights using two techniques. In the first, the final weight is the sum of the two weights. In the second, the weights were multiplied. The multiplicative weights allow a high (low) value on one weight to expand (diminish) the influence of the other. The values reported in the text and tables are the simple average of additive and multiplicative weighted averages.

13. Given that we had data on the population of Michigan charter schools, we did not employ confidence intervals, significance tests, or other tools of statistical inference.

9

Customer Satisfaction

In Chapter 8, we saw that results from the Michigan Educational Assessment Program (MEAP) examinations suggest that while there is considerable variation across schools, achievement gains in most Michigan charter schools lag behind comparable schools at most grade levels and in most subject areas. There is, however, legitimate debate over whether scores on standardized tests are an appropriate—or certainly the best—indicator of school quality. Critics of standardized tests argue that the tests often fail to capture the important nuances of student learning and reflect schools' decisions about what to teach as much as students' mastery of skills. Proponents of school choice, for their part, often argue that in an open market system, the best indicator of a school's quality is its ability to attract, satisfy, and retain its customers. Thus, whereas the chapter on test scores assesses Michigan charter schools' accountability for academic performance (performance accountability), this chapter assesses their market accountability.

Ultimately, market accountability is about a school's (or other institution's) ability to get people to "vote for it with their feet." Accordingly, some studies have attempted to ascertain charter schools' market accountability through examination of enrollments and—especially—waiting lists (see, e.g., Miron & Nelson, 2000). Given that we were unable to obtain copies of reliable waiting lists for a large proportion of Michigan charter schools, we examine instead key stakeholders' opinions about student performance and other aspects of school quality. Presumably, satisfied students and their families are more likely to remain in a charter school. The findings reported in this chapter are based on survey instruments designed specifically for charter schools.[1]

The importance of these alternative indicators of school quality is twofold. First, some commentators, particularly the proponents of market account- ability, consider them ends in themselves. Others, however, view them as necessary prerequisites to the ultimate goal of increasing student achievement. On this view, even if a charter school has not demonstrated gains in student achievement, its ability to change student attitudes toward learning and school climate might augur well for future improvements in achievement. In short, such outcomes might serve as "leading education indicators" of potential educational performance in much the same way that the Index of Leading Economic Indicators serves as a way to predict future economic performance.

The chapter begins by considering nontest indicators of student performance, including student and teacher perceptions of academic gains. The chapter's second section reviews evidence of customer satisfaction with schools' accomplishment of their missions. The third and fourth sections cover satisfaction with curriculum, instruction, and resources. Finally, the last section explores the relationship between market and performance accountability; specifically, the relationship (or, as we shall see, lack thereof) between satisfaction indicators and gains in MEAP scores.

Nontest Indicators of Academic Performance

One nontest indicator of student performance or student achievement is students' own ratings of their performance. Such ratings are obviously subjective and should not be taken as definitive indicators of performance. However, it is likely that such ratings pick up at least some aspects of student learning not captured by objective standardized tests. Our primary interest in this indicator lies in students' comparisons of their performance at the charter school and at their previous school.

Students

One question on the student surveys asked students to rate their performance at their previous school as either Excellent, Good, Average, Poor, or Unsat- isfactory. Another question immediately following the first asked students to rate their current (charter school) performance on the same scale. Figure 9.1 summarizes the student self-ratings graphically, with the lighter bars representing self-ratings of performance at previous schools and the darker bars representing self-ratings of performance at the charter school. As the figure clearly shows, on the whole students rated their current performance as higher than performance at their previous school. For instance, 27 percent of students rated their current performance as "excellent," compared with 22 percent in their previous schools. Similarly, the percentage of students rating

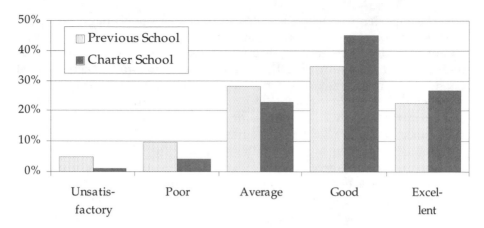

Figure 9.1 Student Self-Rated Academic Performance at Previous and
           Current School

their performance as "good" increased from 35 to 45 percent. At the low end
of spectrum, only 4 percent of students rated their current performance as poor,
compared with 10 percent for the previous school. These differences are
statistically significant ($p < 0.01$).[2]

These aggregate numbers, however, mask considerable variation among
Michigan charter schools. In some schools, the difference between assessments
of previous and current performance was even greater. In one school, for
instance, no students rated their past performance as excellent, while more than
41 percent rated their current performance as excellent. The trend from
previous to current schools was not always positive, however. In 11 of the 47
schools with responses on these questions, the shift was negative. At one
school, for instance, 52 percent of students rated their past performance as
good, compared with only 32 percent who rated their current performance as
good.

Ideally, we would compare perceived performance gains among charter
school students with those among students in traditional public schools. Since
we were unable to administer surveys in noncharter schools, we compared
Michigan charter school students to a composite comparison group of charter
school students in three other states (Pennsylvania, Illinois, and Connecticut).[3]
Here we find that perceived student gains in Michigan charter schools are
similar to those in the other states. In the composite comparison group, the
percentage of students rating themselves as excellent increased from 23 to 26
percent, and the percentage of students rating themselves as "good" increased
from 37 to 44 percent.

In addition to drawing comparisons with students in other states, we
sought explanations for variations in perceived gains among Michigan charter

school students. For instance, we found that students coming from public schools reported larger performance gains than those who previously attended non-public schools (including private, parochial, home schools, and others). Whereas the average perceived improvement in performance was 0.4 points (on a 5-point scale) for former public school students, the improvement was only 0.1 points for students who were formerly enrolled in non-public schools, a statistically significant difference ($p < 0.01$). However, most of the difference in perceived gains appears to stem from the fact that former public schools students gave lower ratings to their past performance and thus had more room for growth. Whereas the typical student coming from a non-public school gave herself/himself a rating of 3.9 for previous performance on the 5-point performance scale, the typical student coming from a public school gave herself/himself a 3.5, again, a statistically significant difference ($p < 0.01$). Figure 9.2 illustrates the public/non-public differences.

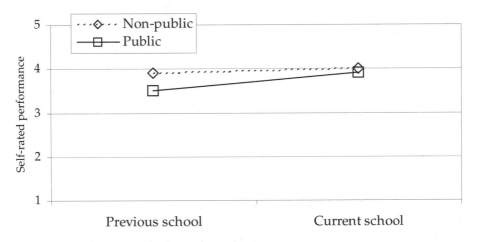

Figure 9.2 Student Self-Rated Academic Gains: Former Public and Non-public Students Compared

We also tested for differences between students enrolled in EMO-managed schools and other charter schools. Students in charter schools run by EMOs reported smaller performance improvements than students in other schools. The average perceived gain among students in EMO-run schools was 0.2, compared with 0.6 in non-EMO schools, thus confirming Chapter 8's finding that EMO student gains on the MEAP lag behind those in non-EMO schools. As with the public–non-public differences, we found that EMO and non-EMO students report different levels of performance in their previous schools, but similar levels in their current charter schools (see Figure 9.3). Indeed, the typical EMO student reported his/her previous performance as "good" (3.7)

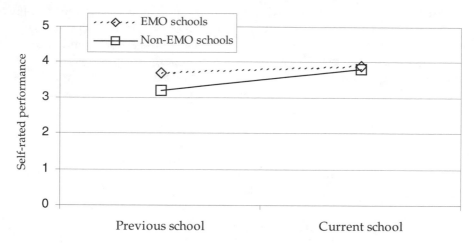

Figure 9.3 Student Self-Rated Academic Performance Gains: EMO and
Non-EMO Students Compared

while the typical non-EMO student rated his/her previous performance as
"average" (3.2), a statistically significant difference ($p < 0.01$). This finding is
interesting since it provides some confirmation (albeit based on subjective
student self-ratings) of claims that EMO schools tend to attract academically
stronger students.

We also found a racial gap in perceived gains, with the average white
student reporting a 0.4 point increase (on a 5-point scale) and the average
nonwhite student reporting virtually no change. Both the pre- and posttest
between-group differences are statistically significant ($p < 0.01$). Interestingly,
however, white and nonwhite students gave themselves similar ratings for
performance in their previous schools (3.6 and 3.7, respectively, on the 5-point
scale).

Next, we tested for differences in perceived improvements across grade
levels. Perceived differences were substantially higher among high school
students than among elementary and middle school students. These differences
are statistically significant ($p < 0.01$). We also tested for the effect of gender and
number of years enrolled in the charter school, but found no statistically
discernible differences among these groups.

One might suspect that at least some of the public-private and EMO-non-
EMO differences might be due to differences in the types of students choosing
to attend the schools. Demographic factors might also account for some of the
observed differences across grade levels, given that most schools serving
Grades 10, 11, and 12 are alternative high schools. To test this, we estimated a
more sophisticated multivariate model capable of simultaneously determining

the impact of grade level and EMO and public status, while controlling for demographic factors. This analysis confirms the earlier finding that former public school students and those in high schools report higher gains and that students in EMO-run schools report lower gains. In addition, nonwhite students report lower gains than white students. As before, the impact of gender on student self-rated gains was small and statistically insignificant.[4]

Teachers

Students' overall perceptions of their academic gains are confirmed by an analysis of a similar item on the teacher survey. Sixty-nine percent of teachers responding said that the statement "The achievement levels of students are improving" was true. Another 29 percent said that the statement was partly true. However, when we asked teachers to compare their initial expectations about achievement with their current perceptions, survey responses indicate that teachers have seen less improvement than they initially expected. The difference between expectations and current perceptions was statistically significant ($p < 0.01$). Most of the downward movement was from "true" to "partly true."

As with the students, we explored differences in ratings according to grade levels taught. While the relationship between perceptions of student learning and the grade level was statistically significant, the nature of the relationship was less clear. The highest levels of agreement came from teachers who work primarily with second and tenth graders, while the lowest levels of agreement came from those working primarily with eighth and ninth graders. Unlike student responses, then, there is no clear evidence that perceived gains are higher or lower in the high school grades. As with student ratings, we compared teacher responses from EMO and non-EMO schools. This time, however, we found no notable differences.

Parents

We also asked parents to report their perceptions of their children's academic progress. Sixty-seven percent of parents surveyed said that the statement "My child's achievement level is improving" was true. Another 26 percent said that the statement was partly true, while 7 percent said that the statement was false. Parents' assessments of student academic progress, then, were very similar to those of teachers (see Figure 9.4). As with teachers, when parents were asked to compare their initial expectations and current perceptions of their children's learning, most suggested that the children were learning somewhat less than they expected. The difference between initial expectations and current perceptions was statistically significant ($p < 0.01$). As with teachers, most of the downward movement was from "true" to "partly true."

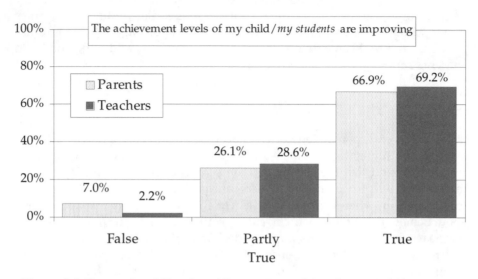

Figure 9.4 Parents' and Teachers' Perceptions of Academic Achivement

It is conceivable, however, that some parents might have chosen a charter school primarily on the basis of factors other than achievement. This might be true, for instance, if a student has a history of severe discipline problems. In such cases, parents might select a school they believe will help their child develop socially. For such parents, lackluster academic gains might not necessarily be a sign that the school is failing. To evaluate this hypothesis, we asked parents to indicate how important past academic performance was in the choice of a charter school. The average response to the item "My child was performing poorly at previous school" as a reason for choosing a charter school was 2.5 on a 5-point scale of perceived importance. More concretely, 45 percent of respondents chose the lowest value on the scale, indicating that this factor was not important, while only 20 percent chose the highest scale value (Very Important). Thus, relatively few parents indicated that poor past performance was a driving factor in their choice.[5]

As with the student and teacher data, we explored a number of explanations for variations among parents' assessments of student progress. As with the teachers, there were no clear patterns in the relationship between grade level and parents' assessments of student progress. Other comparisons (e.g., EMO vs. non-EMO) also yielded no significant differences.

Satisfaction With and Accomplishment of Mission

School mission statements are central to charter school accountability. In addition to results on standardized tests, charter schools are, in theory, held accountable for the goals set out in their charters and accompanying documents. Accordingly, we asked charter school parents and teachers to judge how well their school had accomplished its own particular mission.

Before asking about the accomplishment of mission goals, however, we sought to determine whether parents and teachers were aware of their school's mission. As discussed in the first chapter, an important aspect of the school choice idea is that parents and teachers will sort into schools based on their agreement on core educational goals and methods. Agreement on these issues, according to the theory, will leave schools with more time to focus on educational issues (as opposed to managing internal political conflicts) and allow for efficiency gains through specialization and focus (Chubb & Moe, 1990; Hill, Pierce, & Guthrie, 1997).

Some 93 percent of parents and 97 percent of teachers reported that they were aware of their school's mission. While this certainly suggests wide knowledge of, and perhaps support for, charter school missions, it is unclear from the survey instruments just how deep this familiarity and support run. Students appear to be less aware of school missions, with only 55 percent reporting that they either agreed or strongly agreed with the statement "I am aware of the mission of my school."[6]

Having established whether respondents were aware of their school's mission, we asked them whether they thought the school had succeeded so far in fulfilling that mission. Parents were somewhat more likely than teachers to say that their school's mission was being followed well or very well. Indeed, whereas 85 percent of parents said their school's mission was being followed well or very well, only 79 percent of teachers said so—a statistically significant difference ($p < 0.01$).

Once again, we explored a number of explanations for variations in respondents' opinions on the fulfillment of school missions. First, since new organizations often take time to accomplish their missions, we hypothesized that respondents from older charter schools would be more likely to believe that their school's mission had been fulfilled. However, we found no clear relationship between these variables.[7] Data limitations prevented us from investigating the same relationship among parent responses.

Second, we explored the impact of past school experience on perceptions of mission fulfillment. We found that teachers with more experience in public than private schools were less sanguine about the extent to which their school had fulfilled its mission. Once again, data limitations prevented us from investigating the same relationship among parent responses.

Finally, as with the other variables, we sought to compare perceptions of mission fulfillment in EMO and non-EMO schools. While there were no discernible differences among parents, teachers in EMO-run charter schools were slightly more sanguine about mission fulfillment than teachers in non-EMO schools. Eighty-one percent of teachers in EMO schools said that their school had fulfilled its mission either well or very well, compared with 74 percent in non-EMO schools. This relationship bordered on statistical significance ($p = 0.09$).

In summary, most parents and teachers and approximately half of students, report being aware of their school's mission. Of these, more than three fourths of parents and teachers reported being satisfied with the extent to which that mission is being accomplished.

Satisfaction With Curriculum and Instruction

Our survey research indicates that quality of curriculum and instruction is a very important factor driving parents' decisions to enroll their children in a charter school. Indeed, when asked how important "good teachers and high quality of instruction" were in deciding to enroll their child in a charter school, the average response among parents was 4.5 on a 5-point scale. More concretely, nearly 90 percent of parents surveyed chose the top rating of 5, indicating that this factor was "very important." Given the importance of curriculum and instruction to charter school parents, we sought to assess students', teachers', and parents' levels of satisfaction with these aspects of the schools. We begin with students' perceptions, moving next to the perceptions of parents and teachers.

Students

Our student surveys included a number of items related to satisfaction with instruction. In order to facilitate exposition, we generated an index of closely related items.[8] Items in the index include questions on the availability of teachers, the extent to which teachers encourage students to think about their future, and so on. Given the construction of the student survey, the student index relates to teaching and instruction, not curriculum and instruction. Table 9.1 includes a complete list of questions included in the index. All of the items in the index were on a 5-point scale. The index, in turn, is simply an average of all of those items. The average value on the student satisfaction index was 3.9 on a 5-point scale, indicating a moderate-to-high level of satisfaction. This is virtually the same as the average for the three states in the composite comparison group.

As with many of the variables discussed in the previous section, there is considerable school-to-school variation in scores on the satisfaction index. In some schools, the average index value was as low as 2.8 on a 5-point scale, indicating only a middling level of satisfaction. In other schools, the score was as high as 4.4.

As before, we sought to test a number of explanations for these variations. Students enrolled in charter schools operated by EMOs generally reported lower levels of satis-faction than students in non-

Table 9.1 Questions Included in Index of Student Satisfaction With Teachers and Instruction

Item	Average Score (SD)
My teachers encourage me to think about my future	3.6 (1.3)
Almost every assignment that I turn in to the teacher is returned with corrections and suggestions	3.5 (1.3)
Teachers and administrators know me by name	4.3 (1.1)
My teacher is available to talk about academic matters	4.1 (1.2)
Index	3.9

Note: Cronbach's alpha = 0.7

EMO schools (3.8 vs. 4.0). Students in schools operated by National Heritage Academies reported even lower satisfaction scores, with an average value of 3.5. These differences are statistically significant ($p < 0.01$). (As before, NHA is singled out because it is the largest EMO operating in Michigan.)

Once again, we sought to explore differences by grade level. Generally, we found that students in charter high schools reported higher levels of satis-faction with teaching and instruction than students in elementary and middle charter schools. For high school students the average index score was 4.1, compared with 3.8 for other students—a statistically significant difference ($p < 0.01$).

As with the analyses in the previous section, we also sought to determine whether students' responses were sensitive to their comparison groups. We found no appreciable difference between the responses of former public and former non-public school students. However, we did find that students who plan to pursue higher education were generally more satisfied with their schools' curriculum and instruction than students without such aspirations. For instance, students who reported planning to complete high school only had an average satisfaction score of 3.6, compared with 3.8 for students who reported planning to get a four-year college degree. Given that the index is on a 5-point scale, these differences are not particularly large; however, they are statistically significant ($p = 0.01$). Interestingly, students in EMO-run schools tend to have slightly higher educational aspirations than those in other schools. Fifty-seven percent of EMO students plan to get a four-year or graduate degree compared with 54 percent for non-EMO students.[9]

Parents

We devised a similar index of parents' satisfaction with charter school curriculum and instruction. The index included items on teaching, the curriculum, staff accountability, and expectations for student performance. The specific items are listed in Table 9.2. All of the items in the index were on a 5-point scale. The index, in turn, is simply an average of all of those items. The average value on the student satisfaction index was 4.1 on a 5-point scale, indicating a reasonably high level of satisfaction. This is virtually indistinguishable from the mean index value for parents in the composite comparison group states. Readers might also notice that the average value on the parent index for satisfaction with curriculum and instruction is slightly higher than the average value on the student index for teaching and instruction. It is important to bear in mind, however, that the two indices cannot be compared in any rigorous fashion, since they are based on different items.

Table 9.2 Index of Parents' Satisfaction With Curriculum and Instruction

Item	Average Score (SD)
This school is meeting students' needs that could not be addressed at other local schools	4.0 (1.1)
I am satisfied with the school's curriculum	4.1 (1.1)
I am satisfied with the instruction offered	4.1 (1.0)
I think the school has a bright future	4.4 (0.9)
This school has high standards and expectations for students	4.3 (1.0)
Teachers and school leadership are accountable for student achievement/performance	3.9 (1.1)
Index	4.1

Note: Cronbach's alpha = 0.87

As with the student index, there is considerable variation across schools in the values represented by the parent index. In some schools the average value was as high as 4.5 and in others as low as 3.1. We tested for such variations by grade level of the children, volunteerism, and EMO status. However, we found that none of these explanations account for a significant amount of the variation in index scores. Overall, the mean score of Michigan parents' satisfaction with instruction was very similar to the group of charter school parents from other states (rounded to 4.1 for both groups).

In order to account for the possibility that parents' responses were sensitive to their comparison group, we asked parents what type of school their child previously attended, but found no relationship between this and level of satisfaction with instruction. Similarly, there was only a very small negative relationship between the grade levels of parents' children and their level of satisfaction. While the relationship was statistically significant ($p < 0.01$), the magnitude was extremely small.

As before, we also examined differences between EMO-run and other charter schools. While we found no discernible difference between parents in EMO and non-EMO schools, we found that parents with children enrolled in National Heritage Academy schools were more satisfied with curriculum and instruction than parents with children in other schools (4.4 vs. 4.1 on a scale of 1 to 5). The difference was statistically significant ($p = 0.01$).[10]

Teachers

As with parents, we devised an index of teachers' satisfaction with curriculum and instruction. The index included items on teaching, the curriculum, staff accountability, and expectations for student performance. The specific items are listed in Table 9.3. All of the items in the index were rated on a 5-point scale. The index, in turn, is simply an average of all of those items. The average value on the student satisfaction index was 4.0 on a 5-point scale, indicating a fairly high level of satisfaction. This value was comparable to, although statistically significantly different from, that of our group of charter school teachers from other states, which was 3.9 ($p < 0.01$).

Readers might note that the average value on the teacher index is about the same as the average value on the parent index. The two indices, however, are not comparable, since they include some different items. Fortunately, there is enough overlap in items that we can construct comparable satisfaction indices with the same

Table 9.3 Index of Teachers' Satisfaction With Curriculum and Instruction

Item	Average Score (SD)
This school has high standards and expectations for students	4.2 (0.9)
I think this school has a bright future	4.2 (1.0)
Teachers are challenged to be effective	4.2 (0.9)
I am satisfied with the school mission statement	4.1 (0.9)
I am satisfied with the school's ability to fulfill its stated mission	3.7 (1.0)
Teachers and school leaders are accountable for student achievement/performance	4.0 (0.9)
This school is meeting students' needs that could not be addressed at other local schools	4.0 (1.0)
Parents are satisfied with the instruction	3.9 (0.8)
I am satisfied with the school's curriculum	3.6 (1.0)
Index	4.0

Note: Cronbach's alpha = 0.87.

items. Comparison of the two comparable indices confirms that parents and teachers have a similar level of satisfaction on matters of curriculum and instruction. For teachers, the mean value was 3.9 on a 5-point scale. Once again, Michigan teachers' average index score is virtually the same as that for the composite comparison group of teachers in other states. As with the student and parent indices, there is considerable variation in the average value across charter schools. In some schools the average value was as high as 4.7 and in others as low as 2.8. Among the explanations we tested for these variations were type of previous school, grade level of children, EMO status, and level of experience. While we found no differences according to type of previous school, grade levels taught, and experience, teachers in EMO-run schools were, on average, slightly more satisfied with curriculum and instruction than teachers in other schools. The average satisfaction score for teachers in schools managed by National Heritage Academies was higher than in other schools. The average score for teachers in NHA schools was 4.4, compared with 3.9 in other schools. This difference was statistically significant ($p < 0.01$).

In summary, most parents, students, and teachers in Michigan charter schools reported moderate to high levels of satisfaction with curriculum and instruction. Levels of satisfaction for all three groups were very similar to those in the composite comparison group.

Satisfaction With Facilities and Available Resources

A final dimension we examine in this chapter is satisfaction with facilities and resources. Facilities and resources are consistently cited by charter school operators as significant barriers to effective implementation of school missions. As we might expect, parents and teachers do appear to be less satisfied with these aspects of their charter schools.

Parents

Our surveys of charter school parents included two items designed to address issues of facilities and resources. First, we asked parents whether they agreed with the statement, "This school has sufficient financial resources." The average response to this question was 3.2 on a 5-point scale, with 43 percent either agreeing or strongly agreeing with the statement. Second, we asked parents to indicate whether they agreed with the statement, "This school has good physical facilities." Here, answers were slightly more positive, with an average value of 3.4 on a 5-point scale and 48 percent of parents either agreeing or strongly agreeing with the statement. These figures place Michigan parents at about the same level of satisfaction as parents in one comparison state and considerably higher than those in the other two comparison states.

As with most other survey items, we assessed differences between parents with children in elementary, middle, and high school grades. However, we found little, if any, evidence of any significant differences across the grade levels.[11] We also tested for differences between EMO and non-EMO schools. While we found no significant differences on the question of financial resources, we found that parents from EMO-operated schools were more satisfied with their school's facilities than other parents. Specifically, the average score for EMO parents was 3.5 on a 5-point scale, compared with 3.1 for other parents. The difference was statistically significant ($p < 0.01$). An even more striking difference emerges when one compares National Heritage Academies (NHA) schools with other schools. The average score for NHA parents was 4.0, compared with 3.1 for others. This difference is also statistically significant ($p < 0.01$).

Teachers

Our teacher surveys included several items pertaining to satisfaction with facilities and resources, which we combined into an overall index. The index included items on quality of facilities, sufficiency of resources, and access to computers. The specific items are listed in Table 9.4. All of the items in the index were rated on a 5-point scale. The index, in turn, is simply an average of all of those items. The average value on the index of teacher satisfaction with resources was 3.2 on a 5-point scale, indicating a middling level of satisfaction. This mean was similar to, but statistically discernible from ($p < .05$), the mean of our comparable group of charter school teachers from other states (3.1).

Table 9.4 Index of Teachers' Satisfaction With Resources

Item	Average Score (SD)
I am satisfied with the availability of computers and other technology	3.6 (1.3)
I am satisfied with school buildings and facilities	3.3 (1.2)
The school has good physical facilities	3.2 (1.3)
I am satisfied with resources available for instruction	3.2 (1.3)
The school has sufficient financial resources	3.0 (1.3)
Index	3.2

Note: Cronbach's alpha = 0.80.

When we examined variations in responses, we found no differences according to the grade level with which teachers work most, or according to amount of experience in public versus private schools. We did find that, contrary to parents, teachers at EMO-run schools were, on average, less satisfied with facilities and resources than teachers from other schools (3.5 vs. 3.1 on a 5-point scale). The difference is statistically significant ($p < 0.01$). In spite of the generally negative findings for EMO schools, however, teachers at National Heritage Academy schools reported being slightly more satisfied with facilities and resources than other teachers (3.6 vs. 3.5 on a 5-point scale). This difference, however, is not statistically significant ($p = 0.29$). Satisfaction with resources among teachers with less than five years of experience versus teachers with five or more years of experience was explored but, as with satisfaction with instruction, no significant differences were found.

The Relationship Between Market and Performance Accountability

On the whole, it appears that charter school parents, students, and teachers are relatively satisfied with Michigan charter schools. This comports with the picture provided by studies from other states (see e.g., Finn, Manno, & Vanourek, 2000; Miron & Nelson, 2000). In this section, we explore two questions that arise from the survey findings. First, how strong is the relationship between the levels of student, parent, and teacher satisfaction across the schools. Put another way, do schools with satisfied students also tend to have satisfied parents and teachers? The second question is motivated by the observation that the generally high level of satisfaction in Michigan charter schools stands in sharp contrast to the more negative view of school success painted in the chapter on student achievement tests. Specifically, to what extent do these two measures of charter school quality track together? That is, do schools scoring higher on the MEAP also have happier parents, teachers, and students?

To explore answers to the first question, we simply examined the correlations among the three satisfaction indices. The correlations are shown graphically in Figures 9.5 through 9.7. The strongest relationship is between the parent and teacher indices, with a correlation coefficient (Spearman's rho) of 0.70, indicating a moderately strong relationship (see Figure 9.5).[12] The other relationships were considerably weaker, with the correlation between the student and parent indices at 0.56 (Figure 9.6) and the correlation between students and teachers at 0.41 (Figure 9.7), both indicating only modest relationships. Although not particularly strong, all correlations were statistically significant. However, these findings may be influenced by the relative

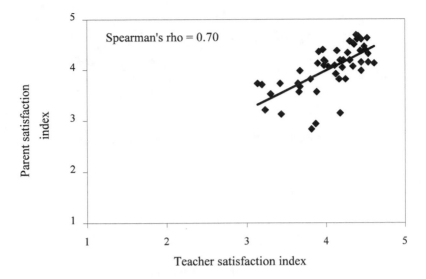

Figure 9.5 Relationship Between Parent and Teacher Satisfaction With Curriculum and Instruction

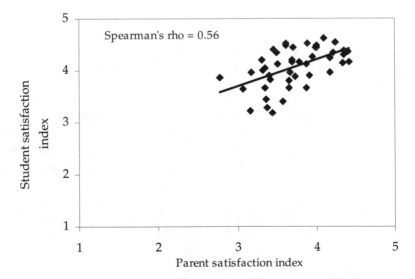

Figure 9.6 Relationship Between Student Satisfaction With Teachers and Instruction and Parent Satisfaction With Curriculum and Instruction

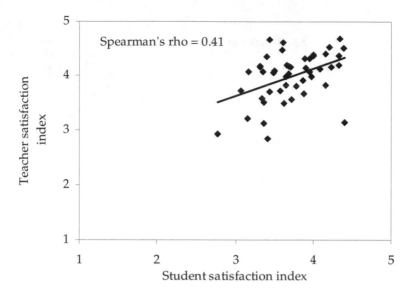

Figure 9.7   Relationship Between Student Satisfaction With Teachers
and Instruction and Teacher Satisfaction With Curriculum
and Instruction

similarities of the surveys given to the parents and teachers, in contrast with
the survey given to the students, the items of which were substantially different
from those on the other two surveys. Overall, it appears that, to a certain
extent, schools that manage to satisfy one clientele are generally able to satisfy
the others.[13]

In exploring an answer to the question about the relationship between
satisfaction and test scores, we compared each school's relative gain scores[14]
with its scores on the indicators of perceived gains and satisfaction with
curriculum and instruction described above. Given the large number of subject
areas and grade levels covered by the MEAP, we calculated a MEAP index
score for each school. The index is the average of the fourth, fifth, seventh, and
eighth grade results reported in Chapter 8. Readers should remember that the
scores reported in Chapter 8 are themselves the difference between each
charter school's average annual gain and that of its host district.

Somewhat surprisingly, we found little or no relationship between students' self-ratings of academic gain and the more objective assessments of achievement gains represented by the MEAP index. Indeed, the correlation between the two was indistinguishable from zero.[15]

Similarly, we found little or no relationship between satisfaction (of parents, students, and teachers) and average MEAP performance. As Table 9.5 illustrates, the correlation coefficients between MEAP scores and the three satisfaction indices were extremely small—especially for parents

Table 9.5 Correlations Between Average MEAP Scores and Satisfaction Indices

Stakeholder group	Correlation coefficient (p-value)
Students	–0.25 (0.13)
Parents	0.04 (0.78)
Teachers	0.00 (0.99)
Average	–0.07 (0.66)

Note: Spearman rank correlation coefficients are used.

and teachers—and not statistically significant. The only relationship of any magnitude is with student satisfaction. Interestingly, the coefficient is negative, suggesting that schools with higher levels of student satisfaction have lower MEAP scores. However, the relationship was not statistically significant and was very small.

Since we found earlier that levels of student satisfaction vary with EMO status and grade level, we suspected that the correlation between student satisfaction and performance might be contaminated by the influence of these other factors. Thus, we tested the relationship using a multivariate model. After controlling for EMO status and average grade level in each school, we found that student satisfaction with curriculum and instruction does, in fact, have a statistically significant—though still negative—relationship with MEAP scores. Specifically, for each 1-point increase in the 5-point satisfaction index, there is an 11-point decrease in the MEAP index.[16]

In summary, we found a moderately strong relationship between parent and teacher satisfaction with curriculum and instruction in Michigan charter schools. That is, schools with higher levels of parent satisfaction tend also to have higher levels of teacher satisfaction. Conversely, schools with lower levels of parent satisfaction tend to have lower levels of teacher satisfaction. Levels of student satisfaction with teachers and instruction were positively, but only weakly, related to teacher and parent satisfaction with curriculum and instruction. Somewhat surprisingly, we found an even weaker relationship between satisfaction among all groups and schools' performance on the MEAP tests. Only student satisfaction was related to MEAP scores, and here the relationship was negative. In concrete terms, schools with higher levels of student satisfaction tend to perform more poorly on the MEAP. Conversely, schools with lower levels of student satisfaction tend to perform better on the MEAP.

Summary and Conclusion

Proponents and opponents of charter schools continue to debate how the schools ought to be held accountable. Part of this debate revolves around the question of "accountability for which outcomes?" While most observers agree that standardized test scores must play some role in charter school accountability, many believe that these scores capture only part of the picture. This chapter has examined two alternative indicators: self-rated academic performance and overall satisfaction with the schools.

Generally, students in Michigan charter schools report that their performance has improved since switching to a charter school. There was, however, considerable school-to-school variation in these self-assessments, with students in high schools reporting larger gains. Students coming from public schools, however, were more likely to report lower performance in their previous school and larger gains since moving to a charter school. Similar differences in reported growth existed between students in EMO and non-EMO schools, with EMO students reporting higher past performance. This finding provides some support (albeit based on subjective ratings) for claims that EMO schools engage in cream-skimming. Students in EMO schools also reported lower perceived gains than those in non-EMO schools, which confirms the test score analysis in Chapter 8. There also appears to be a racial gap in perceived gains, with nonwhite students reporting lower gains than white students. Unlike the public–non-public and EMO-non-EMO analysis, however, we found no differences between white and nonwhite students' perceptions of prior performance. Students' self-assessments are largely borne out by charter school teachers and parents, with the exception that we found no significant differences among parent and teacher perceptions by EMO status, grade level, and other factors.

Along with self-rated academic performance, we also assessed various aspects of customer satisfaction with charter schools. One such aspect was schools' missions. Most parents and teachers reported being aware of their school's mission, with only slightly more than half of students reporting such awareness. Of those aware of their school's mission, the overwhelming majority of parents and teachers reported that their school's mission was being fulfilled adequately. Similarly, most parents, students, and teachers reported being satisfied with the curriculum and instruction at their schools, with satisfaction levels similar to those in other states for which we have similar data. Parents and teachers, however, were less satisfied with their school's level of resources than they were with curriculum, instruction, and overall mission fulfillment.

Given the debates over whether charter schools should be held accountable for test scores, customer satisfaction, or both, we investigated the statistical relationship among these indicators of school quality. While there were modest correlations among the satisfaction indices, there were generally no notable relationships between the satisfaction indices and the MEAP index (which compares charter school students' achievement gains to those in host districts). Moreover, where there was a relationship (between student satisfaction and the MEAP index), it was negative. This suggests that charter schools' ability to satisfy customers bears little or no relationship to their ability to produce gains in achievement that show up on standardized tests. While satisfaction may be considered important in and of itself, these findings raise questions about claims that customer satisfaction is a meaningful indicator of academic quality in charter schools.

Notes

1. The surveys were administered in 51 charter schools during the 1997-98 academic year. The sample excludes schools in the Detroit metropolitan area. More extensive results from the surveys, as well as a discussion of these results, can be found in Horn and Miron (1999).

2. Unless otherwise noted, Wilcoxon signed-rank tests were used to assess statistical significance on pre-post comparisons. Comparisons across groups (e.g., EMO vs. non-EMO schools) were evaluated using the Mann-Whitney rank sum test. Finally, we used Kruskal-Wallis tests for comparisons against variables with multiple categories. Throughout, readers are encouraged to bear in mind that statistical significance does not necessarily imply substantive or policy significance. Statistical significance is based on the probability of observing a given difference between groups by chance alone (the lower the probability, the more certain we may be that the difference is not due to sampling or other error). In large samples, however, even small differences (and ones that may be insignificant from an educational policy perspective) are often statistically significant. We have attempted to distinguish statistical and policy/educational significance throughout the chapter.

3. See endnote 6 in Chapter 5 for more information about the composite comparison group.

10

The Effects of Education
Management Organizations

"Charter schools will provide a fertile ground for companies
waiting to penetrate the K-12 education market."

Education Industry Review

One of the most striking and unique aspects of Michigan's experiment with
charter schools is the prominent role of private education management
organizations (EMOs). As we have noted in earlier chapters, EMOs manage or
operate approximately three fourths of the state's charter schools—a much
higher percentage than in any other state.

EMO involvement in charter schools comes against the backdrop of a
larger movement toward the privatization of educational services.[1] Proponents
of this movement often claim that privatization will bring a much needed dose
of entrepreneurial spirit and a competitive ethos to public education. In many
respects, private involvement in public schools is not new. What is new,
however, is that private companies are moving beyond providing specific or
partial services to schools (e.g., busing, food services, etc.) and are now
increasingly providing full management and operation of schools.

Charter schools have provided a particularly effective path for private
EMOs to enter the public school sphere. Close behind the EMOs are venture
capitalists and private investors. Since the K-12 education market in the United
States is estimated to be more than $400 billion per year,[2] and since it repeats
itself every year, it is no wonder that the private sector is so interested in this
traditionally public domain. Even though only one large EMO that works
primarily with public schools has reported profits so far (i.e., National Heritage
Academies),[3] the number of EMOs entering the market suggests that many
more anticipate that profits are just over the horizon.

The number of EMOs and their share of the education market is increasing rapidly in the nation, both in the charter school sector and elsewhere. Edison Schools Inc. is now the largest EMO, operating more than 120 schools with close to 75,000 students enrolled. Aside from public schools, EMOs are also capturing market share in other education service areas, including tutoring, after-school care, summer schools, vocational programs, juvenile services, and so on. Although the growth and expansion of EMOs is most obvious in the United States, there are also signs of EMO growth in the United Kingdom, Canada, and elsewhere.

A discussion of EMOs is important, not only because of their prevalence in Michigan, but also because they throw into relief many of the key public-private issues we have sought to explore in this book. Up to this point, the book has focused on the functionalist definition of public-ness, according to which schools are public inasmuch as they serve important public functions, irrespective of who owns, operates, or controls them. The formalist definition, by contrast, focuses on issues of ownership and control. In this chapter we assess evidence for the formalist definition of public-ness through examining the role of EMOs.

The chapter begins by describing the variety of roles EMOs play in charter schools and chronicles their remarkable growth in Michigan. Next, the chapter provides an in-depth examination of ownership and control in EMO-run schools. The chapter concludes by exploring the controversial issue of profit-making in charter schools.

The findings presented in this chapter are based on interviews conducted during 1998 and 2000 with charter school directors (over 50 in total), and representatives from EMOs, school districts, authorizers, and the Michigan Department of Education. These findings are supplemented by a review of literature and documentation from or about EMOs. Some of this documentation came from a 1998 request to all EMOs operating in Michigan for documentation and sample contracts. In 2000, we requested additional documents from both charter schools and EMOs. While these data collection activities yielded many interesting insights on the role of EMOs, our efforts have been limited by the increasing difficulty in obtaining information from EMOs, the charter schools they operate, and even from the authorizers that must approve the contracts. Thus, readers should bear in mind that the material presented in this chapter is more preliminary in nature than the data presented in other sections of the book.

The Growth of EMO Involvement in Charter Schools

The expansion of private, for-profit EMOs in charter schools has gone more quickly in Michigan than anywhere else. Our own best estimate suggests that between 20 and 25 percent of all charter schools across the country are operated by EMOs.[4] While some states have few or no for-profit EMOs, the Michigan initiative stands out, with 74 percent of all the charter schools contracting out all or part of their services to EMOs. Indeed, the extensive involvement of EMOs often comes as a surprise to state policymakers.[5]

As depicted in Figure 10.1, the number of EMOs has risen rapidly to a total of 44 in the state during the 2000-01 school year. The actual number may be larger. Indeed, there are indications that a few schools recently established companies for the sole purpose of providing payroll and benefits, which allows teachers to become private employees and avoid the restrictions of the state retirement system. Of the 44 known EMOs, two are actually nonprofit organizations that manage, altogether, three very small schools.

Of the 44 EMOs, 28 operate only one school, while nine companies operate between two and four different schools and seven companies operate five or more charter schools across the state. The largest private operator of charter schools in Michigan is National Heritage Academies (NHA), with 22 schools. The Leona Group had more than 20 schools, but a few schools switched companies in recent years, so the total number of schools they operated during the 2000-01 school year was 19. The next largest company is Beacon Education Management Inc., which operates 15 charter schools in Michigan. Other key management companies involved in Michigan include Charter School Administration Services (9 schools), Helicon & Associates (8 schools), and Mosaica Education Management Inc. (Mosaica had 5 schools in 2000, but their takeover of Advantage Schools in July 2001 brought an additional three schools to their portfolio). The only large EMO that provides only partial services is Educare. This company had agreements with four schools in 2000-01 and employs the teachers and staff at the school and handles payroll and personnel

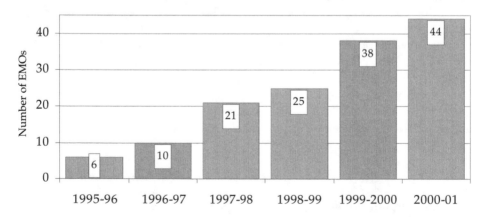

Figure 10.1 Number of Education Management Organizations by Year

matters. Beyond this, the company does not involve itself in the business of the school. Educare lost contracts with 5 schools in recent years. All 5 schools switched to another EMO, and at least 3 of these were full service operators. The last large EMO that should be mentioned is Edison Schools Inc. which, even though it operated only five charter schools in the state during 2000-01, has the largest concentration of its contract schools in Michigan.[6]

The larger EMOs are national companies, but many got their start in Michigan. Some, such as NHA, started in Grand Rapids but expanded to other Michigan locations before opening schools in New York and North Carolina. The Leona Group also operates charter schools in Arizona. Many of the Beacon schools were originally operated by a Michigan-based company, JCR & Associates, which specialized in the management of private Christian schools, before moving into the charter school market. JCR & Associates merged with Beacon, a Massachusetts-based firm, in January 2000. Appendix C contains a list of EMOs and the number of schools they operated in Michigan during the 2000-01 school year.

As the number of EMOs has grown rapidly, so too has the number of Michigan charter schools contracting with them (see Figure 10.2). During the 1995-96 school year, 16.7 percent of the schools had contracts with EMOs. Two years later, just over 50 percent of the schools were contracting out services to EMOs; and in 2000-01, 73.9 percent of the schools had contracts with EMOs. Figure 10.2 illustrates the growth in the proportion of schools that have contracts with management companies. It is important to note that since the EMOs tend to work with large schools, they actually account for an even larger portion of all charter school students. In fact, during the 2000-01 school year, more than 85 percent of all Michigan charter school students were enrolled in schools operated by EMOs.

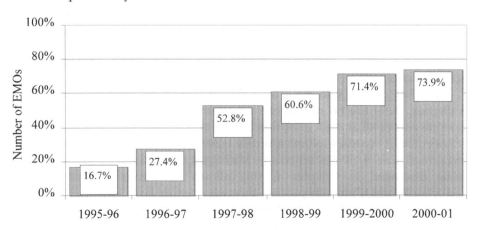

Figure 10.2 Percentage of Charter Schools Operated by EMOs by Year

received fees for services that were equivalent to between 10 and 15 percent of the schools' revenues. Some of the larger full-service EMOs simply guarantee a positive ending balance. In the case of National Heritage Academies, the contracts between the board and the EMO state that the EMO will receive an annual capitation fee equivalent to 98 percent of all per pupil expenditures from all sources after deducting the amount retained by the authorizing agency (i.e., 3 percent of state funds). NHA in turn is responsible for paying for all services and educational programs specified in the contract, including the lease on the facility (National Heritage Academies, 1996). The company retains all money remaining after paying for the specified services.[7]

EMO-charter school relationships vary on a number of dimensions, including for-profit status, the number of schools operated, and full-service versus partial service companies. Two of those dimensions—for-profit status and the number of schools operated—are represented in Figure 10.3 in a 2x2 matrix. It is immediately clear that most charter schools (78 percent) fall into Category 4, which includes schools that contract with for-profit companies that operate more than one charter school. Some of the 15 companies represented in this category manage schools around the country and even abroad, while others are limited to managing schools in Michigan. Moreover, most, if not all, of the companies operating only in Michigan have expressed a desire to expand operations to other states with permissive charter school legislation. These EMOs typically have substantial financial resources to help schools locate, renovate, or build a school facility. Examples of companies in this category are National Heritage Academies, the Leona Group, Edison Schools Inc., Advantage Schools, Mosaica, Beacon Education Management, and so on.

Type 4 EMOs differ widely in their approach to providing services. Some have an *à la carte* approach where schools can pick and pay for only those services they wish, while others require full-service agreements. The EMOs in the latter group have extensive—if not total—control over curriculum and school design, resulting in schools with little autonomy and almost identical curriculum, instructional practices, and school organizations. The

	Single School	Multiple Schools
Nonprofit	**1** (0.7%)	**2** (1.4%)
For-Profit	**3** (19.9%)	**4** (78.0%)

Figure 10.3 Typology of EMOs Operating in Michigan

Note: The approximate percentage of EMO-operated charter schools in each category is designated in parentheses. These figures are based on 136 of 184 charter schools that were operated by EMOs in 2000-01.

EMOs in this category also vary depending on whether they take over management of an existing charter school or whether they involve themselves only with schools they start from the beginning.

Operating only 20 percent of Michigan's charter schools, Type 3 EMOs represent a much smaller share of the market for management services. However, given that these companies each manage only one school, this category includes 27 EMOs. In many cases, Type 3 EMOs are contracted only for employing and supervising the personnel. In such cases, the EMO has limited involvement in the school and is typically established for the sole purpose of providing a private entity to employ the existing teachers. In many cases, single-school EMOs have eventually taken on management of other schools, suggesting that the number of companies and schools in Type 4 may increase in the years to come.

Nonprofit EMOs—found in Categories 1 and 2—compromise only a small share of the market for management services. The one school in Category 1 (single-school nonprofit) closed during the summer of 2001, reducing the number of nonprofit EMO-board relationships in the state to two.[8]

We have already mentioned the third dimension on which EMO-charter school relationships vary: full-service versus partial-service agreements. Unfortunately, our attempts to get good estimates of the proportion of schools with full- or partial-service agreements has been hindered by a paucity of information and schools' and EMOs' unwillingness to share such information.[9] In spite of these limitations, we were able to arrive at some estimates of the proportion of full- and partial-service agreements, as shown in the bottom row of Table 10.1.

The observations provided in the remainder of the chapter focus mainly on Type 4 schools—the larger EMOs involved in full-service agreements with several charter schools. Readers should bear in mind, then, that our conclusions do not apply equally well to the remainder of the EMOs. Since large, full-service EMOs comprise a growing and overwhelming majority of cases, our focus on these EMOs seems justified.

Table 10.1 Estimated Numbers of Charter Schools With Full-Service or Partial-Service Agreements (2000-01)

	No EMO	Full-Service	Partial-Service	Total
Number of charter schools	48	109	27	184
% of all charter schools	26.1%	59.2%	14.7%	100%
% of all EMO charter schools	--	80.1%	19.9%	100%

Ownership of Charter Schools and the Problem of Bundling

Having described the range and scope of EMO involvement in Michigan charter schools, we move now to an evaluation of EMOs' role based on the public-private framework developed in Chapter 1. Our analysis of the public and private aspects of Michigan charter schools has been based on a distinction between *functionalist* and *formalist* definitions of public-ness (see Chapter 1). Up to this point, we have focused primarily on the functionalist definition, which suggests that a school is public if it serves valued social functions. Thus, we have examined the extent to which Michigan charter schools have served public goals on equity, teacher professionalism, innovation and impact, achievement, and customer satisfaction, as delineated in the state's charter school law (see Chapter 3) and in the charter school concept (see Chapter 1).

In this section we turn to the formalist view of public-ness. As we suggested in Chapter 1, the formalist view is perhaps the more traditional of the two. According to this perspective, a school or other institution is considered public if it is owned or controlled by citizens and their duly elected representatives. Assessing public-ness with this definition requires an investigation of who owns the means of educational production and to what extent charter schools and their activities are susceptible to oversight by elected bodies.

Issues of control and ownership are relevant for all charter schools. Nonetheless, these issues are particularly salient in EMO-run charter schools. Thus, while we focus on EMO-run schools, readers should bear in mind that most of these issues pertain—though perhaps to a lesser degree—to non-EMO schools. We begin with the issue of ownership.

Ownership of Facilities and Equipment

Many of the large EMOs such as National Heritage Academies own the school buildings. The school in turn, leases the building from the EMO or from a sister company of the EMO. In most of the private school conversions, the building is leased from the previous private school owner (who, in most cases, still leads the school) or the EMO that was established to operate the school. The school facilities provide an excellent opportunity for private companies to accumulate equity (see endnote #7 in this chapter as well as our analysis of facilities costs in Chapter 4).

While visiting charter schools during 1998, we asked each director about the ownership of facilities, equipment, and furniture. In the EMO-operated schools the equipment was often reported as belonging to the company. In some cases we asked the school representative to clarify how computers and equipment purchased with federal start-up money could be the property of the private company. The typical answer was that the equipment was being leased from the EMO. Put another way, the equipment and often facilities were being purchased by the private company—often using the school's tax-exempt status—with public monies. In a few schools operated by partial service EMOs, we were informed that the school was making arrangements to purchase and own the building in its own name rather than lease it from a company.

An interesting, though unresolved, question is whether these properties, purchased with public funds, will be returned to the state. In one case an EMO-run school was closed with a deficit. Since the school was in debt to its EMO, the company claimed all equipment and materials. As with some of the other issues raised in this chapter, information on ownership is scant. However, information on a limited number of cases raises a number of concerns and issues in need of further exploration.

Ownership of Curriculum

The issue of ownership also extends to curriculum. In many EMO schools, the instructional models and materials used are the property of the management company. Indeed, a number of the contracts we reviewed even insisted that any lesson plans or materials developed by the teachers were proprietary in nature and belonged to the EMO rather than to the public charter school. The NHA contract for Vista Charter Academy (NHA, 1996, p. 11), for instance, stipulates that the charter school

> shall treat all such proprietary information as though it were a trade secret and copyrighted, and shall use efforts as may be reasonably requested by [National Heritage Academies] to assure that no Academy personnel or agent disclose, publish, copy, transit, alter or utilize [NHA's] proprietary information.

In an earlier evaluation of Michigan charter schools, Horn and Miron (1999) found that EMO ownership of curriculum and materials was a source of concern among some school directors. One principal cited such concerns as a primary reason the school had decided not to contract with an EMO. Moreover, we noted in Chapter 7 of this book that the proprietary nature of these materials is a hindrance to the transfer of charter school innovations to other schools.

During our site visits to charter schools in 1998, we asked school directors and teachers about the influence teachers and staff had in terms of curriculum and the direction and steering of the schools. We found extensive variations across the schools. In some schools, it appears that the teachers and staff had influence on both the curriculum and in the general steering of the school. Responses from schools operated by EMOs (both from interviews as well as questionnaire responses), however, suggested that teachers in EMO-operated schools had less influence in the curriculum and on the steering of the school than in non-EMO schools. Differences in questionnaire responses were statistically significant (see also Nelson & Miron, 2001). At one school we visited, the principal noted that the management company had a very strong presence and that the top decision maker at the school was the president of the management company.

Another cause for concern in EMO ownership is that even school brand names may be proprietary and severing ties with an EMO is further complicated by the need to rename the school (Lin & Hassel, 1999). Since many charter schools recruit largely on the basis of reputation and word-of-mouth, such a name change may be far from trivial.

EMOs and the Bundling of School Services

The fact that EMOs often own school facilities, curricula, and the brand name used by the school suggests that these schools are not public according to the formalist definition, which emphasizes ownership of facilities and materials by citizens and their elected representatives. Proponents of EMOs and privatization might point out, with some justification, that while true, our observations are beside the point. Charter schools, they might argue, are a different kind of public school—one that emphasizes results over methods, function over form.

Our concerns with ownership, however, go beyond formal legal arrangements. The extensive involvement of full-service EMOs in the state's charter schools threatens the concepts of autonomy, flexibility, and site-based management that are at the core of the charter concept. Charter schools, to be sure, can voluntarily choose whether to contract with an EMO and, if so, which company to employ. It is less clear, however, whether such schools, having once employed an EMO, are in a good position to sever the relationship should they become dissatisfied with it. EMO-run schools are in theory free to fire the companies. However, if firing a company implies losing a building, equipment, curriculum, and brand name, then many such schools may be effectively unable to exercise this option.

The situation is quite similar to current allegations against Microsoft. Just as this company is accused of trying to capture and hold market share by bundling e-mail, Internet and other services into its operating system, EMOs often bundle their charter school services in a way that makes the costs of firing or switching companies unbearable. This is at odds with the atmosphere of open competition that advocates of privatization seek to create in the public education system.

This is not to deny that EMOs offer valuable services to charter schools. As we pointed out earlier in this chapter, much of the impetus for EMOs in Michigan and elsewhere came from charter school founders' inability to manage schools on their own. There is growing evidence, however, that EMOs are becoming a golden straightjacket for the schools. Chapter 11 briefly summarizes some safeguards that charter school boards might employ to benefit from EMO services while retaining their autonomy and flexibility.

Control and Governance of Charter Schools: Is the Tail Wagging the Dog?

The formalist view requires that public schools are not only owned by citizens and their elected representatives (discussed in the previous section) but that they are controlled by those same citizens and representatives. As we pointed out in Chapter 1, the charter concept seeks a transformation in educational governance from one based on majority control of schools (through school boards and state legislatures) to one based on consumer sovereignty. Yet, most charter school laws (Michigan's included) do not seek to *replace* democratic control with consumer sovereignty. Instead, the laws envision a balance between the two forms of control and accountability (Bulkley, 2001a). Thus, in addition to the control that charter school parents exercise through choice, there should be a chain of influence that leads from the schools back to the larger citizenry and its representatives on school boards, in legislatures, and in the executive branch of state governments. At the very least, the principle of public control requires that charter school boards be effective and independent. As we shall see, many EMO-run charter schools appear to violate these principles of control.

The Relationship Between EMOs and Charter School Boards

As we noted in Chapter 3, just over 80 percent of Michigan charter schools are chartered by public universities. In theory, this arrangement preserves the public nature of the schools (according to the formalist definition), since members of university boards of trustees appoint members of charter school boards who in turn retain legal control of the schools. In short, somewhere down the line, the "appointers" of the "appointees" are either democratically elected or are appointed by someone who was democratically elected. Our research on the appointment process, however, raises a number of concerns.

Our first concern relates to the process by which university authorizers select charter school board members. Interviews with charter school principals, teachers and some board members suggest that while university boards often conduct routine interviews of board candidates, lists of candidates for board positions is largely self-selected by the founding group or EMO that is starting the charter schools.[10] There is also evidence that in some instances EMOs, which are nominally agents of charter school boards, are heavily involved in the selection of charter school board members. In one case, we were informed by a business leader that he was called directly by J. C. Huizenga, owner of National Heritage Academies, and invited to serve on the board of one of his schools. In these instances, it is unclear whether there is the sort of arms-length relationship typically present in the relationship between contractors and those who hire them. Indeed, in the recitals section of the management contract between NHA and Vista Charter Academy, it is stated that the EMO "was instrumental in the creation of the Academy, having incorporated the Academy, [and] recruited its initial Board of Directors" (NHA, 1996, p. 1). This contract even noted that NHA had prepared the charter application to the state university authorizer. Prior personal relationships between EMOs and board members might well compromise boards' willingness or ability to objectively evaluate an EMO's performance and, if necessary, sever the relationship.

Our second concern is that there is evidence that state universities in some instances have failed to follow proper procedures in selecting charter school board members. For example, in some instance charter contracts are signed without a functioning board. This is crucial because charter school boards are responsible for making decisions on such issues as the selection of an EMO and the terms of the contract between the charter school board and the EMO. A few of the contracts we reviewed were actually signed by an EMO representative on behalf of the school rather than a board member. A closer look at the application materials from EMO-initiated charter schools suggests that in some cases fewer than the required number of board members are identified and involved during the start-up and application phase.[11] These incidents suggest that the public board for some start-up schools is merely an item to check off on a list and is not a driving force in establishing the school, and presumably in operating the school down the road.

The tight control and lack of autonomy of charter school boards in EMO-operated schools might best be illustrated by board meetings for schools started and operated by Charter Schools Administrative Services (CSAS). A representative of one of the authorizers reported that CSAS hosts at its company office the board meetings of its numerous charter schools simultaneously. Holding joint board meetings might lead to greater efficiency, since meeting protocols can be easily modified and duplicated for each charter school in attendance, but it might impinge on the autonomy of the separate school boards. While NHA charter schools hold their individual board meetings at each school, several principals indicated that extensive planning and decision making takes place at monthly meetings of school principals held at the corporate headquarters. These instances exemplify the extensive involvement of EMOs in establishing school policy and steering the development and operation of the charter schools.

In part, this shift in control might be a consequence of the national character of many of the larger EMOs. Edison, for instance, advertises itself as the first national school system. Indeed, the company reports that its school system is larger than many large citywide school systems. National Heritage Academies, Beacon Education Management, Advantage, and others are also establishing national networks/systems of charter schools. This movement results in some of the local decision making being replaced by decisions made in corporate headquarters halfway across the country. This might stand in conflict with the notion that charter schools would be responsive to the particular needs of local communities.

Finally, and perhaps more strikingly, a number of school officials and stakeholders we interviewed told us that the original impetus for their charter school came not from a local group of parents or educators but from EMOs. More generally, by the 1996-97 school year, EMOs were involved in opening more new schools than they were assuming control of. In most of these cases, the strategic planning interests of the EMO was the impetus for starting the school. After selecting a promising community, the EMO organized informational meetings (several of which we attended), and then sought out a few local persons who could sign on as the founding group. The establishment of the school was driven by the EMO that completed the application materials and submitted them to a state university charter school office. Indeed, our review of contracts verified this when we found that EMO officials were signing application materials and even charter school contracts with the authorizing agency on behalf of the charter school.

Managing Charter School Teachers

Another important area of control relates to the employment of teachers and staff. While in some states charter school boards are by law responsible for hiring and firing teachers, this is not the case in Michigan. In fact, data collected in 1998 and 2000 revealed that more than 85 percent of the teachers in Michigan charter schools are actually private employees of management companies rather than employees of charter schools.[12]

Teachers and principals are key employees in a school, so the board is at a disadvantage when it comes to steering the school if it does not have control and oversight of them. In a few cases, the management company provides a job description for the principal that states that the principal is responsible for the hiring and firing at that particular site on behalf of the management company. This arrangement at least assures the principals that they can have greater control of instruction in the school. To be sure, principals are likely to have providing specific or limited services (e.g., janitorial or food service) or products (e.g., textbooks or photocopy machines) for schools. This trend is especially pervasive among Michigan's charter schools. The extensive EMO ownership and control of charter schools we have described in this chapter allow decisions about spending and educational programing to be steered by EMOs that have profit motives. In this section, we review evidence we have presented throughout the book on the impact of EMO involvement in Michigan charter schools with an eye toward identifying the strategies EMOs use in seeking profits and the consequences of such profit-seeking.

Chapter 4 showed that one impediment to profit-making in Michigan charter schools is the fact that charter schools generally get less money than noncharter public schools. Thus, EMOs wishing to profit from running charter schools must find ways to cut costs. As noted in Chapter 4, a large share of the variable costs of education are related to student characteristics. Most notably, high school students are more expensive to educate than other students, given the need for laboratory and technical vocational equipment, the greater diversity of course offerings, and—in many cases—the need to provide extracurricular activities. Likewise, students with special educational needs can be substantially more costly to educate. Thus, it seems clear that restricting the focus of charter schools to less expensive students is one way to cut costs and increase profitability.

In-depth financial case studies presented in Chapter 4 suggest that charter schools do, in fact, realize cost savings by offering a more limited range of services than noncharter public schools. Moreover, Chapter 5 (Figure 5.1), which is based on data from all Michigan charter schools, shows quite clearly that EMO schools are much less likely to serve high school students than non-EMO schools. Similarly, we found that charter schools as a group enroll substantially fewer students with special educational needs, and that the students with special needs enrolled in EMO-run charter schools typically had disabilities that were milder in nature and less-costly to remediate than the special education students in non-EMO schools. Finally, we found that students in EMO-run charter schools are more likely to come from homes with higher incomes, two parents living at home, and better educated parents who volunteer more at school, than students in non-EMO schools. While we emphasized in Chapter 5 that we have no direct evidence that any charter school is engaging in intentional cream-skimming, enrollment patterns are certainly compatible with a cost-reducing, profit-making approach to education.[16]

As discussed in Chapter 1, the role of for-profit entities in public education has been characterized as an attempt to harness private interests in the service of the public interests. According to this line of thinking, the presence of private interests—and profit-making—in education is ultimately justified by the outcomes it produces. Thus, profit in education is neither intrinsically good nor intrinsically bad, but should be evaluated in terms of its consequences.

Before summarizing the outcomes produced by EMO schools, we should note that available evidence is not sufficient for drawing clear causal connections between the strategies outlined above and outcomes. Nonetheless, the connections are sufficiently compelling to warrant mention and to merit attention from policymakers and stakeholders.

As we have seen throughout the book, charter school performance in Michigan is reasonably strong in some areas. Generally, the schools appear to be doing a good job of attracting like-minded teachers, of leveraging at least modest changes in surrounding districts, and of satisfying customer preferences. On customer satisfaction, EMO-run charter schools enjoyed advantages in a number of areas. However, we often found disagreement among stakeholder groups in these areas. For instance, while parents in EMO-run charter schools were more likely to be satisfied with the schools' facilities, teachers were less satisfied. Similarly, while teachers in EMO-run charter schools were more likely to be satisfied with instruction and teaching, students were generally less satisfied. Interestingly, parents in charter schools operated by NHA gave particularly high marks to school facilities.

In other areas, however, charter schools lag behind noncharter public schools. In these areas EMO-run charters often lag even further behind. For example, while charter school achievement gains on average lag behind those of noncharter public schools, gains in EMO-run schools are weaker yet. In other words, relative gains (charter and host district gains compared) in EMO-run schools were lower than in non-EMO schools in all subjects and grades except Grade 7 math, with particularly weak results coming from schools operated by the Leona Group. While data limitations preclude hard and fast conclusions, these findings cast doubt on privatization advocates' claims that introducing the discipline of the bottom line into education will lead to greater efficiencies. (We provide a more in-depth discussion of charter schools' efficiency in Chapter 11.) Interestingly, the test score findings are largely matched by students' self-reported gains, with students in EMO-run schools reporting smaller gains than those in non-EMO schools.

The EMO effect also extended to some of the charter concept's intermediate outcomes. While our data did not allow for systematic EMO/non-EMO comparisons on innovation and systemic impact, many EMOs' centralized structures suggest that EMO-run charter schools are not particularly well designed for innovation. Moreover, the proprietary nature of EMO curricula and materials likely makes it difficult for these practices to spread to other schools—or, at least, to those who do not choose to purchase their services. Indeed, we have found elsewhere that teachers in EMO-run schools are less likely to report having autonomy, opportunities to innovate, and professional

Oversight by authorizing agencies might hold EMOs in check. Yet, as we described in Chapter 3, the state universities that grant charters have promoted and in some cases requested the involvement of EMOs in the charter schools they approve and oversee. Further, the extensive involvement and influence of EMOs in the state charter school association (see Chapter 3 for more details) also ensures their position and standing in Michigan.

Advocates of privatization have claimed that the school system will benefit from efficiency gains and that private agents would be more accountable and more effective at raising student performance levels. Michigan has gone farther than other states at privatizing their schools through the involvement of EMOs. The results, however, do not suggest that the EMOs are increasing overall efficiency gains in the system. Likewise, the evidence suggests that EMO-operated schools are often less accountable to the public. Finally, in Michigan we have found that the EMO-operated schools are not as successful as the non-EMO charter schools in raising student performance levels.

These findings, should not come as a surprise, since earlier research has suggested that efforts to privatize have not been successful as yet. For example, Ascher, Berne, and Fruchter (1996) examined the early experiments with vouchers and with district contracts, which they characterized as "hard lessons," largely based on the reforms' disappointing outcomes. The EMO they studied that was involved with contracting was Education Alternative Inc. This company ultimately lost its contracts with districts and, after a name change and an attempt to enter the charter school market, went bankrupt. Similarly, papers presented at a conference sponsored by the National Center for the Study of Privatization in Education (Levin, 2001) raised questions about the outcomes of privatization in terms of efficiency, equity, and social cohesion. In terms of student achievement, there is still no evidence—aside from the studies that EMOs conduct themselves—that EMOs are successful in raising student achievement results relative to similar comparison groups.[18]

We emphasize that our findings should not necessarily be construed as an indictment of the *idea* of profit in education. While some stakeholders certainly find the idea morally repugnant, we proceeded on the assumption that the appropriateness of for-profit entities in charter schools should be evaluated in terms of its consequences. The evidence we have presented raises serious concerns about those consequences. However, as we suggest in the next and final chapter of the book, these consequences seem to follow from weaknesses in the state's charter school law and the incentives it creates for educational entrepreneurs.

In the final analysis, readers should bear in mind that this chapter has provided a preliminary analysis of a very rapidly changing aspect of charter schools. Further study—including better access to information on the inner-workings of EMOs and the schools they run—will be needed to fully understand EMOs' impact on charter schools.

Notes

1. Efforts to privatize education have come in many forms. Fitz and Beers (2001) identified several modes of privatization of education, including vouchers, contracting some or all school services to private enterprises, public-private partnerships, takeovers, and tax credits for fees or donations to private schools. In this chapter, we focus on only one mode of privatization: contracting out services to private companies. Both traditional school districts and charter schools can contract with education management organizations.

2. Including higher education and other forms of schooling the entire education market is estimated to be more than $800 billion annually.

3. Novel Learning Communities, Inc. also reports that it is profitable, but this company largely works with private schools and only a small number of its schools are public charter schools.

4. Our estimate is based on figures from 17 states that account for approximately 80 percent of the nation's charter schools. For these 17 states our figures were based on either existing reports or from estimates made by individuals working with charter schools in the state. For the remaining 20 percent of the charter schools—for which we had no basis for making an estimate—we assumed that 7 percent of the schools were operated by EMOs, which seems to us a rather conservative estimate. For the last few years, the Center for Education reform has suggested that only 10 percent of the charter schools in the nation are operated by EMOs.

5. The Request for Proposals (RFP), for our first evaluation of Michigan charter schools, requested that we examine the role of all key stakeholder groups in the reform. There was no mention of EMOs because those preparing the RFP had no idea that they existed.

6. During the summer of 2001, Edison lost its contract with Mid-Michigan Public School Academy in Lansing, which was the state's largest charter school, with more than 1,000 students.

7. Because NHA leases the facilities from a sister company, it also retains any profits derived from the building lease. In fact, the financial arrangement that NHA has with its boards essentially allows NHA extensive leeway to set the terms of the lease. Annual leases on most of the buildings cost between $600,000 and $1 million per year, which is higher than traditional public schools pay (see per-pupil spending on facilities in Chapter 4). NHA doubled the annual lease paid by one of its schools in 1999, which drew questions from the media (Reinstadler, 1999) but not the governing board.

8. In other states, particularly in Pennsylvania, we have seen extensive involvement of nonprofit community foundations/organizations that are establishing charter schools as an extension of their community services (Miron & Nelson, 2000).

9. During the course of both of our statewide evaluations in Michigan, we requested this type of information from both schools and management companies. The response from schools was poor, and the information we received was incomplete. We are aware that the Michigan Department of Education requested information from authorizers about the management companies that work with the

11

Lessons in Choice
and Accountability

Charter schools are a new form of public school—a hybrid that mixes elements traditionally associated with private schools (choice, autonomy, and flexibility) with elements traditionally associated with public or government-run schools (universal access and public funding). The charter school movement is part of a larger set of national and international trends toward subjecting the delivery of public services to market competition.

This book has provided a case study in how one state (Michigan) has operationalized the charter concept. As we have seen, Michigan's experiment with charter schools is in many respects atypical (Chapter 3). Its law is widely regarded as one of the most permissive in the country. Not surprisingly, the state has more charter schools than just about any other in the nation. Of equal interest, Michigan charter schools are unsurpassed in their efforts to employ privatized services, mainly through contracts with education management organizations (EMOs). Thus, Michigan provides not a thumbnail sketch of the national charter movement as it is, but a vision of what a more robust national movement might look like with extensive and comparatively unregulated private involvement. And, inasmuch as the charter concept borrows ideas from other school reforms—decentralization, choice, deregulation, accountability, and use of market forces—Michigan's experiment with charter schools bears important lessons for those considering other reforms as well.

In this final chapter we attempt to articulate some of the main lessons from the Michigan case as detailed in the earlier chapters. We turn first to the question we began with, and that framed our empirical analysis: What's public about charter schools? This discussion provides an opportunity to summarize the book's main findings. We are in many ways quite skeptical that the

16. Based on extensive interviews and field research in 1998 and 2000, Miron (2000) speculates on a wide range of potential profit strategies for EMOs including those listed below:

- Recruit *able, English-speaking students at the elementary level.* The ability level of students and their readiness to learn will affect overall costs as well as overall performance of the school on standardized tests.
- Recruit families with *parents who are charitable, resourceful, and available* to help at the school and help the child with schoolwork at home. The level of parental involvement and the resources they can bring to the school are important and can affect the school's resources negatively or positively.
- Employ *committed, energetic, yet relatively inexperienced teachers.* Teachers' salaries occupy the largest budget item, so having a group of younger/novice teachers who are at the bottom of the pay scale positively impacts the overall budget.
- Identify and appoint *faithful and available board members who have relevant skills* to share.

A number of mechanisms can be used by charter schools to "structure" or "shape" their school community. Some represent savings by themselves, while others represent direct savings as well as a strategy to discourage the enrollment of students who might be deemed more costly to educate. These include the following:

- *Do not provide transportation.* This makes the school less attractive to low-income families or single-parent families who are more likely to find it difficult to drive their children to and from the charter school each day.
- *Provide only elementary grades.*
- *Require that parents volunteer* at the school and back this with parent contracts
- *Require preapplication interviews .*
- *Do not provide a hot lunch program.* This will disqualify the school from the federally-sponsored free and reduced lunch program so low-income families that wish to take advantage of this program will be less interested in the school.
- *Selectively share recruitment information about the school,* both in terms of distribution and language used.

17. Bulkley (2001b) provides evidence based on interviews with EMO officials that levels of autonomy vary across EMOs.

18. One EMO that has captured considerable media attention is Edison Schools Inc. In each of its annual performance reports, Edison claims that its schools are able to make substantial gains on standardized achievement tests (Edison Schools Inc., 2001). Evaluations conducted by districts that contract with Edison or by other researchers have found, however, that gains made in Edison schools are similar to or slightly lower than gains made by comparable groups of students (AFT, 2000; Miami-Dade County Public Schools, 2000; Minneapolis Public Schools, 2000; Miron & Applegate, 2000; Shay, 2000). Our findings also indicate that EMO-operated charter schools perform less well than non-EMO charter schools (see Chapter 8).

11

Lessons in Choice
and Accountability

Charter schools are a new form of public school—a hybrid that mixes elements traditionally associated with private schools (choice, autonomy, and flexibility) with elements traditionally associated with public or government-run schools (universal access and public funding). The charter school movement is part of a larger set of national and international trends toward subjecting the delivery of public services to market competition.

This book has provided a case study in how one state (Michigan) has operationalized the charter concept. As we have seen, Michigan's experiment with charter schools is in many respects atypical (Chapter 3). Its law is widely regarded as one of the most permissive in the country. Not surprisingly, the state has more charter schools than just about any other in the nation. Of equal interest, Michigan charter schools are unsurpassed in their efforts to employ privatized services, mainly through contracts with education management organizations (EMOs). Thus, Michigan provides not a thumbnail sketch of the national charter movement as it is, but a vision of what a more robust national movement might look like with extensive and comparatively unregulated private involvement. And, inasmuch as the charter concept borrows ideas from other school reforms—decentralization, choice, deregulation, accountability, and use of market forces—Michigan's experiment with charter schools bears important lessons for those considering other reforms as well.

In this final chapter we attempt to articulate some of the main lessons from the Michigan case as detailed in the earlier chapters. We turn first to the question we began with, and that framed our empirical analysis: What's public about charter schools? This discussion provides an opportunity to summarize the book's main findings. We are in many ways quite skeptical that the

Michigan charter law has maintained an appropriate balance between private interests and the public goals of education, especially as it pertains to equity, accountability, student achievement, and (to a lesser extent) impacts on noncharter schools. Having made this argument, we expand the discussion somewhat by asking whether, given what we have found, charter schools are a good investment of public funds. In this section, we integrate our findings on charter school finance (Chapter 4) with our findings on equity, teacher professionalism, student achievement, and customer satisfaction. The third section attempts to generalize our findings by providing some preliminary explanations for the weaknesses we have found in Michigan's charter school experiment, and some steps that policymakers in Michigan and elsewhere might take to address them. As yet, we see nothing inevitable in the flaws in Michigan's charter school reform. Rather, we suggest that through changes in law and policy it might be possible for charter schools in Michigan (and elsewhere) to achieve a better balance between private means and public ends. The final section of the chapter returns to larger issues related to school reforms by drawing some more general lessons about the charter school movement.

What's Public About Michigan Charter Schools? A Review of the Evidence

Much of this book has focused on the question of whether and to what degree charter schools in Michigan (and elsewhere) are public and private. As we saw in the first chapter, these concepts are highly contestable and lack clear definitions. Recognizing this, we articulated two definitions of public-ness, each of which has been evident—though not explicitly stated—in court cases on the constitutionality of charter school laws.

Defining "Public"

The first, and perhaps more traditional, definition of public is the *formalist* definition, which focuses on issues of control and ownership. According to this definition, a school (or other institution) is public if it is owned or controlled by citizens or their duly elected representatives. Assessing public-ness with this definition requires an investigation of who owns the means of educational production and to what extent schools and their activities are susceptible to oversight by elected bodies.

Charter school and choice proponents, by contrast, tend to argue for a newer and more flexible definition of public. According to the *functionalist* definition, a school or other institution is public, not by virtue of lines of authority and chains of influence, but by whether it performs important public functions. The functionalist view grants to the larger citizenry and elected officials the authority to define the ends of education and prescribe outcomes, but it largely abjures the need (or the authority) for government institutions to either own or control the means of educational production. Rather, the functionalist definition is content to specify ends and leave it to schools to prescribe the means. Here, the key questions regarding the functionalist definition revolve not around control and ownership but around the outcomes produced by the schools. Put simply, are charter schools producing valuable public services?

Ownership and Accountability

Although we stated the formalist definition first, our analysis of it came last in the book, with Chapter 10's investigation of EMOs. Here the Michigan case is especially interesting given that nearly three fourths of the state's charter schools are managed by these private companies. Our findings raise several concerns about the public-ness of Michigan charter schools according to the formalist definition. Extensive EMO ownership of school facilities, equipment, curricula, and brand name may place significant limits on charter school autonomy and flexibility, thus vitiating notions of site-based management in the charter school concept.

Moreover, the linkages between charter schools and the citizenry they ultimately serve often appear tenuous. First, there is evidence that in many instances EMOs, rather than charter school boards, are in the driver's seat when it comes to school decision making. Thus, the EMO tail appears to be wagging the charter school board dog. Second, the accountability of charter schools is weak when it comes to responding to requests for information and accounting for how public funds are used. While Michigan has detailed financial and other data on schools, information on charter school operations is increasingly subsumed under private management agreements. While at first blush this might seem a minor technicality, use of fair and open accounting standards is a necessary component of accountability.[1] Furthermore, oversight of the schools by their authorizers is often ineffective and authorizers appear to have incentives to conceal rather than reveal weaknesses—and, in some cases, illegalities—in the schools they have chartered (Horn & Miron, 2000; Michigan Office of the Auditor General, 1997).

Charter proponents might respond, with some justification, that the very point of charter schools is to move away from traditional formalist conceptions of public-ness. However, we emphasize that the requirements of the formalist definition go beyond ownership to encompass democratic control and oversight. Democratic control, in turn, requires not just that citizens agree with policy outcomes, but also have an opportunity to influence the *process* by which those outcomes are generated. While the charter school concept certainly seeks to balance democratic political accountability with market accountability (Bulkley, 2001a), in Michigan this balance tips in favor of market accountability.

Equity and Access

Having evaluated Michigan charter schools against the formalist definition of public, we turn now to the functionalist definition. Accordingly, a school is public if it serves a valuable social function. This, however, begs the question of what counts as a *valuable* public function. In operationalizing this concept we were guided by Michigan's charter school law (see Chapter 3) and the more general charter concept from which it springs (see Chapter 1). The specific goals and functions we examined in this book are (a) equity, (b) teacher autonomy and professional opportunities, (c) impact on other schools, (d) student achievement, and (e) choice and customer satisfaction.[2]

Our analysis of the functionalist definition of public-ness began with issues of equity and access. Critics of charter schools often invoke these notions when they charge that the schools lead to further social sorting or even engage in "cream-skimming," which limits access by some students on the basis of family income, race, ability, or other suspect categories. We must emphasize that we have no clear and direct evidence that Michigan charter schools are willfully excluding certain students. Available data tell us only that there are disparities in the types of students attending charter and noncharter schools and do not allow us to determine to what extent this is due to self-selection by families versus charter school practices. Having said this, there is emerging evidence that Michigan's charter school reform is having a negative impact since it promotes further segregation by class, race, and ability.

One possible source of charter/noncharter differences in student composition might come in school location decisions. Given that most charter school students live reasonably close to their schools,[3] founders of charter schools might effectively "choose" their communities ahead of time. An earlier study (based on 1998-99 data) showed that charter schools were locating mainly in districts that are poorer and more racially and educationally diverse than other districts (Glomm, Harris, & Lo, 2000). In more recent years, the trend has been toward schools locating in more affluent areas or on the borders between poor urban and wealthier suburban districts. This trend is especially evident among charter schools operated by EMOs.

The differences persist even after we control for other community characteristics. Comparisons between charter schools and their host districts reveal that while charter schools and their host districts *as a group* enroll roughly equal proportions of low-income and nonwhite students, there are remarkable variations in ethnic and family income representation between charter and noncharter schools. The problem is especially acute among some schools run by EMOs, several of which enroll few or no nonwhite or low-income students.[4] We also found that several charter schools—particularly those managed by National Heritage Academies[5]—enroll many more students from two-parent families than other charter schools in Michigan and in other states for which we have comparable data (Illinois, Pennsylvania, and Connecticut). The largest disparities, however, come in special education. Although a few charter schools enroll high proportions of students with special education needs, most enroll few or none. Such differences also emerge from our data on teacher demographic characteristics, as the state's charter schools generally employ fewer nonwhite teachers than charter schools in other states.

Another form of selectivity among Michigan charter schools is by grade level. As demonstrated in Chapter 5, charter schools overwhelmingly target students in the lower elementary grades, largely avoiding the more-expensive-to-educate high school students. As we saw in Chapter 4, there are clear financial incentives for targeting the earlier grades, given that the state per-pupil foundation grant is fixed and takes no account of these particular variations in educational costs. It is important to note, however, that EMO-run schools account for most of the imbalance in grade levels covered. Non-EMO schools cover all grades more or less equally.

A final equity issue stems from the finding that a large proportion of charter school students (approximately 20 percent) previously attended non-public schools (this figure was much higher for NHA). This implies that a large share of the charter school families were already exercising school choice before the advent of charter schools. While the introduction of charter schools, no doubt, creates lower-cost educational alternatives for many families, policymakers might want to consider whether there are ways to better focus charter school opportunities on those who have not previously had access to educational alternatives.

Teacher Autonomy and Professionalism

Another goal articulated in the charter concept and most charter school laws is enhanced professional opportunities for teachers. As discussed in Chapter 1, the charter concept suggests that allowing teachers to choose schools with educational missions and approaches that closely match their own beliefs and interests will create school communities that can spend less time managing value conflicts among school stakeholders and more time implementing effective educational interventions.

Our evidence suggests that charter schools are, in fact, creating communities of teachers with similar educational perspectives. Teachers reported that important reasons for choosing to work in a charter school included the opportunity to work with like-minded educators, as well as their interest in taking part in an education reform. Finally, the overwhelming majority of teachers surveyed reported being aware of their school's mission, and most believe that they have enough professional autonomy—though not as much as they had initially expected. High attrition rates for teachers, however, tell another story and suggest frustration with working conditions and dissatisfaction with low salaries. The attrition rates also suggest that over time there may be an erosion of the sense of professional community within schools.

However, this sorting process also appears to have a downside, as we saw in the discussion of teacher demographics. Indeed, Michigan charter schools generally have teachers who are younger and less experienced than those in the state's traditional public schools and in other states' charter schools. Among Michigan charter schools, those managed by EMOs (in particular those operated by National Heritage Academies) have the highest concentrations of young teachers. The impact of this youth and inexperience, however, is unclear. From one perspective, young and inexperienced teachers might be more willing to adopt new teaching strategies. On the other hand, young teachers might be more likely to feel overwhelmed by the pressures of starting a new profession in a start-up school. In any case, this trend bears watching.

Student Achievement

Having explored the characteristics of charter school students, families, and teachers, we turned next to a discussion of academic outcome, the most widely discussed of which is student achievement. Here the picture from Michigan is particularly troubling (see Chapter 8). Using a *relative gains* approach, which compares each charter school's gains on the Michigan Educational Assessment Program (MEAP) tests to gains in comparable schools, we found that while there certainly are some charter schools producing impressive academic gains, most of the schools have been outgained by their comparison schools. The single exception to this pattern came in Grade 4 math, where average charter schools gains slightly exceeded those of the comparison schools. With the exception of Grade 7 math, EMO-run schools generally showed smaller gains than other charter schools, with schools run by the Leona Group showing the weakest results. Our findings on student achievement are confirmed by three other studies of Michigan charter schools, each of which used slightly different methods and, in some cases, more restricted samples (Bettinger, 1999; Eberts & Hollenbeck, 2001; Kleine, Scott, & White, 2000).

Impact on Other Schools

As discussed in Chapter 1, charter school proponents contend that the schools' benefits will extend to students in noncharter schools. Accordingly, charter schools will serve as public education's R&D sector, developing innovative practices that can be adopted by other schools. According to theories of school choice, much of the pressure charter schools will exert on other schools will be through competition for students. We found that charter schools do appear to be having financial impacts on some public school districts as they lure away students—and the money that follows them (see Chapter 7). To be sure, schools losing students to charter schools also enjoy some reduction in resource demands. However, the *net* financial impact of these losses is difficult to estimate. Also, it is quite clear that enrollment shifts between charter and noncharter schools are creating a degree of uncertainty that often makes it difficult for school districts to budget and plan effectively.

There is also evidence that these competitive pressures are leveraging at least some changes in traditional public schools' educational practices. Interviews with officials in a sample of districts suggest that traditional public schools are engaging in more vigorous advertising; improving communication with parents and community members; and, in limited instances, adopting new programs such as foreign language programs, all day kindergarten, and before- and after-school programs. While *innovation* is difficult to define in practice, there is considerably less evidence that charter schools are developing educational practices that are innovative in any meaningful sense. Indeed, our findings and those of Mintrom (2000) suggests that most educational practices employed in Michigan charter schools were already quite prevalent elsewhere.

A case can be made that the level of innovation in charter schools is unimportant if the schools' educational practices lead to achievement gains in neighboring districts. However, two fairly rigorous studies have failed to find any evidence that charter schools are leveraging academic improvements (as measured on the state's assessment) in the traditional public schools with which they compete (Bettinger, 1999; Eberts & Hollenbeck, 2001).

Choice and Satisfaction

A final goal of the charter concept is to provide enhanced educational choices within the public school system. While the results in Chapter 7 suggest that the choices offered by charter schools are perhaps less innovative than the movement's architects had anticipated, our evidence suggests that most charter school parents, teachers, and students are quite satisfied with those choices. Most charter school students, for instance, report that they believe that their academic performance has improved since they moved to a charter school—a perception generally corroborated by teachers and parents. Charter school parents and teachers, moreover, generally report that they are satisfied with the extent to which their school's mission is being fulfilled and are satisfied with curricula and instruction. However, charter school parents and teachers were less satisfied with school buildings, facilities, and resources.

Surprisingly, we found that there is little or no relationship between the level of satisfaction with a school's curriculum and instruction and its gains on the MEAP. Moreover, where there is a relationship between student satisfaction and MEAP gains, it is negative. Thus, it appears that charter schools' ability to satisfy customers bears little or no relationship to their ability to produce gains in achievement that show up on standardized tests. While satisfaction may be considered important in and of itself, these findings raise questions about claims that customer satisfaction is a meaningful indicator of academic quality in charter schools.

The Bottom Line

This, then, leaves us to provide an answer to our initial question: What's public about charter schools in Michigan? The answer, perhaps not surprisingly, is mixed. From the formalist perspective, which emphasizes ownership and control, we have serious reservations about the fact that management companies often own the school facilities, equipment, and instructional materials that are being purchased with taxpayers' dollars. This is more often the case when the school is started by an EMO rather than a local group. More important, the fact that in many cases EMOs—not charter school boards—appear to dominate school policy making seems at odds with the principles of democratic control.

From the functionalist perspective, which emphasizes the fulfillment of educational goals that serve the public good, it appears that Michigan charter schools are doing well in some areas but quite poorly in others. The schools appear to be doing a reasonably good job of creating communities of teachers with commonly held educational viewpoints. Moreover, the schools appear to be providing educational alternatives that satisfy their customers, although we have not found the diversity of educational options that were expected. However, the evidence suggests that many of these goals are being accomplished at the expense of equitable access to the schools and student achievement gains. Given this, it is not surprising that Michigan charter schools are also failing to leverage significant changes and improvements in noncharter schools. In a phrase, the answer to the question "What's public about Michigan charter schools" is "Some things, but not others." Table 11.1 summarizes our findings as they relate to the formalist and functionalist definitions of public-ness.

Our claims about the public character of Michigan charter schools must be considered in the context of two very important facts about education in Michigan and in the United States. First, while charter school laws have set out a number of goals for charter schools—goals we have used to evaluate them—there remains much dispute about their relative importance. For some, student achievement is the overriding goal of all schools, charter and noncharter. Others grant the importance of achievement but place more value

Table 11.1   Summary of Findings as They Relate to the Formalist and
             Functionalist Definitions of Public-ness

Formalist: Focus on ownership & control	Public Elements	Private Elements
Facilities (Chapter 10)		Private ownership of materials bought with public funds
Personnel (Chapter 10)		Teachers employed by private EMOs. They can be hired/fired without board consent
Governance (Chapter 10)		EMOs, not boards, drive school decisions
Functionalist: Focus on valuable outcomes		
Equity & Access (Chapters 5, 10)		Disparities in student composition: race, income, special education status, grade level
Teacher Professionalism (Chapter 6)	Creation of communities of like-minded teachers interested in reform	High levels of teacher attrition
Innovation & Impact (Chapter 7)	Changes in district relationships with parents; some new programs	Few innovative practices
Student Achievement (Chapter 8)		Charter school gains lag behind district gains
Customer Satisfaction (Chapter 9)	Most stakeholders satisfied	

on customer satisfaction or equity. This debate is far from academic, since giving greater weight to customer satisfaction would paint a much more sanguine picture of the public-ness of Michigan charter schools than if we were to give more weight to academic achievement and equity. Indeed, one of the things that makes charter school and school choice debates so difficult to resolve is this disagreement over how much weight to give to each of education's many functions. While empirical research, such as that presented in Chapters 4 through 10, can shed light on these issues, research by itself cannot resolve these fundamental questions of value. These questions are most properly addressed through democratic deliberation.

Second, in assessing the public-ness of charter schools we must bear in mind that traditional public (or "government-run" schools) are not entirely public according to our definitions (see, e.g., Labaree, 1997), as many traditional public schools fail to adequately improve their students' academic abilities. And certainly the traditional public school system in this country exhibits serious problems with equity and access, as funding and school quality are largely determined by local property values. In most areas, the price of a high-quality traditional public school is the ability to buy or rent housing in its catchment area. Done properly, school choice reforms—including charter schools—that allow students to move across traditional district boundaries might well alleviate some of the social and economic sorting already present in our educational system. Unfortunately, a number of factors have prevented Michigan charter schools from realizing this promise.

Recognizing the flaws of traditional public schools should not, however, excuse flaws in charter schools. Charter schools, after all, operate according to a unique bargain—increased autonomy in exchange for enhanced account-ability. Thus, it is certainly reasonable to hold charter schools to a higher standard. Charter schools, after all, were not created to reproduce the ills of the traditional public school system, but to leverage change in that system.

In the remainder of this chapter we consider what policymakers and citizens should make of this evidence and what policy actions they might consider to address the concerns we have raised.

Are Charter Schools a Good Public Investment?
The Question of Efficiency

As we have seen, the evidence suggests that Michigan charter schools are public only to a limited extent, according to the formalist and functionalist definitions. First, there are serious concerns about democratic control and ownership. Second, the evidence suggests that the granting of substantial public authority for producing education to quasi-public charter schools and to private management companies has not accomplished many of the public goals set out in the state's charter school law, in spite of the fact that many have been open for six or more years.

But the public-private issue is not the only lens through which policy-makers and citizens should view the issue. Advocates of charter schools, choice, and privatization often cast their arguments in terms of efficiency (see Chapter 1). Charter schools, they argue, will produce superior outcomes at less cost than traditional public schools. Thus, it is appropriate to ask whether, in light of the data presented in this book, charter schools are a worthwhile investment of public funds.

As with so many complicated policy issues, the somewhat frustrating answer to this question is "It depends." As discussed in Chapter 1, efficiency is a rather slippery concept. Because it involves a comparison of inputs and outcomes, discussions of efficiency require agreement on what the appropriate educational outcomes are. As summarized above, Michigan charter schools have a mixed record on the outcomes examined in this book (equity, professional opportunities for teachers, student achievement, innovation, and impact). The efficiency question, then, is this: How do charter school outcomes stack up against charter school costs? Moreover, how does the ratio of inputs to outcomes compare with other educational alternatives, most notably traditional public schools? Comparing the costs and benefits of policy alternatives is a tricky business, since many important costs and benefits are difficult, if not impossible, to measure accurately. In spite of these limitations, we believe that thinking through such an exercise is useful.[6]

Unfortunately, the news is not particularly good for Michigan charter schools on the input side. As part of its examination of charter school finance, Chapter 4 provided in-depth analyses of the cost structures of four charter schools in Michigan—three operated by EMOs.[7] This analysis also considered revenues and expenditures for facilities. In all cases, the charter schools received more money than traditional public schools offering similar services and serving similar student populations (and taking into account expenditures on facilities). Indeed, while charter schools as a group receive less funding than traditional public schools as a group, they typically get *more* than traditional public schools once we control for the types of services offered and students served. We hasten to add that these findings are based on a small sample of schools. However, they do provide cause for concern. Nor do things look any better on the output side, as charter schools as a group have posted weaker gains in student achievement than comparable noncharter public schools.

The news is particularly sobering for charter schools managed by EMOs. As Chapter 4 demonstrated, EMO-run schools tend to spend a considerably lower proportion of their total expenditures on instruction and, not coincidentally, have higher administrative costs. On the output side, we demonstrated in Chapter 8 that relative test score gains in EMO-run schools lag behind those in non-EMO schools.

These findings, if generalizable to the larger population of Michigan charter schools, are particularly interesting in light of the fact that some charter proponents have sold the reform as a lower-cost alternative to traditional public schools. In fact, far from producing more for less, it appears that many Michigan charter schools are, in fact, producing less for more. From this comparison of costs and benefits, we might conclude that Michigan charter schools are not a good investment of state funds. However, a thorough analysis of efficiency assumes we can agree upon and fully measure all relevant benefits and costs. Unfortunately, many relevant costs and benefits are difficult to quantify.

On the cost side, competitive pressures from charter schools have compelled some traditional public schools to make greater investments in marketing and advertising, expenditures that most district officials would rather spend on educational programs. Moreover, the uncertainty created by enrollment shifts between charter and noncharter schools has limited districts' abilities to budget and plan effectively. However, we have as yet no reliable way to place a dollar value on these effects. Nor can we determine whether these competitive pressures might ultimately lead to achievement gains among noncharter school students, though it is clear that they have not as yet.

On the benefits side, we have seen that charter schools are causing some changes for the better in how traditional public schools relate to parents and communities. While these pressures have yet to translate into measurable changes in student performance, such impacts should certainly count in charter schools' favor. Yet, it is difficult to quantify such benefits. More profoundly, it is unclear what value we should place on choice itself. For some, choice of schools is a *good* in itself, regardless of its connection (or lack thereof) with educational outcomes. In any case, a full accounting of the costs and benefits of charter schools must take account of this.

In summary, a simple comparison of the costs and benefits of Michigan charter schools does not look good for the schools, as they appear in many respects to produce inferior outcomes at greater cost than comparable traditional public schools. Nonetheless, this conclusion must be tempered by a recognition that many costs and benefits are difficult to quantify and that a large part of the policy debate focuses—and ought to focus—on such intangibles as the inherent value of choice.

Diagnoses and Prescriptions for Charter School Laws

We stated in the preface of this book that readers should bear in mind that Michigan is, in many ways, an outlier, and that the Michigan case is valuable not so much as a representation of the charter school movement nationwide but as a harbinger of what a larger national charter presence with extensive EMO involvement might look like. In this section we offer some tentative explanations for the weaknesses we find in Michigan's charter school experiment and suggest some recommendations that policymakers might consider in addressing them. In many cases, our observations arise from other states we have studied that, in our opinion, have done a better job of ensuring that charter schools serve important public purposes.

Charter Schools and Policy Theory

As Chapter 1 details, the charter concept relies on a fairly explicit theory about how charter schools should lead to educational improvements among their students and leverage systemic reform in noncharter schools. What we did not discuss in Chapter 1 were the assumptions that the charter concept makes about the actors involved in charter schools. Like nearly all policies, the charter concept makes assumptions—sometimes tacit—about actors' motives, incentives, and capacities (see, e.g., Schneider & Ingram, 1997). In the case of charter schools, these actors include state officials, authorizers, school officials, and consumers.

In most respects, the charter concept is an application of a more general set of policy theories about "contracting out" for educational services (Hill, Pierce, & Guthrie, 1997). Contracting involves a shift from government provision of public services to market-based provision. But the shift is only partial, as it relies on a mix of market accountability and more traditional mechanisms of oversight and political accountability. Thus, policy scholars often refer to this as the theory of "quasi-markets" (see, e.g., Kettl, 1993).

Like other policies that rely on quasi-markets, the charter school concept relies on a web of contracts or agreements among public and private entities. State legislatures and education agencies, which in most states hold ultimate public authority for education policy, contract with charter authorizers and charter schools. (This contract was on full display in the court cases on "delegation" discussed in the first chapter.) Authorizers, in turn, contract with charter schools through the formal charter agreements. And many charter schools contract with EMOs for a variety of administrative and educational services.

A quick read of any introductory economics text suggests that markets assume the existence of certain conditions, and that failure to meet those conditions will lead to "market failure" (see, e.g., Munger, 2000; Weimer & Vining, 1992). The theory of market failure provides useful general guidelines for when and how governments should intervene to fix the market's failures. Quasi-markets also fail in fairly predictable ways (Kettl, 1993; Lowery, 1998). In the remainder of this section we examine some of these quasi-market failures as they pertain to Michigan charter schools. This analysis is useful not only in better understanding Michigan but also in applying Michigan's lessons to similar reforms in other states and nations.

Financial Incentives

All contracts involve risk. In a contract, a person or organization hires a contractor who is supposed to perform some function in accordance with the former's interests.[8] But, as anyone who has ever hired a bad electrical contractor, lawyer, or accountant knows, contractors sometimes act in ways contrary to one's interests. Thus, contracts usually include built-in provisions to ensure that contractors do what they are supposed to.

Like most contracts, charter school laws provide financial incentives for charter schools to provide education to students. These incentives come mainly in the form of a per-pupil payment from the state that follows students to the school in which they enroll. The analysis in Chapters 4 and 5 suggests that this system of financial incentives creates some notable equity problems. In our judgment, the problems issue not so much from any malicious intent on the part of EMOs and other operators as from the incentives built into the state's charter school funding system. As for-profit companies, EMOs seek to make money. Moreover, publicly traded companies such as Edison have a responsibility to their shareholders to produce profits. While some may find the idea of profit-seeking in education distasteful, it is not surprising that these companies would seek to reduce their costs by steering away from high school students, special education students, and others that are more costly to educate (see also Arsen, Plank, & Sykes, 1999).

One perhaps excessive solution to these equity problems is, of course, to ban charter school boards from contracting with for-profit companies. Another would be to require certain proportions of nonwhite, special education, or high school students in management companies' charter school portfolios. Our first recommendation is less drastic and more realistic than either of these:

Recommendation #1: Policymakers should peg the state funding for charter schools to variations in the true cost of educating different groups of students.

By linking state funding to variations in the concentration of more-expensive-to-educate high school and special education students, the law would give management companies and other operators an economic incentive to better serve these previously underserved populations. This solution would also likely require less state-level administrative expense and capacity than a system of student quotas, which would require monitoring and enforcement. It also seems more politically feasible than any attempt to severely curtail the role of EMOs. In short, it is in keeping with the current preference in our nation for policy solutions that harness private interests in the service of public equity goals.

Another problem with the financial incentives in Michigan's charter school reform involves start-up funding. Compared with other states we have studied, Michigan charter schools receive less start-up funding; and the funding they do receive does not come in a timely fashion. The size of start-up grants, moreover, is largely unrelated to enrollment head counts, creating yet another mismatch between the state's charter school funding system and true educational costs.

Both the low amounts and the late arrival of funds in the start-up process create advantages for EMO schools, which have access to capital and administrative capacity that allows them to win out over smaller groups seeking to start charter schools. While there is perhaps nothing inherently wrong with private management of charter schools, these schools' higher administrative costs and standardized curriculum and instruction may undercut the idea that charter schools should provide a broader range of educational choices at less cost than traditional public schools. From this follows our second recommendation:

> *Recommendation #2:* Policymakers should consider linking start-up funding to head count enrollments and providing funds earlier in the start-up process.

Oversight

Problems in Michigan's charter school program, however, go beyond equity and access to include poor student performance. We suspect that lackluster oversight lies beneath both sets of problems. Oversight is another mechanism by which those who enter into contracts can be sure that service providers are doing their jobs. As Bulkley (2001a) points out, the charter concept envisions at least two forms of accountability. Contractual accountability involves authorizers, perhaps with the help of other state and local entities, monitoring charter schools to ensure that they meet the goals embodied in their charter agreements. Market accountability, by contrast, relies on customers "voting with their feet" for or against the schools. In Michigan the balance between market and contractual accountability has tilted well toward market accountability.

While a few Michigan charter schools have been closed by their authorizers (4 percent of the schools have closed thus far and authorizers played an active role in closing less than half of them), overall there is little evidence that charter school authorizers and state officials have provided systematic or vigorous oversight of the schools. Nor is this peculiar to Michigan, as other studies have documented (Bulkley, 2001a; Hill et al., 2001). In part, this may be due to authorizers' reluctance to close schools, most of which have vocal, if sometimes small, groups of supporters (Bulkley, 2001a).

The political disincentives for conducting thorough oversight and closing poor performing schools appear to be greatest for university authorizers in the state. University officials have reported that often they grant charters in response to pressure from the governor. As a result, closing charter schools or releasing information critical of charter schools would undermine the political rationale for chartering in the first place. As described in Chapter 3, the governor has pushed the reform through the persons he has appointed to governing boards of state universities and through incentives (and, in some cases, threats) to these universities. In short, it seems that the threat of closure, which underlies the charter concept's theory of accountability, has thus far been a paper tiger.

Authorizers, however, have at their disposal many tools, short of revoking a charter, in order to ensure that charter schools live up to their contractual obligations. In theory, both charter authorizers and the state department of education provide oversight of the state's charter schools. Yet, compared to other states, the Michigan Department of Education has had very little involvement in the oversight of charter schools. Charter authorizers, for their part, often appear reluctant to make public their oversight practices, to say nothing of *findings* from inspections and monitoring processes. Contracts, as one expert on privatization has observed (Kettl, 1993), are not self-enforcing and require overseers to deploy considerable resources to ensure compliance. The charter concept, like other forms of contracting, places state authorities in the position of steering, not rowing (Osborne & Gaebler, 1992). Steering, however, requires solid information for effective navigation.

To a certain extent, the Michigan Association of Public School Academies (MAPSA) has sought to step into the breach by providing information about the state's charter schools through a series of newsletters and press releases. MAPSA's advocacy role, however, is reflected in the rosy picture it presents of charter schools, which has led us to worry that MAPSA's reporting has given charter schools a false sense that everything is great. While we certainly understand the difficulty of developing representative data on charter schools, such information is not a viable substitute for systematic public oversight. Moreover, the recent appearance of Standard & Poor's school evaluation services has made information about charter schools more accessible. However, the S&P service does not facilitate important comparisons between charter and noncharter schools and thus does not allow users to address questions about the comparative efficiency of charter and noncharter schools.

The failure to properly oversee and, if necessary, close weak charter schools has two negative effects on the charter movement. First, it represents a failure to send appropriate signals to poorly performing schools, allowing them to believe that all is well. Second, the existence of weak schools drags down charter school test averages as well as other indicators of school quality, all of which serves to threaten the credibility of the reform.

To address problems with charter school oversight, we propose a number of policy changes.

Recommendation #3: Policymakers should act to make oversight of charter schools more transparent to the public by requiring that authorizers publicize information on both oversight processes and findings.

The provision of such information would allow interested parties to ensure that authorizers are performing their important accountability function and maintain the link between charter schools and the citizenry at large.

> *Recommendation #4:* Policymakers should adopt clearer and more standardized reporting formats for charter schools, with appropriate incentives for providing the information in a timely manner.

Here, policymakers might look to Connecticut, where charter schools are required to prepare annual reports each year that focus on specified goals and objectives that are unique to each school. These annual reports are then posted on the Web site for the Connecticut Department of Education, so that the public can readily access the information.

> *Recommendation #5:* Policymakers should make appropriate investments in the state's capacity to provide oversight.

While this might involve adding staff at the department of education, it might also involve developing capacity elsewhere. Finally,

> *Recommendation #6:* The state should make use of its authority, under the charter school law, to suspend authorizers who fail to engage in appropriate oversight of their charter schools.

But improving charter school oversight is not simply a matter of developing institutional capacity. There remain important value questions about how to balance the many goals of the charter school program. For instance, Chapters 4 and 5 suggest that the demands of financial solvency and profit often conflict with the requirements of equity and open access for all students. Given the apparent tensions between these goals, how should charter school operators and authorizers weigh these goals? Similarly, how should operators and authorizers balance market accountability against test scores (performance accountability)? Or, more concretely, at what point (if any) should high levels of customer satisfaction offset low test score gains? Until policymakers and stakeholders can provide clearer answers to these questions, it will be difficult for overseers to properly calibrate their oversight efforts.

Role of EMOs

Another one of the "web of contracts"—one especially important in Michigan—is the relationship between charter schools and EMOs. These companies have received their share of criticism in this book, as EMO-run schools produce lower test gains while generating more cause for concern on equity issues. Another concern about EMOs involves the cookie-cutter nature of their curricula. Standardization certainly has its place in the marketplace, given that it reduces some of the uncertainty customers must face when making choices. However, standardization also appears to conflict with the charter school concept's notion that the schools would develop programs that respond to the needs of particular students and communities. Finally, we have raised concerns about EMOs and charter school governance, as there is evidence that in many cases EMOs, rather than duly constituted charter school boards, largely drive important school-level policy decisions (Chapter 10).

None of this is to suggest that those who run EMOs lack good intentions. However, it seems clear that the financial incentives embedded in state law, combined with the need for most of the companies to make a profit, have led EMO-run schools to operate in ways that are often at odds with the program's goals and, ultimately, the public interest. This leads to the following recommendation:

> *Recommendation #7:* Those who contract with EMOs should take concrete steps to engage in "smart buying."

Given their autonomy, charter schools are in the best position to ensure that EMOs serve the public interest by writing strong contracts. Good EMO contracts include the following types of provisions (Horn & Miron, 2000; Lin & Hassel, 1999):

- At least two competing bids from EMOs
- Limits the length of contract to no more than the length of the charter, and preferably less
- Contingency plans so that the option of firing the EMO remains viable and realistic
- Full disclosure of financial information and test scores to citizens, authorizers, and state officials
- Budgeting for internal and external evaluations of school and EMO performance
- Ensuring that the EMO hired has no personal or professional connections with charter school board members

Charter authorizers and state officials should consider providing further technical assistance to would-be charter operators to help implement these and other safeguards.

Consumer Information

One of the more striking findings of this book is the disconnect between customer satisfaction with charter schools and test score gains (Chapter 9). While this issue certainly deserves further exploration by researchers, it might be an indication of problems with market accountability. Parents report that academic performance is among the most important criteria they use in selecting charter schools (Chapter 5). Yet, schools with high levels of satisfaction are no more likely than others to post gains on the state's achievement test. While we have no direct evidence, it is likely that some of this disconnect is the result of poor information. In order to work efficiently, markets must provide cheap and reliable information about products to potential consumers (see, e.g., Stiglitz, 1988). This leads to the following recommendation:

> *Recommendation #8:* State officials should create or support the creation of an information clearinghouse on charter schools.

Such a clearinghouse could build upon the newly instituted Standard & Poor Web-based information system. However, given the widely discussed "digital divide" in the nation, any such system should be complemented by a system that does not require access to the Internet. As noted above, the Standard & Poor system is currently deficient in that it does not facilitate comparisons between charter schools and noncharter schools. Also, any system should rely heavily on *gains* in MEAP scores, not just absolute levels. The MEAP index, detailed in Chapter 8, might provide an easy-to-interpret method for conveying information about how charter schools' gains stack up against comparable schools. It is important to note, however, that this index is limited by the fact that the state provides no data on year-to-year individual student gains, leaving no way to rule out definitively the possibility than observed gains and losses in MEAP scores are the result of changes in student composition.

Ensuring Smart Growth

Based on more than 50 years of scholarly work in the field, Husén (1990) outlined a number of rules for implementing school reforms. Using these rules to measure the likely success of the Michigan charter school reform suggests that the reform is likely to fail. The reasons for this are related to the rapid implementation of the reform with little or no pilot testing, the top-down manner in which the reform was implemented, the lack of sufficient resources to help in start-up, and the inherent weaknesses in oversight.

Essentially, Michigan succeeded in rapidly establishing a large number of charter schools, yet the rapid proliferation of choices may have come at the expense of quality. Indeed, the push to open schools has allowed little time for taking stock and learning from mistakes. Authorizers have had little time to develop the institutional capacity and skill needed to oversee wholly new organizations. Consumers have had little time to learn how to properly evaluate competing educational options. State officials have had little time to learn how to ensure that this new form of public schooling truly serves the public interest—all the while laboring under staff cutbacks and retrenchment. And charter operators, perhaps, have been too willing, under the pressure of time, to reach for cookie-cutter educational models, thus limiting the reform's ability to generate innovative practices. These observations lead to our final recommendation:

> *Recommendation #9:* The state legislature should retain the cap on university-sponsored charter schools pending further exploration into the reasons for poor performance in most of the state's charter schools.

We stress that this should not stop the process of creating new charter schools. It does, however, require a weeding process by which the poor-performing charter schools are closed in order to make way for others with promising ideas. It could also include efforts to encourage district-sponsored charter schools, which are not subject to legislative caps.

The Future of Choice and Accountability

The charter concept is part of a larger set of school reforms taking place across the nation and in many Western countries. Like other similar attempts at school restructuring, it blends elements of decentralization, deregulation, choice, and the use of market forces. It is also an intriguing mix of elements usually associated with both public and private schools. As such, it is one of several reforms—in education policy and elsewhere—that seeks to harness market-like forces in the service of public interests. Given that these ideas comport with the general suspicion of government and reverence for the private sector currently prevalent in the nation, we can expect continuing debate on the subject.

We chose to focus our discussion of charter schools on Michigan because it has one of the oldest and most permissive charter laws in the nation. As such, it provides a glimpse of what might happen in other states that choose to pursue a similar course. Michigan is also noteworthy in the pervasiveness of private management companies in charter schools. Thus, we have sought to provide lessons about privatization in education. We have argued that, in many respects, Michigan provides a lesson in how *not* to implement the charter concept and privatization in education. As we have detailed in other chapters, we have serious concerns about equity and academic performance in Michigan charter schools, particularly among the privately operated schools. The Michigan story, then, is a cautionary tale (Fiske & Ladd, 2000).

We do *not* argue, however, that the charter concept is fundamentally or fatally flawed. Indeed, we have seen it work better in other states and have provided a number of suggestions for strengthening and improving Michigan's law. We must caution, however, that scholarly understanding of the causes of charter school success and failure is very much in its infancy and that our diagnoses and prescriptions should be taken as preliminary. We intend to continue exploring these causes and hope and expect that our colleagues in the research community will do the same.

As policymakers and citizens consider reforms to charter school laws, however, they should bear in mind that while many questions can be resolved by more and better data analyses, many cannot. Such questions involve the balance between individual rights and the collective welfare, the relative importance of equity and efficiency, and the proper balance between customer satisfaction and performance on objective indicators in assessing school quality. In the end, charter school policy—indeed, all school reforms—must be informed by both sound research and vigorous public debate. By both highlighting important normative issues and providing key data, we hope to have made a sound contribution to this debate.

Notes

1. It is no accident that *accounting* and *accountability* share the same etymological root.

2. These goals correspond to those set out in Michigan's charter school law: (a) improving student achievement; (b) stimulating innovative teaching methods; (c) creating new professional development opportunities for teachers; (d) achieving school-level accountability for educational performance; (e) providing parents and pupils with greater choices among public schools; and (f) determining whether state funds may be more effectively, efficiently, and equitably utilized by allocating them on a per-pupil basis and directly to schools (Section 511 Michigan Revised School Code).

3. Approximately three fourths of the parents we surveyed reported living within 10 miles of their charter school.

4. As discussed in Chapter 5, limited participation by Michigan charter schools in the federal free and reduced-price lunch program forces us to draw conclusions about income based on a sample of approximately half the charter schools.

5. Readers should recall that findings from NHA schools are often highlighted throughout the book because NHA is the largest EMO in Michigan and because it is the first EMO in the nation that serves exclusively public schools to report profits.

6. At least two other studies have explicitly addressed the question of whether charter schools are efficient uses of public resources. Solmon, Paark, and Garcia (2001) find that charter schools in Arizona produce greater improvements in test scores, and at less cost, than traditional public schools. Nelson and Hollenbeck (2001), however, call into question these authors' methods for calculating efficiency. Similarly, Gronberg and Jansen (2001) find that in Texas most charter schools operate more efficiently than traditional public schools.

7. This reflects the three fourths of schools statewide that are managed by EMOs.

8. See Wood and Waterman (1994) for an introduction to the theory of principals and agents, which has been used to describe such contractual relationships in the public and private sectors.

Appendix A

Key Historical Developments in Michigan That Have Affected the Public and Private Nature of Schooling

Year	Development/Milestone
1921	*Private, Denominational and Parochial School Act.* Gave the state superintendent of Public Instruction supervision over private, denominational, and parochial schools. Required teachers at nonpublic schools to obtain the same certification as public school teachers.
1929	*CL 1929, 7379.* Revision of the school code forbade districts from providing money to schools of a "sectarian character."
1963	*New state Constitution approved.* The language regarding education was deliberately vague on the subject of state aid to nonpublic schools, which later fueled a debate about public resources for private schools.
1963	*Public Act 241.* This Act required free transportation for students in nonpublic schools. This was challenged in court and upheld as constitutional.
1966	*Bill enacted in 1966* allowed for tuition grants to students who seek entrance to nonpublic colleges and universities.
1965	*Public Acts 341 and 343.* These acts extended indirect assistance to nonpublic school students by mandating that auxiliary services such as medical services, crossing guards, and health services for mentally and physically disabled children, be provided for students attending nonpublic schools. These laws were challenged in federal court in the mid-1960s and upheld as constitutional.
1970	*Public Act 100, Parochiade.* The Michigan legislature decided that the state would provide direct support to nonpublic schools by paying for up to 50 percent of the salaries of lay teachers teaching secular subjects.
1970	*Proposal C, Parochiade Ammendment to Article VIII of the Michigan Constitution of 1963.* This is reportedly the most restrictive language in the country and prohibited any form of public support (both direct and indirect) for nonpublic schools. The impetus for Proposal C was Public Act 100, approved earlier the same year. The amendment was approved by 57 percent of voters.

Year	Development/Milestone

1971 *Michigan Supreme Court Ruling*: *Traverse City School District v. Attorney General.* This ruling struck down language that would deny support to a nonpublic school student attending a public school part-time and maintained that the state could not prohibit the use of state funds for auxiliary services such as special education, general health, and welfare measures in nonpublic schools.

1978 *Proposal H.* Proposal to prohibit the use of property taxes for school operating expenses and to establish a voucher system for financing education of students at public and nonpublic schools. This was defeated with 74 percent of voters against it.

1993 *Public Act 362 (Part 6a of the School Code).* This act allowed a wide range of public educational bodies to authorize charter schools. The number of new charter schools was unlimited except for a cap of 150 on schools sponsored by state universities. This cap was met in 2000. Public Act 416 of 1994 modified the language of PA 362 since this was being challenged in the courts. In 1997, the Michigan Supreme Court ruled that PA 362 was constitutional.

1994 *Proposal A.* Guaranteed funding for school districts on a per-pupil basis for school operating costs and shifted the source of school funding from the property tax to the sales tax. The state's sales tax was increased from 4 percent to 6 percent to accommodate this.

1996 *Schools of Choice Program.* Permitted pupils to transfer from the public school district of their residence to another school and allowed state aid resources to move with them. During the first year of operation, pupils could move only within the intermediate school district. After the first year, students could attend schools of choice in contiguous intermediate school districts. School districts have the ability to refuse participation in the Schools of Choice Program.

1997 *Universal Tuition Tax Credit Plan.* This plan, which was prepared by The Mackinac Center, was never formally developed as a proposal and never brought to a vote. The plan suggests a constitutional amendment that would allow Michigan taxpayers to claim a tax credit against certain state taxes for tuition paid on behalf of a pubic or nonpublic K-12 student. The state of Michigan already allows for tuition tax credit for university-level students.

2000 *Proposal 00-01. Michigan's School Choice Initiative.* This proposal would have changed the state constitution by prohibiting indirect aid to nonpublic schools. It would also have established a new school choice program that included nonpublic K-12 schools and provided vouchers to pupils attending these schools. In order to qualify, students must have been in districts with a graduation rate under 2/3 in 1998-99, or districts that had approved vouchers through school board vote or a public referendum. The proposal would have required teacher testing in public schools and nonpublic schools that redeem vouchers. Finally, the proposal would have also guaranteed that state funding to districts would not drop below levels in FY 2001. This was defeated with 70.1 percent of the voters rejecting it.

Appendix B

Background and Supporting Documentation for Analysis of Student Achievement

Description of Other Studies of Michigan Charter Schools' Impact on Student Achievement

Three other studies have examined Michigan charter schools' impact on student achievement. Because the study by Public Sector Consultants (1999) was limited to schools in southeastern Michigan, we chose not to focus on these findings. Two additional studies provide more in-depth, and in many ways more sophisticated, analyses of student achievement, but only in a limited number of grades and subjects. Bettinger's (1999) study examined math and reading MEAP scores for Grades 4 and 7 and included data from 1996 through 1999. Eberts and Hollenbeck (2001) examined Grade 4 math and reading scores along with Grade 5 writing and science scores. The latter two studies address some of the methodological limitations of that data.

The methodological strengths of the studies by Bettinger and Eberts and Hollenbeck lie in the fact that they include statistical controls in addition to the charter-host district comparisons we made. In both cases, the findings are very similar to our own. In Bettinger's strongest statistical models, he found that, controlling for race and income, charter schools are outgained by the population of host districts. Similarly, Eberts and Hollenbeck found that, controlling for a large number of background factors, charter schools consistently score below host districts.

These studies differ from our own only in that they failed to find the slight positive impact on Grade 4 math scores. The most plausible explanation for this small discrepancy is "positive selection" into charter schools. Positive selection exists when students and families with greater resources are more likely to choose to attend charter schools. If this is the case, then our own comparisons between charter schools and their host districts are too "easy" on the charter schools, since they have fewer at-risk students than their host districts. In the end, the similarities between our study and these others far outweigh the differences.

Table B.1 Correlations Among Grades and Subject Areas

	Grade 4 Math	Grade 4 Reading	Grade 5 Science	Grade 5 Writing	Grade 7 Math	Grade 7 Reading	Grade 8 Science	Grade 8 Writing
Grade 4 Math	1.00							
Grade 4 Reading	0.51	1.00						
Grade 5 Science	−0.03	−0.03	1.00					
Grade 5 Writing	0.18	0.19	−0.05	1.00				
Grade 7 Math	0.17	0.08	−0.12	0.23	1.00			
Grade 7 Reading	0.13	0.22	−0.17	0.24	0.63	1.00		
Grade 8 Science	−0.01	−0.25	0.07	−0.38	0.51	0.18	1.00	
Grade 8 Writing	0.17	0.20	−0.07	−0.28	0.17	−0.02	0.57	1.00

Table B.2 Charter Schools' Impact on MEAP Pass Rates

Grade and Subject	Relative Gain Score*	Number of Schools
Grade 4 Math	0.4	91
Grade 4 Reading	−1.9	91
Grade 5 Science	−0.6	61
Grade 5 Writing	−6.2	62
Grade 7 Math	−1.0	54
Grade 7 Reading	−2.2	55
Grade 8 Science	−0.6	35
Grade 8 Writing	−5.8	35

* The average of the additive and multiplicative weighted values

Table B.3 EMO and Non-EMO Schools Compared

Grade–Subject	Relative Gain Score		Difference (EMO Minus non-EMO)
	Non-EMO Schools*	EMO Schools*	
Grade 4 Math	5.0	−0.7	−5.7
Grade 4 Reading	1.7	−2.7	−4.4
Grade 5 Science	0.6	−0.9	−1.4
Grade 5 Writing	−1.9	−6.9	−5.1
Grade 7 Math	−2.7	−0.6	2.2
Grade 7 Reading	−1.6	−2.3	−0.7
Grade 8 Science	0.7	−1.2	−1.9
Grade 8 Writing	−4.2	−5.0	−0.8

* Values are the average of the additive and multiplicative weighted values

Appendix C

List of EMOs and the Number of Schools They Operated in 2000-01

EMO Name	Number of charter schools
National Heritage Academies	22
The Leona Group	19
Beacon Education Management Inc.	15
Charter School Administration Services	9
Helicon & Associates	8
Edison Schools Inc.	5
Mosaica Education Management Inc.	5
Educare	4
Advantage Schools (merged with Mosaica in 2001)	3
American Institutional Management Services Inc.	3
Choice School Associates	3
Schoolhouse Services and Staffing	3
Smart Schools	3
Foundation for Behavioral Resources	2
Hamadeh Educational Services Inc.	2
Synergy Training Solutions	2

The following list of companies operated only one school during the 2000-01 school year: 777 Management Company, Advance Staff Leasing, Inc., Advanced Employment Services, Alpha-Omega Education Management, Black Starr Education Management, Chatfield Management Foundation, Childcare Connections, Design Administrative Resources, Educational Resources of Michigan, Eagle Point, EightCap Inc., Family Institute Early Childhood, Global Educational Excellence, Global Learning Associates, Innovative Education Programs, Innovative Teaching Solutions, Learning Solutions Unlimited LLC, Learning Facilitators, Inc., Matrix Human Services, Midland Charter Initiative, Northstar Educational Management, Orbis Management Group, L.L.C., PEAK Performance Educational Management Co., Petra Learning Systems, SABIS, Sankofa Watoto, Solid Rock, and Technical Management Group.

References

Ahearn, E. M. (1999). *Charter schools and special education: A report on state policies.* Alexandria, VA: National Association of State Directors of Special Education.

American Federation of Teachers. (2000). Trends in student achievement for Edison Schools, Inc.: The emerging track record in an ongoing enterprise. [On-line]. http://www.aft.org/research/edisonproject/index.htm.

Antonucci, R.V. (1997). 1997 test results from Massachusetts charter schools. [On-line]. http://www.doe.mass.edu/cs.www/reports/1997/toc.html.

Apple, M.W. (1996). *Cultural politics and education.* New York: Teachers College Press.

Apple, M.W. (2001). *Educating the "right" way: Markets, standards, God, and inequality.* New York: Routledge Falmer.

Arsen, D., Plank, D. L., & Sykes, G. (1999). *School choice policies in Michigan: The rules matter.* East Lansing, MI: Michigan State University Educational Policy Center.

Ascher, C., Berne, R., & Fructher, N. (1996). *Hard lessons: Public schools and privatization.* New York: Twentieth Century Fund Press.

Basheda, V. (1993, October 6). Student is singled out by governor—For you, Rory: Plan would allow schools of choice. *The Detroit News*, p. 8A.

Beadie, N. (1999). Market-based policies of school funding: Lessons from the history of the New York academy system. *Educational Policy, 13*(2), 296-317.

Bettinger, E. (1999). *The effect of charter schools on charter students and public schools.* National Center for the Study of Privatization in Education, Occasional Paper, No. 4. New York: Teachers College, Columbia University.

Bierlein, L. A. (1997). The charter school movement. In D. Ravitch & J. P. Viteritti (Eds.); *New schools for a new century: The redesign of urban education.* New Haven, CT: Yale University Press.

Bowles, S., & Gintis, H. (1976). *Schooling in capitalist America: Educational reform and the contradictions of economic life.* New York: Basic Books.

Boyd, W. L. (1993). The politics of choice and market-oriented school reform in Britain and the United States: Explaining the differences. In G. Miron (Ed.); *Towards free choice and market-oriented schools: Problems and promises* (Skolverkets rapport nr.2). Stockholm: National School Agency.

Budde, R. (1988). *Education by charter: Restructuring school districts.* Andover, MA: Regional Laboratory for Educational Improvement of the Northeast and Islands.

Bulkley, K. (1999). *Telling stories: The political construction of charter schools.* (Unpublished Dissertation.) Stanford University.

Bulkley, K. (2001a). Educational performance and charter school authorizers: The accountability bind. *Education Policy Analysis Archives, 9*(37), [On-line]. http://epaa.asu.edu/epaa/v9n37.html.

Bulkley, K. (2001b). Education management organizations and charter school autonomy. Paper prepared for the CPRE Educational Issues in Charter Schools Conference, Washington, DC.

Charter Friends National Network. (2001) *Charting a clear course: A resource guide for building successful partnerships between charter schools and school management organizations.* St. Paul, MN: Author.

Chubb, J. E., & Moe, T. (1990). *Politics, markets and America's schools.* Washington, DC: Brookings Institution.

Church, R. L., & Sedlak, M. W. (1976). *Education in the United States: An interpretive history.* New York: Free Press.

Cibulka, J. G. (1990). Choice and the restructuring of American education. In W. L. Boyd & H. J. Walberg, (Eds.), *Choice and education: Potential and problems.* Berkeley, CA: McCutchan Publishing Company.

Cobb, C. D., & Glass, G. V. (1999). Ethnic segregation in Arizona charter schools. *Education Policy Analysis Archives, 1*(7).

Coleman, J. S., Campbell, E., Mood, A., Weinfeld, E., Hobson, D., York, R., & McPartland, J. (1966). *Equality of educational opportunity.* Washington, DC: U.S. Government Printing Office.

Colorado Department of Education. (1997). *The Colorado charter schools evaluation.* Denver, CO: University of Colorado-Denver.

Colorado Department of Education. (1998). *1997 Colorado charter schools evaluation study: The characteristics, status, and student achievement data of Colorado charter schools.* Denver: Author.

Colorado Department of Education. (1999). *1998 Colorado charter schools evaluation study: The characteristics, status, and student achievement data of Colorado charter schools.* Denver: Author.

Colorado Department of Education. (2000). *1998-1999 Colorado charter schools evaluation study: The characteristics, status, and performance record of Colorado charter schools.* Denver: Author.

Colorado Department of Education. (2001). *The state of charter schools in Colorado: 1999-2000: The characteristics, status, and performance record of Colorado charter schools.* Denver: Author.

Cookson, P. W., Molnar, A., & Embree, K. (2001). *Let the buyer beware: An analysis of the social science value and methodological quality of educational studies published by the Mackinac center for public policy.* Tempe, AZ: Educational Policy Studies Laboratory, Arizona State University.

Crain, R. L. (1993). New York City's career magnet high schools: Lessons about creating equity within choice programs. In M. E. Rasell & R. Rothstein (Eds.), *School choice: Examining the evidence.* Washington, DC: Economic Policy Institute.

Dale, R. E. (1999). *The politics of special education policy in charter school legislation: Lessons from Pennsylvania.* Pennsylvania State University.

DeWeese, P. (1994). The process of educational reform in Michigan. *Journal of Education, 2*(176), 29-35.

Durant, W. C. (1997). The gift of a child: The promise of freedom: Creative approaches to learning, teaching, and schooling. *The Freeman, 47*(6), 360-364.

Eberts, R. W., & Hollenbeck, K. (2001). *An examination of student achievement in Michigan charter schools.* Upjohn Institute Staff Working Paper 01-68.

Edison Schools Inc. (2001). Fourth annual report on school performance. New York: Author. [On-line]. http://www.edisonschools.com/.

Engler, J. (1993a). *Our kids deserve better. The Governor's address on school reform.* Lansing, MI: State of Michigan.

Engler, J. (1993b). *To strengthen the family of Michigan.* The Governor's 1994 state of the state address. Lansing, MI: State of Michigan. [On-line]. http://www.migov.state.mi.us/gov/speeches/StateoftheState_1994.html.

Englund, T. (1993). Education for public or private good. In G. Miron (Ed.); Towards free choice and market-oriented schools: Problems and promises (Skolverkets rapport nr.2). Stockholm: National School Agency.

Evaluation Center, Western Michigan University. (2000). *The impact of charter schools on public and parochial schools: Case studies of school districts in western and central Michigan.* Kalamazoo, MI: Author.

Finn, C. E., Manno, B. V., & Vanourek, G. (2000). *Charter schools in action: Renewing public education.* Princeton, NJ: Princeton University Press.

Fiske, E. & Ladd, H. (2000). *When schools compete: A cautionary tale.* Washington, DC: Brookings Institution.

Fitz, J., & Beers, B. (2001). *Education management organizations and the privatization of public education: A cross-national comparison of the USA and the UK (Occasional Paper #22).* New York: National Center for the Study of Privatization in education, Teachers College, Columbia University.

Golden, D. (1999) Old time religion gets a boost at a chain of charter schools. *Wall Street Journal.* September 15, 1999.

Grissmer, D., Flanagan, A., Kawata, J., & Williamson, S. (2000). *Improving student achievement: What NAEP state test scores tell us.* [Online]. http://www. rand.org/publications/MR/MR924/.

Gronberg, T., & Jansen, D. (2001). *An analysis of Texas charter school performance.* Austin, TX: Texas Public Policy Foundation.

Guthrie, J. W., & Koppich, J. E. (1993). Ready, A.I.M., reform: Building a model of education reform and "high politics". In H. Beare & W. L. Boyd, (Eds.), *Restructuring schools: An international perspective on the movement to transform the control and performance of schools.* London: Falmer Press.

Hanushek, E. (1997). Assessing the effects of school resources on student performance: An update. *Educational Evaluation and Policy Analysis, 19*(2), 141-161.

Hassel, B. C. (1999). *The charter school challenge: Avoiding the pitfalls, fulfilling the promise.* Washington, DC: Brookings Institution.

Henig, J. (1994). *Rethinking school choice: Limits of the market metaphor.* Princeton, NJ: Princeton University Press.

Higgs, R. (1987). *Crisis and leviathan: Critical episodes in the growth of American government.* New York: Oxford University Press.

Hill, P., Lake, R., Celio, M. B., Campell, C., Herdman, P., & Bulkley, K. (2001). *A study of charter school accountability.* Seattle, WA: Center on Reinventing Public Education, University of Washington.

Hill, P., Pierce, L. C., & Guthrie, J. W. (1997). *Reinventing public education: How contracting can transform America's schools.* Chicago: University of Chicago Press.

Hirschman, A. O. (1970). *Exit, voice, and loyalty: Responses to decline in firms, organizations, and states.* Cambridge, MA: Harvard University Press.

Horn, J., & Miron, G. (1999). Evaluation of the Michigan Public School Academy Initiative. Kalamazoo, MI: Evaluation Center, Western Michigan University. [On-line]. http://www.wmich.edu/evalctr/charter/michigan/.

Horn, J., & Miron, G. (2000). *An evaluation of the Michigan charter school initiative: Performance, accountability, and impact.* Kalamazoo, MI: The Evaluation Center, Western Michigan University. [On-line]. http://www.wmich. edu/evalctr/charter/michigan/.

Hoxby, C.M. (2000). Does competition among public schools benefit students and taxpayers? Evidence from natural variation in school districting. *American Economic Review,* 1209-1239.

Husén, T. (1990). "Strategy rules for education reform: An international perspective on the Spanish situation." In T. Husén (Ed.), *Education and the Global Concern.* Oxford: Pergamon.

Illich, I. (1971). *Deschooling society.* New York: Harper and Row.

Johnston, B. J. (1990). Considerations on school restructuring. *Educational Policy, 3*(4).

Kaestle, C. F. (1983). *Pillars of the republic: Common schools and American society, 1780-1860.* New York: Hill & Wang.

Kane, T., & Staiger, D. (2001). *Improving school accountability measures.* National Bureau of Economic Research Working Paper No. 8156, Washington, DC.

Katz, M. B. (2001). *The irony of early school reform: Educational innovation in mid-nineteenth century Massachusetts.* New York: Teachers College Press.

Kemerer, F. R., & Maloney, C. (2001). The legal framework for educational privatization and accountability. *West's Education Law Reporter, 150,* 589-327.

Kettl, D. F. (1993). *Sharing power: Public governance and private markets.* Washington, DC: Brookings Institution.

Khouri, N., Kleine, R., White, R., & Cummings, L. (1999). *Michigan's charter school initiative: From theory to practice.* Lansing, MI: Public Sector Consultants.

Kingdon, J. W. (1995). *Agendas, alternatives, and public policies.* New York: HarperCollins.

Kleine, R., Scott, C., & White, R. (2000). *Issues in Michigan's public school academy initiative phase II.* Lansing, MI: Public Sector Consultants.

Kolderie, T. (1990). *Beyond choice to new public schools: Withdrawing the exclusive franchise in public education* (8). Washington, DC: Progressive Policy Institute.

Labaree, D. F. (1997). Public goods, private goods: The American struggle over educational goals. *American Educational Research Journal, 34*(1), 39-81.

Ladner, M., & Brouillette, M.J. (2000). *The impact of limited school choice on public school districts.* Midland, MI: Mackinac Center for Public Policy.

Lange, C. M. (1997). *Charter schools and special education: A handbook.* Alexandria, VA: National Association of State Directors of Special Education.

Lee, V. & Smith, J. B. (1996). Collective responsibility for learning and its effects on gains and achievement and engagement for early secondary students. *American Journal of Education, 104*(2), 103-147.

Legislative Office of Education Oversight. (2001). *Community schools in Ohio: Second-year implementation report.* Columbus, OH: Author.

Levin, H. M. (2000). *The public-private nexus in education.* Occasional Paper #1. New York: National Center for the Study of Privatization in Education, Teachers College, Columbia University.

Levin, H. M. (Ed.). (2001). *Privatizing education: Can the marketplace deliver choice, efficiency, equity, and social cohesion?* Boulder, CO: Westview Press.

Lin, M., & Hassel, B. (1999). *Contracting for charter school success: A resource guide for clear contracting with school management organizations.* St. Paul, MN: Charter School Friends National Network. [On-line]. http://www.charterfriends.org/partnerships.html.

Louis, K. S., Marks, H. M., & Kruse, S. (1996). Teachers' professional community in restructuring schools. *American Educational Research Journal, 33*(4), 757-798.

Lowery, D. (1998). Consumer sovereignty and quasi-market failure. *Journal of Public Administration Research and Theory, 8*(2), 137-172.

Lubienski, C. (1998). *Public goods and private ends in the reform of education.* Paper presented at the 1998 annual conference of the Sociology of Education Association, Monterey, CA.

Lubienski, C. (2000). Wither the common schools? A critique of home schooling. *Peabody Journal of Education, 75*(1), 207-232.

Lubienski, C. (2001). Redefining "public" education: Charter schools, common schools, and the rhetoric of reform. *Teachers College Record, 103*(4), 634-666.

Marks, H. M., & Louis, K. S. (1997). Does teacher empowerment affect the classroom? The implications of teacher empowerment for instructional practice and student academic performance. *Educational Evaluation and Policy Analysis 19*(3), 245-275.

Miami-Dade County Public Schools (2000). *Evaluation of the Edison project school third interim report: 1998-99 school year.* Miami: Author.

McCubbins, M. D., Noll, R. G., & Weingast, B. R. (1987). Administrative procedures as instruments of political control. *Journal of Law, Economics and Organization, 3*(2), 243-277.

McEwan, P. J., & Carnoy, M. (2000). The effectiveness and efficiency of private schools in Chile's voucher system. *Educational Evaluation and Policy Analysis, 3*(22), 213-239.

Michigan Association of Public School Academies (MAPSA). (2000, March). News about Michigan's charter schools. *Progress.*

Michigan Compiled Laws 380.502.

Michigan Compiled Laws 380.504(2).

Michigan Compiled Laws 380.507(1).

Michigan Court of Appeals. (1996). Council of Org. & Others for Educ. About Parochiaid v. Governor. 216 Mich. App. 126; 548 N.W. 2d 909. Decided, March 29, 1996.

Michigan Department of Education. (1999a). *1996-97 report to the House and Senate Committees on Education: A description of Michigan public school academies (charter schools).* Lansing, MI: Author.

Michigan Department of Education. (1999b). *The MEAP handbook.* Lansing, MI: Author.

Michigan Office of the Attorney General (1989). Attorney General's opinion No. 6581. May 8, 1989.

Michigan Office of the Auditor General (1997) *Audit report: Performance audit of charter schools office and Michigan Resource Center for Charter Schools, Central Michigan University.* Lansing, MI: Author.

Michigan Supreme Court. (1997). Council of Org. & Others for Educ. About Parochiaid v. Governor. 455 Mich. 557; 566 N,W. 2d 208. Decided, July 30, 1997.

Mill, J. S. (1989). *On liberty and other writings.* New York: Cambridge University Press.

Millot, M.D. (1994). *Autonomy, accountability, and the values of public education: A comparative assessment of charter school statutes leading to model legislation.* Santa Monica, CA: Rand.

Minneapolis Public Schools. (2000). *Edison project school information report.* Minneapolis: Author.

Mintrom, M. (2000). *Leveraging local innovation: The case of Michigan's charter schools.* East Lansing, MI: Michigan State University.

Mintrom, M., & Vergari, S. (1998). *Charter school laws across the United States: A policy report–1998 Edition.* East Lansing, MI: Public Policy and Social Research, Michigan State University.

Miron, G. (1993). Choice and the use of market forces in schooling: Swedish education reforms in the 1990s. *Studies in Comparative and International Education,* No. 25, Stockholm: IIE.

Miron, G. (Ed.). (1997). *Restructuring education in Europe: Country reports from the Czech Republic, Denmark, Germany and Sweden.* Stockholm: Humanities and Social Science Research Board.

Miron, G. (2000). What's public about Michigan's charter schools: Lessons in school reform from statewide evaluations of charter schools. Paper presented at the American Educational Research Association annual meeting, New Orleans, LA.

Miron, G., & Applegate, B. (2000). *An evaluation of student achievement in Edison schools opened in 1995 and 1996.* Kalamazoo, MI: The Evaluation Center, Western Michigan University.

Miron, G., & Nelson, C. (2000). *Autonomy in exchange for accountability: An initial study of Pennsylvania charter schools.* Kalamazoo, MI: The Evaluation Center, Western Michigan University.

Miron, G., & Nelson, C. (2001). *Student academic achievement in charter schools: What we know and why we know so little.* National Center for the Study of Privatization in Education, Occasional Paper, No. 41. New York: Teachers College, Columbia University.

Moe, T. (1989). The politics of bureaucratic structure. In J. Chubb & P. Peterson (Eds.), *Can the government govern?* Washington, DC: Brookings Institution.

Molnar, A., Morales, J., & Vander Wyst, A. (2001). *Profiles of for-profit education management companies.* Milwaukee, WI: Center for Education Research, Analysis, and Innovation, University of Wisconsin-Milwaukee.

Moore, D., & Davenport, S., (1990). School choice: The new school sorting machine. In W. Boyd & H. Walberg (Eds.), *Choice in education: Potential and problems.* Berkeley, CA: McCutcheon Publishing.

Mulholland, L. (1999). *Arizona charter school progress evaluation.* Phoenix: Morrison Institute for Public Policy, Arizona State University.

Munger, M. (2000). *Analyzing policy: Choices, conflicts, and practice.* New York, NY: W.W. Norton.

Naim, M. (1993). *Paper tigers and minotaurs: The politics of Venezuela's economic reforms.* Washington, DC: Carnegie Endowment for International Peace.

Nathan, J. (1996). *Charter schools: Creating hope and opportunity for American education.* San Francisco: Jossey-Bass.

National Center for Education Statistics. (2000). *State profiles of public elementary and secondary education, 1996-97.* Washington, DC: Government Printing Office.

National Heritage Academies. (1996). *Management agreement for Vista Charter Academy.* Grand Rapids, MI: Author.

Naudi, J. (2001). "Lessons in economics." Grand Rapids Press (December 2, 2001).

Nelson, C., & Hollenbeck, K. (2001). *Does charter school attendance improve test scores? Comments and reactions on the Arizona achievement study.* Upjohn Institute Staff Working Paper 01-70. Kalamazoo, MI: W.E. Upjohn Institute for Employment Research.

Nelson, C., & Miron, G. (2001). *Professional opportunities for teachers: A view from inside charter schools.* Paper prepared for the CPRE Educational Issues in Charter Schools Conference, Washington, DC.

Nelson, F., Muir, E., & Drown, R. (forthcoming). *Paying for the vision: Charter school revenue and expenditures* (Study funded by the U.S. Department of Education under contract Number ED98-CO-0029).

Nelson, F., Muir, E., & Drown, R. (2000). *Venturesome capital: State charter school finance systems.* Washington, DC: Government Printing Office.

New Jersey Supreme Court. (2000). In re Englewood on the Palisades Charter School. 164 N.J. 316; 753 A.2d 687; 2000.

Olson, M. (1965). *The logic of collective action: Public goods and the theory of groups.* Cambridge MA: Harvard University Press.

Osborne, D. E., & Gaebler, T. (1992). *Reinventing government: How the entrepreneurial spirit is transforming the public sector.* Reading, MA: Addison-Wesley.

Prince, H. (1999). Follow the money: An initial view of elementary charter school spending in Michigan. *Journal of Education Finance, 25,* 175-194.

Public Agenda. (1999). *On thin ice: How advocates and opponents could misread the public's views on vouchers and charter schools.* New York: Author.

Ravitch, D. (1978). *The revisionists revised: A critique of the radical attack on the schools.* New York: Basic Books.

Reinstaldler, K. (1999). Charter school's rent nearly doubles. *Grand Rapids Press* (September 3, 1999).

Reynolds, K. (2000). *Innovations in charter schools: A summary of innovative or unique aspects of Michigan charter schools.* Kalamazoo, MI: The Evaluation Center, Western Michigan University.

Richmond, G., & Lin, M. (2001). Putting the "public" into charter schools: The important role of charter school authorizers. *ECS Governance Notes.* [Online]. http://www.ecs.org/clearinghouse/31/68/3168.doc.

Rofes, E. (1998). *How are school districts responding to charter laws and charter schools?* Berkeley, CA: Policy Analysis for California Education, University of California, Berkeley.

Rogers, E. M. (1995). *Diffusion of innovations* (4th ed.). New York: Free Press.

RPP International. (1998). *A national study of charter schools, second-year report.* Washington, DC: U.S. Department of Education.

RPP International. (2000). *The state of charter schools, national study of charter schools, fourth-year report.* Washington, DC: U.S. Department of Education

RPP International. (2001). *Challenge and opportunity: The impact of charter schools on school districts.* Washington, DC: U.S. Department of Education.

Sanders, W. L., & Horn, S. P. (1993). *The Tennessee value added assessment system: Mixed model methodology in educational assessment.* Kalamazoo, MI: Western Michigan University Evaluation Center.

Savoie, D. J. (1994). *Thatcher, Reagan, Mulroney: In search of a new bureaucracy.* Pittsburgh, PA: University of Pittsburgh Press.

Schneider, A. & Ingram, H. (1997). *Policy design for democracy.* Lawrence, KS: University Press of Kansas.

Schulz, K., & Golder, E. (2000). Unlocking school records. *The Grand Rapids Press* (March 26, 2000).

Schultze, C. L. (1977). *The public use of private interest.* Washington, DC: Brookings Institution.

Shay, S. A. (2000). A longitudinal study of achievement outcomes in a privatized public school: A growth curve analysis. Unpublished doctoral dissertation, University of Miami, Coral Gables, Florida.

Solmon, L., Block, M. K., & Gifford, M. (1999). *A market-based education system in the making: Charter schools.* Phoenix, AZ: The Goldwater Institute.

Solmon, L., Paark, K., & Garcia, D. (2001). *Does charter school attendance improve test scores? The Arizona results.* Phoenix, AZ: Goldwater Institute.

Stiglitz, J. E. (1988). *Economics of the public sector* (2nd ed.). New York: W.W. Norton.

Stone, D. A. (1988). *Policy paradox and political reason.* Glenview, IL: Scott, Foresman.

Teske, P., Schneider, M., Buckley, J., & Clark, S. (2000). *Does charter school competition improve traditional public schools?* New York: Manhattan Institute.

Walford, G. (Ed.). (1996). *Oxford Studies in Comparative Education: School choice and the quasi-market.* Oxfordshire, UK: Triangle Journals Ltd.

Weimer, D., & Vining, A. (1992). *Policy analysis: Concepts and practice.* Upper Saddle River, NJ: Prentice Hall.

Wells, A. S., Artiles, L., Carnochan, S., Cooper, C. W., Grutzik, C., Holme, J. J., Lopez, A., Scott, J., Slayton, J., & Vasudeva, A. (1998). *Beyond the rhetoric of charter school reform: A study of ten California school districts.* Los Angeles: UCLA Charter School Study.

Wells, A. S., Grutzik, C., Carnochan, S., Slayton, J., & Vasudeva, A. (1999). Underlying policy assumptions of charter school reform: The multiple meanings of a movement. *Teacher's College Record, 100*(3), 513-535.

Whitty, G., Power, S., & Halpin, D. (1998). *Devolution and choice in education: The school, the state, and the market.* Birmingham: Open University Press.

Wohlstetter, P., & Griffin, N. (1998). *Creating and sustaining learning communities: Early lessons from charter schools* (OP-03). Philadelphia, PA: Consortium for Policy Research in Education.

Wohlstetter, P., Wenning, R., & Briggs, K. L. (1995). Charter schools in the United States: The question of autonomy. *Educational Policy, 9,* 331-358.

Wolf, C., Jr. (1988). *Markets or governments: Choosing between imperfect alternatives.* Cambridge, MA: MIT Press.

Wolfram, G. (1999). *Report of Hillsdale Policy Group on Michigan charter schools.* Hillsdale, MI: Hillsdale Policy Group. [On-line]. http://www.s2f.com/mapsa/whatsnew/pr/hillsdale1.html.

Wood, B. D., & Waterman, R. (1994). *Bureaucratic dynamics: The role of bureaucracy in a democracy.* Boulder, CO: Westview.

Wood, M. T. (2000). Letter delivered to State Superintendent Ellis and the state board of education. October 25, 2000.

Wylie, C. (1994). *Self-managing schools in New Zealand: The fifth year.* Wellington: New Zealand Council for Educational Research.

Index

CORWIN
PRESS

The Corwin Press logo—a raven striding across an open book—represents the happy union of courage and learning. We are a professional-level publisher of books and journals for K-12 educators, and we are committed to creating and providing resources that embody these qualities. Corwin's motto is "Success for All Learners."